Stress-Free Documentation

for Mental Health Therapists

Stress-Free Documentation
for Mental Health Therapists

The Complete Guide to Progress Notes,
Treatment Planning, and Medical Necessity

Maelisa McCaffrey, Psy.D.

Stress-Free Documentation for Mental Health Therapists:
The Complete Guide to Progress Notes, Treatment Planning, and Medical Necessity
This edition first published 2024
© 2025 by Maelisa McCaffrey, Psy.D.

Edited by Christina Kaake
Proofread by Danielle Van Voorst
Cover Design, Book Design, and Illustrations by Stephen Crowe / My Digital Maven
Author Photograph by Angie Mitchell

All rights reserved. Except as noted below, no part of this book may be reproduced, transmitted, stored in a retrieval system or distributed in any form or by any means, except as permitted by U.S. copyright law, without prior written permission from the author.

Limited Single-User License
Reproduction and adaptation of the templates, forms, and other handouts in Chapters 5, 7, 10, and 12 is provided to the individual purchaser for individual professional use with clients. All pages are copyrighted. Permission to reproduce and adapt these templates, forms, and handouts is granted only to the individual purchaser for their individual professional use and under a limited single-user license, unless otherwise agreed upon in writing with permission from the author.

This publication is intended to provide educational information for the reader on the covered subject. It is not intended to take the place of legal advice or clinical supervision. Always consult an attorney, applicable laws, ethical guidelines, and other relevant clinical standards when needed. Confirm all information is current and correct at time of use.

ISBN: 979-8-9917505-2-3
Ebook ISBN: 979-8-9917505-3-0

Published by QA Prep
Gig Harbor, Washington, USA

Discounted university copies and other bulk discounts available when purchased in bulk directly from QA Prep, Inc. Contact maelisa@qaprep.com for university and other bulk orders.

Dedication

This book is dedicated to every clinician who:

Thought about leaving the profession
because the paperwork was too overwhelming,

Asked for help from a supervisor
and didn't get the understanding, training, or support they needed,

Worried they were "a bad therapist"
because they couldn't manage documentation.

It's not you.

Struggling with documentation doesn't make you a bad therapist.
Here's the book you needed.

Contents

Website Resources and Bonus Content — 1
Introduction — 2

CHAPTER 1: HOW TO USE THIS BOOK — 4

Guidance for Your Clinical Role — 7
An Important Note About Clinical Language — 10
Identify Goals for Reading and Using This Book — 13
What to Focus on First — 14
Limitations of This Book — 15
The Top 2 Time Saving Tips From This Book — 16
Accessing the Online Resources — 17
Quick Read Chapter Summary — 19

CHAPTER 2: FOUNDATIONS OF ETHICAL DOCUMENTATION — 22

Documentation in Various Settings — 24
Ethical Guidelines for Documentation — 25
Creating Your Documentation Policies — 28
Electronic Health Records (EHRs) in Various Settings — 29
A Quick Review of HIPAA — 32
Client Access to Records — 33
Cultural Considerations for Documentation — 34
Documentation in Your Own Style — 35
Working Within the Context of an Organization — 37
Quick Read Chapter Summary — 40

CHAPTER 3: INSURANCE AND MEDICAL NECESSITY — 42

Types of Mental Health Insurance Coverage — 43
What is Medical Necessity? — 45
Using the Clinical Loop of Documentation — 46

Discussing Insurance With Clients (Even if You're Private Pay)	49
Mental Health Services Covered by Insurance	51
Why Couples Therapy is Different for Insurance Clients	52
Dealing With Insurance Audits	55
Audit Red Flags	57
Quick Read Chapter Summary	59

CHAPTER 4: INTAKE ASSESSMENT — 62

Policies and Forms	64
What is Informed Consent for Treatment?	64
What Goes in a Client Record?	65
Connecting Policies to Forms	67
Setting the Stage for a Great Intake Interview	69
One Tip to Save Hours of Documentation Time	70
How to Ask Great Assessment Questions	71
Intakes With Minors, Couples, and Families	72
The Mental Status Exam	74
Case Conceptualization and Diagnosis Justification	75
Finalizing the Intake Assessment Process	76
Quick Read Chapter Summary	80

CHAPTER 5: INTAKE ASSESSMENT FORMS — 82

Guidance on Using Templates	83
Client Intake Form: Adult	85
Client Intake Form: Child or Adolescent	93
Progress Note Template: Intake Assessment	103
Problems Questionnaire	106
Diagnostic Symptoms Cheat Sheet	107
Diagnosis Justification Form	109
Consent for Audio / Video Recording	110
Consent for Services	111
Consent for Telehealth	119
Consent to Treat a Minor	121
Minor Consent to Treatment	122
Agreement to Confidentiality in Group Therapy	123

Notice of Privacy Practices (USA Specific) 124

CHAPTER 6: TREATMENT PLANNING — 132

Treatment Planning as Client Empowerment 135
Writing Easy and Meaningful Treatment Goals 136
When to Use "SMART" Goals 138
The Most Important Thing About Treatment Plan Interventions 140
Integrating Strengths and Supportive Factors 141
When and How to Update Treatment Plans 141
Quick Read Chapter Summary 144

CHAPTER 7: TREATMENT PLAN TEMPLATES — 146

Guidance on Using Templates 147
Potential Treatment Plan Components 149
Treatment Plan Example: Insurance 156
Treatment Plan Example: Simple 161
Treatment Plan Example: Narrative 165
Treatment Plan Example: Child 167
Treatment Plan Example: Couples 171

CHAPTER 8: PROGRESS NOTES — 176

What Goes in a Progress Note? 177
Psychotherapy Notes Versus Progress Notes 179
Making Notes Simple and Meaningful 180
The Perfect Progress Note Template 181
Different Types of Progress Notes 183
Collaborative Documentation 185
Amending Progress Notes 188
Documenting Risky Situations 190
Documenting Ethical Dilemmas 194
Quick Read Chapter Summary 196

CHAPTER 9: COMMON PROBLEMS WITH PROGRESS NOTES — 198

- Using the QUOTE Framework to Identify Problems and Solutions — 200
- Questioning Yourself While Completing Documentation — 200
- Understanding What to Include in Notes and When — 203
- Other People Who Read Progress Notes — 204
- Time Management in Real Practice — 207
- Emotionally Charged Documentation and Burnout — 210
- Common Struggle: How to Catch Up on Progress Notes — 212
- Quick Read Chapter Summary — 215

CHAPTER 10: PROGRESS NOTE TEMPLATES — 218

- Guidance on Using Templates — 219
- Potential Progress Note Components — 221
- Progress Note Example: Simple — 237
- Progress Note Example: Insurance — 242
- Progress Note Narrative Starter Phrases — 248
- Progress Note Example: Narrative — 251
- Progress Note: Child/Play Therapy Additions — 253
- Progress Note Example: Child — 255
- Progress Note: Couples Therapy Additions — 262
- Progress Note Example: Couples — 264
- Progress Note: Group Therapy Additions — 269

CHAPTER 11: COORDINATING CARE AND ENDING TREATMENT — 272

- Ethically Coordinating Care With Other Professionals — 273
- Seeking Consultation and Whether or Not to Document It — 277
- Writing Objective and Helpful Letters for Clients — 279
- Considerations When Releasing Client Records — 280
- Documenting the End of the Therapeutic Relationship — 282
- Managing and Destroying Records Beyond Treatment — 284
- Quick Read Chapter Summary — 285

CHAPTER 12: FORMS FOR COORDINATING CARE AND ENDING TREATMENT — 288

- Guidance on Using Templates — 289
- Authorization to Release Information — 291
- Progress Note Example: Collateral Contact — 293
- Progress Note Example: Consultation — 295
- Case Summary Example — 297
- Letter Template: Summary of Treatment — 299
- Letter Template: Case Coordination — 300
- Letter Template: Case Closing — 301

APPENDIX — 304

- Your Documentation Journey: Where to Go From Here — 305
- References — 306
- Index — 312
- Acknowledgments — 314
- About the Author — 316

Website Resources and Bonus Content

Use the QR code below, or go to **QAPrep.com/SFD-Resources** to access all the templates and forms in this book, along with bonus content. Bonus content includes full example client files, bonus video trainings, and extra templates and forms.

Example Client Files

- Example Adult Client File: Belle Marchand
- Example Child Client File: Simba King

Bonus Video Trainings

- How to Use the Templates in Google Drive
- How to Use the Templates in an EHR
- How to Adapt the Templates for Your Organization
- Reviewing Your Documentation for Quality

Bonus Forms and Templates

- Client Email Templates
- Letter Template: No Show Follow Up
- Letter Template: Delinquent Payment
- Paperwork Catch Up Plan

Graduate Course Supplements

- Learning Objectives
- Learning Assessments

Scan QR code with your phone

or visit
QAPrep.com/SFD-Resources

Introduction

On the surface, I am the last person who "should" write a book about clinical documentation. I have ADHD, reject structure and rules, dislike the parameters set forth by insurance, and still struggle with administrative tasks for my business. However, it was these very things that led me to become a documentation expert and to start a business, QA Prep, whose sole purpose is helping clinicians with mental health documentation.

Organization hasn't always come naturally to me. I learned early in my career that it was difficult to manage the competing priorities of clinical work, professional development, documentation, and other administrative tasks. I refined this process through trial and error while working in a variety of clinical settings.

It was burnout, not a love for documentation, that eventually led me to work in quality improvement. Thankfully, I worked on an amazing team where we focused more on training clinicians than on reviewing client charts. I loved turning a traditionally boring topic into an engaging training and began hearing the same thing from clinicians over and over: "I never learned any of this in grad school!"

The clinicians and clinical supervisors in the agency had a direct line to ask me documentation questions as they came up in real life, and questions came up every day. That got me wondering whether or not clinicians in other settings, especially those in private practice, had similar documentation questions but no expert readily available to answer those questions. A quick survey of friends in private practice revealed that they had no one to turn to with their documentation questions - and yes, they had many documentation questions!

That encouraged me to start QA Prep in 2014. I continued working in quality improvement programs simultaneously as I discovered what private practice clinicians most needed help with regarding documentation. It was surprising to learn that most clinicians needed reassurance just as often as they needed specific guidance. And they all needed non-judgmental support above anything else.

It is hard to believe that, over 10 years later, I am still training clinicians on documentation, but now I'm doing it full-time through QA Prep. For me, that highlights two things: 1) Documentation is still a mysterious subject that creates significant stress for many clinicians throughout their careers, and 2) Most clinicians are conscientious and caring people who have a genuine desire to learn about all the aspects of their job, including documentation, so they can do those things well.

My hope is that after reading this book you will feel more comfortable navigating the gray areas of documentation and have a clear definition of your own documentation standards, tailored to your specific needs and goals. These are everlasting changes that will help with any documentation goal you identify while reading this book and throughout your career.

Chapter 1

How to Use This Book

IN THIS CHAPTER

Guidance for Your Clinical Role 7
An Important Note About Clinical Language 10
Identify Goals for Reading and Using This Book 13
What to Focus on First 14
Limitations of This Book 15
The Top 2 Time Saving Tips From This Book 16
Accessing the Online Resources 17
Quick Read Chapter Summary 19

> *Your present circumstances do not determine where you can go, they merely determine where you start.*
>
> *- Nido Qubein*

Documentation is a practice, not a set of rules. This can be both relieving and stressful. Most clinicians would prefer to learn how to document "correctly" because documentation is so closely associated with justifying clinical work in some way. It is also unlikely that a love for paperwork was your motivation for attending graduate school and becoming a mental health clinician. Therefore, you may have picked up this book hoping for a quick set of do's and don'ts you can memorize and then get back to the "real" clinical work.

Unfortunately, this book will not provide you that list (for the most part). However, this book will teach you how to think about documentation differently, so that it actually becomes a more natural part of the other clinical work you do and ironically, becomes something you can spend less time worrying about.

You will learn principles and ethics in a very practical and clinical sense. This includes ethical principles related to documentation and how to manage the purposely vague documentation requirements (Wiger, 2009) included in the major five ethics codes for mental health professionals - AAMFT, ACA, AMHCA, APA, and NASW. Just as importantly, you will also access:

- Examples of problem-solving common documentation struggles with fictional clinicians based on real-life scenarios (through the Clinician Spotlights),

- "Top Tips" for saving time and mental effort on documentation,
- Curated information about ethical and legal requirements for documentation in common mental health practice, along with guidelines to use when there appear to be many options with no clear "right" path,
- Templates that are created to meet ethical and insurance requirements, but also to meet the needs of clinicians providing outpatient psychotherapy,
- Other helpful tools for creating high quality documentation that is individualized to each client without needing to reinvent the wheel each time you write a progress note.

Use the book along with the online resources available at **QAPrep.com/SFD-Resources**. The online resources include all of the templates within this book in a digital and editable format, along with additional handouts, video training, and specific resources for graduate schools.

Clinician Spotlight: Abby

Abby booked a consultation with me because she was struggling with documentation, spending hours each week on paperwork and yet consistently falling more and more behind in her progress notes. When I met with Abby she admitted feeling very embarrassed about being behind in her progress notes and that I was the first person she had told. I discovered Abby was spending about 25-35 minutes per progress note and seeing 20 clients a week. That's 10 hours each week on progress notes alone! No wonder she couldn't keep up with treatment plans, intake assessments, and other work, as well.

Abby admitted that she had never received training on documentation and when she asked her supervisor for help, the supervisor said her progress notes "are fine, but maybe I could write a little less." She had no idea what information was okay to remove and was overwhelmed by how to catch up on notes from weeks prior.

After explaining to Abby how common this experience is and offering some compassion, we got to work creating some cheat sheets with common phrases she could use in progress notes. We identified what components she should include in each section of her notes and discussed strategies for making treatment plans and intake assessments more efficient. We also reviewed her schedule and identified the best times for her to complete paperwork and times for catching up on the older progress notes. I suggested she try all these strategies for two weeks before making any adjustments to the templates or her schedule, to allow time for her to adapt to the new process and become familiar with her new resources.

> She emailed me a few weeks later to say she was already down to about 10 minutes per progress note. More importantly, she was less stressed about documentation and felt more confident about the feedback she received from her supervisor. She had admitted to the supervisor that she was behind in notes. She was able to present her plan for catching up and the supervisor was helping her stay accountable. Abby felt much more confident and was relieved of the secret shame she had been carrying for months.

GUIDANCE FOR YOUR CLINICAL ROLE

Documentation is a journey for all clinicians throughout their career, and this book is written to guide you regardless of where you are in that process. Below is guidance based on needs unique to each position.

 ### Student / Intern

If you are reading this book in graduate school or post-graduate training, it is likely you will receive multiple and competing suggestions about clinical documentation in your various placement settings. This is normal and expected.

Each agency or placement has various considerations when creating documentation policies. Likewise, each supervisor has different preferences, along with their own varied training and experience. Sadly, many supervisors do not feel confident in their own documentation experience and may not offer clear guidance. Others may have specific expectations.

Use this book as a foundation for how to *think* about documentation, and as guidance for translating clinical practice into clinical language. Always follow the directives of your supervisors, but use this as a resource when you need practical examples.

For example, the therapy interventions listed with the progress note template in Chapter 10 provide the foundation for you to create a more personalized "cheat sheet" to help with progress notes, regardless of your clinical placement. Chapter 4 guides you in how to discuss informed consent with clients, and Chapter 6 provides a formula for writing SMART treatment goals.

Lastly, save the online resources at **QAPrep.com/SFD-Resources** as a browser bookmark and keep that ready for when you move into a position with more flexibility in how you document.

You will find that as you move through your career, different resources will be helpful, and things that do not apply now may prove useful in the future.

Professor

One of the most common things clinicians say to me is *"How come we never learned this in grad school?"* Thank you for reading this book! It is an excellent resource for students in or about to start practicum or internship, since they have opportunities to implement the information.

As with many ethics topics, documentation is a practice that requires critical thinking and principles, rather than clearly spelled out rules. It is an extremely relevant topic for exercises that include ethics, theory, case conceptualization, and practical application. And thankfully, documentation is very easy to practice in a classroom setting, whether in person or virtually.

The more you include exercises that relate to the experiences of students, the more they will be able to apply these ethical principles and anticipate problems common to clinicians. There are Clinician Spotlights throughout this book that highlight real life examples, but I would encourage you to have students use their own experience. If you are working with students who have no clinical experience yet, bring in your own stories or have them create sample clients they hope to work with soon.

Access the online resources at **QAPrep.com/SFD-Resources** for course handouts based on discipline. Each course handout has learning assessments with correlating competencies for that profession. There are also reflection questions, practice exercises, and suggestions for adapting the content to various settings.

I am available for contracted question and answer sessions specific to documentation. Lastly, I would love to hear feedback about how you are using this book in a training setting, practical applications, and further resources needed for future editions. Please complete the feedback form available at **QAPrep.com/SFD-Resources**.

Clinical Supervisor

Although this book is written with clinical practice in mind, clinical supervisors are the most important readers. As a supervisor, you have the power to create a positive experience in all aspects of clinical practice, and this includes the often neglected but stressful area of documentation.

You must be able to explain a clinical intervention, why it is relevant for a particular client, and how to document that after the session. The overused example of putting on your own oxygen mask before supporting others applies here, too. If there are any aspects of documentation that cause you stress, start there.

Then jump ahead to Chapter 9 to learn about the most common mistakes clinicians make with progress notes and strategies for how to address those mistakes. If you are a supervisor for any amount of time, you will absolutely see these mistakes in action. Be prepared with resources and a non-judgmental attitude.

Beyond that you will want to be familiar with the documentation basics - informed consent, gathering biopsychosocial history for a client, treatment planning, and writing progress notes. If you work in a context that includes billing to insurance, understanding medical necessity is also important.

The provided templates will give you practical resources to use with supervisees, and the content chapters will guide you in when to use each resource. Combine all of this with your own experience to adapt and personalize the resources provided in this book and online.

Each clinician you supervise will have a more positive experience with documentation as a result of your reading this book. Know that your investment in time, effort, and money can last for decades through each supervisee's ongoing work.

 ## Private Practice Clinician

Reading this book as a clinician, you have the advantage of choosing which portions apply to you. While it may be tempting to skip ahead to the templates, I encourage you to also read the related chapters so you fully understand what you can take out and what is important to include when creating your own templates.

Focus on the specific areas that cause stress or confusion in your current documentation practice. Start with the reflection questions from the quiz in this chapter to identify specific goals for reading this book. Start with those goals and slowly implement the different strategies for that topic area, making sure you feel confident about what you have implemented before moving on to the next chapter or topic.

For example, if you purchased this book to save time on progress notes because it takes you 30 minutes to write a note, start with Chapter 9. You will be able to identify which strategies are most relevant to you. Make a plan to start with one of those strategies *today*. Then revisit other strategies as needed, and build upon your progress.

However, if you purchased this book because you are about to start a private practice and want guidance in creating your intake paperwork and practice policies, start with Chapter 2 and then move on to Chapter 4. This will help you determine your policies, and then guide you in creating the appropriate documents to support that.

Documentation needs change over time with your experience and life circumstances. New laws or tools emerge, and this will continue throughout your career. Keep this book and the online resources as a continual reference guide you can refer to as needed, rather than something to digest quickly.

AN IMPORTANT NOTE ABOUT CLINICAL LANGUAGE

The mental health field includes many types of professional licenses and degrees. In most clinical settings beyond graduate school, these various license types all do similar work, but may use different language when describing various aspects of this work.

This book seeks to use clinical language that is applicable to all professions. However, many clinical terms are both common *and* interchangeable. To avoid confusion when many terms describe the same thing, one word or phrase will be identified and described, then used consistently. The most frequently used terms are described below.

Clinician

For example, the word "clinician" is used throughout this book to describe any mental health professional, licensed or unlicensed, who works directly with clients and identifies as any of the following:

- Counselor
- Intern, associate, or trainee
- Psychiatric nurse practitioner

- Psychiatrist
- Psychoanalyst
- Psychologist
- Psychotherapist
- Social worker
- Therapist

Client
The word "client," rather than "patient" is used throughout this book to describe any recipient of psychotherapy services provided by any of the above professional clinicians.

This is not meant to endorse using one term over the other. Both terms are acceptable and common among various mental health professionals, and based largely upon preference and professional tradition. It is also acceptable to use the word "person" or "individual," or simply to use the client's name in documentation.

Intake assessment
Another commonly confused phrase is "intake assessment." This refers to the first session in which a clinician meets with a client, usually to gather relevant historical data and determine the best fit for treatment. Other terms used for this initial client meeting include "diagnostic assessment," "biopsychosocial assessment," or even just "assessment" or "intake."

To confuse things further, these names may also change based on whether the clinician is describing the actual meeting itself or the form completed in that meeting. For example, it is common to say something like, *"I met with the client for an intake and completed the biopsychosocial."* It is just as common to hear, *"I need to complete the DA (diagnostic assessment) from the client's intake."*

Throughout this book you will see the phrase "intake assessment" used to describe the actual client meeting and intake process. The word "biopsychosocial" will be used in conjunction when discussing the form associated with the intake process.

Psychotherapy
While this book does cover documentation for other related topics, such as consultation, it is primarily focused on documentation related to the process of psychotherapy. In practice, there is significant crossover with the terms "therapy," "psychotherapy," and "counseling."

For the purpose of this book, the term "psychotherapy" includes any of the following:

- Psychotherapy for individuals, families, couples, and groups,
- Short and long-term psychotherapy,
- Mental health treatment such as traditional "talk therapy," as well as more directive modalities,
- Psychotherapy that is combined with medication management and provided by a licensed mental health professional, such as a psychiatrist.

The index at the back of this book outlines when different phrases or words are interchangeable and indicates which one is used throughout the text.

IDENTIFY GOALS FOR READING AND USING THIS BOOK

Use the quiz to evaluate your own beliefs and feelings about documentation so you have a frame of reference.

Quiz - My Relationship with Documentation

Answer each question with true or false. There is no right or wrong answer. The goal is to assess where you are currently and to identify your objectives for reading this book.

1. I know what time of day is best for me to reflect and be quiet.
2. When I sit down to write progress notes, I have no idea what to say.
3. My clients are often frustrated with having to fill out so much paperwork at the outset of therapy.
4. I know how to calm my mind when my thoughts are racing.
5. I feel comfortable talking with clients about goals for therapy and translating this into a treatment plan.
6. I had a clinical supervisor who regularly reviewed client documentation with me and took time to explain related concepts.
7. I feel anxious or angry when I think about writing notes.
8. While a subpoena would be a bit unnerving, I know my client's files are ready to be reviewed.
9. I would have difficulty putting into words what "progress" looks like for my clients.
10. I know my intake forms inside and out and can easily answer questions on practice policies.
11. I have cried about or lost sleep over documentation in the last year.
12. I have a clear process for saving client documentation and feel confident it is securely stored.
13. I understand what to include in documentation for medical necessity criteria.
14. If a client asked to see their records, I would feel uncomfortable letting them read their progress notes.
15. I know how long it takes me to write a progress note.

Now let's take some time to reflect on your answers:

1. *What triggered you emotionally? Was there a question that elicited fear, guilt or resentment? Anxiety or hopelessness?*

    If so, take a moment to write down what those feelings are and why. Perhaps you had a prior negative experience with documentation. Many clinicians were chastised by a supervisor or felt overwhelmed by paperwork requirements at an agency. Acknowledging these negative experiences is crucial to creating a new reality and forming a different relationship with documentation.

2. *Was there an area in which you felt confident?*

Perhaps you have trouble staying on top of writing progress notes, but you are very comfortable with your policies and procedures. Identify these positive experiences as well!

Take about five minutes to reflect on what came up for you - any experiences, thoughts, feelings. Once you have completed the reflection, picture yourself after reading this book and using the templates provided.

- What changes would you like to see happen?
- How will you know you've made a good investment (in both time and money)?
- Choose 1-2 goals for yourself to achieve and write those down.

Now you have an end game for reading this book. You have something to work towards and to guide you along the way. There is a lot of information in this book. Whenever you start to feel overwhelmed, go back to those 1-2 goals and focus on what will help you get there.

WHAT TO FOCUS ON FIRST

It may be tempting to jump straight to the progress note templates or example files. However, the intention of this book is to teach you how to think about documentation, as well as offer practical examples so you can see the overarching principles in action. One without the other is not nearly as useful.

Options for where to start

Consider your reason for purchasing this book and your answers from the quiz in the previous section. Begin with chapters related to those topics. While this book does follow the common psychotherapy journey, starting with intake and ending with discharge, the chapters do not need to be read in order. However, if the entire book feels overwhelming but you are unsure where to start, below are some suggestions.

- Even if you don't bill for insurance, reading Chapter 3 about medical necessity will help with formulating treatment plans based on what your client identifies as their goals at intake. If you work in an agency or community mental health center, this chapter will be especially important.
- Chapter 4 includes information that relates to every clinician working with clients. While

you may not conduct in-depth intake assessments, all clinicians have a first session with each client. This chapter walks you through more than just documentation. It helps you establish therapeutic rapport, while making sure you can practically apply one of the most important ethical concepts - informed consent.

- Chapters 8 and 9 both focus on progress notes. Chapter 8 provides guidance on the ethics of progress notes, common components, and how to document various common scenarios. Chapter 9 dives into the common problems that come up for clinicians of all experience levels. It offers advice for a variety of problems and scenarios - with a focus on managing the struggles that tend to become patterns negatively impacting both documentation and work satisfaction. If your first thought related to documentation is "I hate progress notes," then Chapter 9 may be a great place to start.

There is really no bad place to start. Any of the chapters identified above will give you real-world tips and knowledge you can implement with clients immediately.

LIMITATIONS OF THIS BOOK

Ethics, not rules

This book prioritizes ethical clinical practice, which rarely identifies "one right way" to practice. Whenever I provide a documentation training I always warn the participants that my answer to almost every question starts with, "It depends." Ethics provide principles and guidelines for a reason - because there is no way to outline every potential scenario when real life humans are involved.

While this book does provide examples, cheat sheets, and breaks down complex concepts such as informed consent into a literal checklist for intake assessment, you will only find this book as good as your clinical judgment. You may have to evaluate which principles apply to you specifically, based on not only your profession, but also your clinical specialty. A clinician who works with couples, for example, will have different things to consider than someone who works with children. Likewise, a psychologist may have different standards than a social worker or a marriage and family therapist.

Clinical setting and location

This book uses the most recent ethical guidelines set forth by AAMFT, ACA, AMHCA, APA, and NASW. It also uses my 10 years of clinical consulting experience working with clinicians in settings such as mental health agencies, group and individual private practice, college counseling, and other community-based settings. While I have experience working with clinicians across the world, the ethical principles and laws mentioned are specific to the United States.

Your country may have different expectations and requirements. Likewise, your specific setting may set limits or guidelines that conflict with some of the guidance in this book. Always follow relevant laws and requests from supervisors and management, but also show them the strategies in this book and ask how you might be able to implement some of the practices suggested. It is worth asking!

Insurance billing

Medical necessity requirements are an essential component of this book and covered in Chapter 3. However, documentation for insurance requirements is not the same as billing. Billing is a specialty to itself, and this book does not cover aspects specific to billing, aside from a review of the CPT codes. Concepts of reviewing informed consent related to insurance, audits and records reviews, documenting the need for extended sessions, etc. are covered in Chapter 3, but focus on the clinical documentation, not billing practices.

I recommend Barbara Griswold's book, *Navigating the Insurance Maze* (2022), for those who want a resource that is tailored specifically to all things insurance related. She provides in-depth explanations and examples, along with interviews from a billing expert.

Therapeutic modalities

This book reviews a variety of psychotherapy practices and interventions but is not specific to any modality or population. Some of this is purposeful. There are many workbooks available for EMDR, CBT, and almost any other popular psychotherapy modality. These books offer pages and pages of interventions and examples. They rarely offer guidance on the underlying principles, and they often provide so many examples that the options become overwhelming.

You will find the treatment planning and psychotherapy interventions in Chapters 7 and 10 cover a variety of modalities. While this may be a limitation if you were expecting to create an "EMDR template" from this book, many modalities use similar language. You are likely to find multiple helpful options. My experience has also shown me that most clinicians prefer to include options from multiple modalities in their templates.

THE TOP 2 TIME SAVING TIPS FROM THIS BOOK

There are two phrases I find myself saying in almost every training that I facilitate:

1. *Never write anything twice.*
2. *Any note is better than no note.*

Remember these two phrases throughout this book. They serve as both time saving tips, and reminders to focus on what is necessary, rather than guessing at what might be necessary and including every possible piece of information.

Never write anything twice.

This phrase is especially helpful to keep in mind when completing intake paperwork and treatment plans. If you wrote about symptoms in one form, there is no need to write them again. Simply reference where the information is located (e.g. "See intake assessment"). This saves so much time, especially when it feels like templates from an electronic health record (EHR) or other resource are asking for the same information over and over. Simplify the process for everyone and only write it once.

Any note is better than no note.

This phrase speaks to the fact that many clinicians let perfectionism keep them from writing progress notes at all. If you find yourself sitting in front of a computer screen and avoiding documentation, keep this phrase in mind. A progress note with a grade of C+ is worth far more than a blank progress note. Not every note will be your best documentation or represent your best clinical work. And that's okay.

ACCESSING THE ONLINE RESOURCES

You likely purchased this book for not only the guidance, but the templates! All of the templates included in Chapters 5, 7, 10, and 12 are available for personal download online at **QAPrep.com/SFD-Resources**.

Also included with your purchase and available at **QAPrep.com/SFD-Resources**:

- **Example client files** that have all the forms and multiple progress notes to provide an example of what a full client file looks like over time. There are two example client files, one adult file and one child file.
- **Video trainings** on how to download and edit the templates for personal use, how to integrate the templates with your electronic health record (EHR), and how to adapt the templates to an organizational setting.
- **Bonus training on reviewing records,** with a review tool that you can download and use, regardless of your clinical setting.

- **Graduate coursework resources** such as handouts, exercises, and learning assessments specific to each mental health discipline.
- **Bonus templates and forms,** such as a sample client letter, email communication templates, and a Paperwork Catch Up Plan.

You will need an email address to access the online resources, but they are all complimentary. All of the templates are available as Google Docs so that updates are integrated and accessible seamlessly.

Quick Read Chapter Summary

- This book offers guidance for clinicians in all clinical roles, from student to clinical supervisor to private practice owner.

- Identify your goals for using this book by completing the reflective quiz in this chapter.

- Focus on the aspects that relate to your goals first, since this book can be read out of order to better suit your needs.

- This book offers guidance based on ethical principles but does not provide details about aspects like insurance billing or modality-specific interventions.

- There are two major time-saving tips in this book (and in all my workshops):

    - *Never write anything twice.*

    - *Any note is better than no note.*

NOTES

NOTES

Chapter 2

Foundations of *Ethical Documentation*

IN THIS CHAPTER

Documentation in Various Settings	24
Ethical Guidelines for Documentation	25
Creating Your Documentation Policies	28
Electronic Health Records (EHRs) in Various Settings	29
A Quick Review of HIPAA	32
Client Access to Records	33
Cultural Considerations for Documentation	34
Documentation in Your Own Style	35
Working Within the Context of an Organization	37
Quick Read Chapter Summary	40

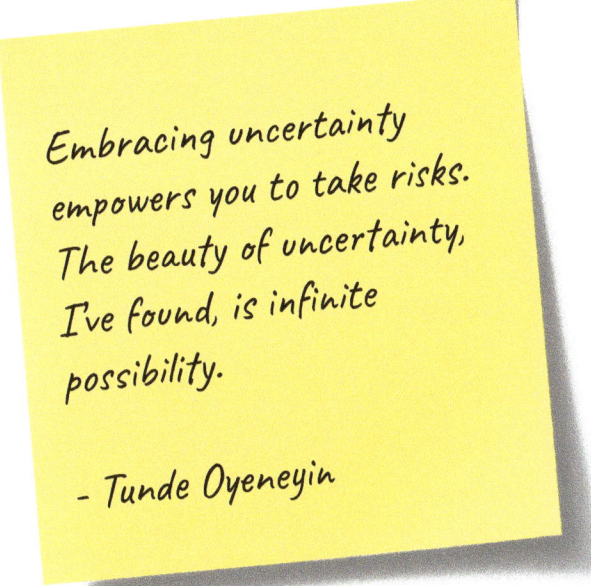

"We have to do it this way."
If you've worked in more than one clinical setting, you have likely heard at least more than one way to document the same circumstance. Documentation varies greatly based on the setting, but more importantly, it also varies *within similar settings.* This creates confusion for newly trained and seasoned clinicians alike.

What leads to this variety of interpretations on documentation requirements? Here are just a few potential reasons:

1. Professional associations offer very little guidance to provide freedom, or may offer specific guidance that becomes outdated in practice due to shifts in technology.
2. Quality Assurance Departments in organizations may adopt a sweeping standard in order to simplify training many employees at once.
3. Some agencies create specific policies as a reaction to poor audit results, rather than base policies on vague criteria identified in contracts. For example, an agency may require three interventions in every progress note, but this is not actually a rule identified by any insurance company.
4. Some supervisors have a personal preference for how things are written.
5. Insurance standards change over time and insurance companies do not always communicate these changes well, especially to clinicians in private practice.

6. Many clinicians have worked across multiple settings and for many years, but policies or laws have been updated since their initial training.

DOCUMENTATION IN VARIOUS SETTINGS

While this variation in documentation can be frustrating, it is actually a very good thing. Work settings for mental health professionals are too broad for any professional association or state licensing board to dictate the specifics of documentation.

For example, as a psychologist I have worked in 1) a community college disabled students center, 2) a field-based county crisis response team, 3) a school-based therapy setting, 4) a large outpatient mental health agency, 5) an in-patient psychiatric hospital, 6) an income-based work assessment program, 7) a federally mandated evaluation program in skilled nursing facilities, and 8) my own private practice.

The documentation within these jobs ranged from extremely detailed multi-page reports to two sentence notes. Sometimes documentation was shared within a team of other professionals who were not licensed clinicians, but were actively working with the same client. Sometimes the documentation was written for the client, and other times it was written for another entity with the goal of helping the client.

Later in this chapter, we will detail the main considerations for documentation policies regardless of clinical setting, along with how to integrate your own personal writing style into an organization that may have predetermined standards.

Clinician Spotlight: Lisa

Lisa was excited to leave her agency job, specifically because the administrative paperwork was overwhelming. Finally, she could just focus on seeing clients and not on paperwork!

However, when Lisa scheduled her first client she panicked. She knew that since this client was private pay she didn't need to complete all the forms she used to complete for clients in the agency, but she had no idea which forms she did need. That's when Lisa scheduled a consultation with me.

Lisa and I identified what was the minimum standard for her private practice documentation, but also what aspects of documentation felt meaningful to her. For example, Lisa hated writing detailed treatment plans that needed to be updated every three months, as she did in her agency job. However, she knew having some form of a treatment plan would be useful for tracking progress and encouraging clients.

We created a treatment plan template that was simple enough to complete with clients in session, so Linda would not need time for paperwork after sessions. We also identified an internal policy of when she would complete these treatment plans with clients (after the first session), and how often she would review them with clients (every six months).

When I worked with Lisa again years later, she did not feel overwhelmed by her paperwork and actually enjoyed using her templates because they improved or aided the clinical work she was doing in session. This is always my goal when working with therapists - to make the paperwork meaningful to the work you are doing in person with real clients.

ETHICAL GUIDELINES FOR DOCUMENTATION

As mentioned in Chapter 1, ethical guidelines for documentation are purposely vague and provide little clarity about what to actually include in a client file. For that reason, this section summarizes the concepts that relate to documentation, rather than specific standards. Understanding the broad concepts and similarities among the different professional codes of conduct provides a better framework for documenting ethically.

You will also find ethical principles from the various codes of conduct integrated throughout this book when reviewing more specific topics such as informed consent, treatment planning, progress notes, releasing records, and more.

The concept of beneficence
One concept that guides all mental health clinicians, regardless of discipline or client population, is that of *beneficence* (AAMFT, 2015; ACA, 2014; AMHCA, 2020; APA, 2017; NASW, 2021). This principle ensures that the clinician's actions always benefit the client first.

One part of beneficence is monitoring ourselves so we always provide the best treatment to clients. Regarding documentation, that means carefully evaluating your practices, beliefs, and feelings about documentation (and sometimes about insurance or other payors). This concept also reminds clinicians that documentation practices can shift based on client need.

Most importantly though, beneficence reminds us that forms, progress notes, and treatment plans are all meant to help us serve our clients. We are not guided to serve paperwork; the paperwork serves us.

This can be difficult to remember when trying to finalize a complex intake assessment, responding to an insurance audit, or completing 10 progress notes for clients from the last two days of intense clinical work. While I would argue that your in-depth psychotherapy session was absolutely more valuable for the client than the related paperwork, this is a "both and" situation. Yes, the majority of benefit to clients relates to the session itself, AND the related documentation is still relevant, important, and potentially beneficial for both you *and* the client.

For example, a client's personalized and up-to-date progress notes provide invaluable information when you are feeling "stuck" with a client. Reading through notes from 3-6 months ago has often helped me to identify specific progress the client has made, and helped me communicate that effectively with clients when they were feeling as though progress in treatment had stalled.

What do the ethics codes say about documentation?

If I were to sum up what the five major ethical codes of conduct for mental health professionals (AAMFT, 2015; ACA, 2014; AMHCA, 2020; APA, 2017; NASW, 2021) say about documentation in the *most simplified* terms, it would be this:

- Document all interactions with clients.
- Inform clients of their rights as early as possible.
- Inform clients of the nature of the therapeutic relationship as early as possible.
- Involve clients in treatment and respect their autonomy and agency.
- Clarify multiple roles as early as possible.
- Provide clients access to their treatment records except under extreme circumstances.
- Consider continuity of care when deciding what to document.
- Consider third party payors and comply with regulations.
- Consider potential readers of documentation. Be accurate and objective.
- Protect client confidentiality through practice and through physical and digital security methods.

There is actually quite a bit of guidance about documentation practices throughout *all* sections of the ethics codes, not just in the "Documentation" or "Record Keeping" sections. This speaks to the fact that documentation is truly a part of the entire client journey, not just at intake or when writing progress notes. To more adequately review these principles, details about each of the previous points are discussed in the relevant chapters, rather than expanded upon in this section.

Ethics versus laws

While ethics provide guiding principles, laws more often provide specific criteria and required actions. Most laws relating to mental health clinicians are state specific and therefore outside the scope of this book. The major exception is the Health Insurance Portability and Accountability Act (2013), a federal regulation more commonly abbreviated to HIPAA, which is discussed later in this chapter.

Licensing boards

Ethics and law often combine when licensing boards are involved. The purpose of a licensing board is to regulate services for the protection of the public. When there is an accusation or suspicion of misconduct by a clinician (or any other licensed professional), the relevant state licensing board investigates.

Investigations that involve mental health clinicians consider both law and ethics to determine 1) whether or not the clinician acted inappropriately, and 2) what consequences are appropriate for the situation. Documentation becomes crucial to these investigations. Client records are often requested and become a critical piece of evidence that can support the clinician's actions, particularly if the investigation is the result of a client complaint.

For this reason, I rarely recommend the "less is more" strategy for progress notes, and especially when any potential ethical dilemma or high risk scenario is involved. Board actions taken against mental health clinicians are public information. Visit the website for your licensing board to read some of the cases and see the common scenarios that arise and how documentation plays a supporting (or condemning) role.

Also notice that investigators always reference both the relevant state laws *and* the guiding ethical principles for that profession and related to the scenario. Ethics and law are separate but integrated. Much like the heart and the brain, they are both necessary for professional life and work in their own way toward the same goal - safe and supportive psychotherapy services.

CREATING YOUR DOCUMENTATION POLICIES

There are many potential documentation policies to consider based upon things like client need, clinical setting, state laws, and professional ethics guidelines. This section includes a review of common documentation policies, along with guiding principles and suggestions. Reference the provided intake forms in Chapter 5 for more details.

Identify which of these important considerations apply to your situation when deciding on record-keeping policies:

- State laws for length of record-keeping for adults and children
- Professional ethics guidelines for length of record-keeping for adults and children
- HIPAA *and* state laws on access to records for clients
- HIPAA *and* state laws on access to records for minors
- Insurance requirements for records (reference insurance contract or other guidelines)
- Accreditation or other regulatory requirements for records (more common for agencies)

Most or all of these considerations may be relevant to your situation and it is worth spending the time and energy to identify them. Let's review some of these specific policies to create more closely.

Top Tip

Always default to the most stringent requirement for any policy. In some circumstances that is your professional code of ethics, whereas in others it may be state law or even HIPAA.

Length of record keeping

One important consideration is how long you are required to keep records. As a psychologist, for example, the APA's *Ethical Principles of Psychologists and Code of Conduct* (2017) suggest maintaining records for adults for seven years after termination. However, some state laws have no specific requirement while other states require maintaining records longer.

Keep in mind that this requirement is very different for children versus adults. For children, the requirement for the number of years usually applies after the age of 18. For example, if you see a seven-year-old client for a few months you may be required to keep their records until they reach age 21, or even age 25 in states such as California. That's potentially 18 years of maintaining their records!

Identifying the timeframe for record keeping and adhering to a record keeping policy is equally important for a few reasons:

1. Clients may need access to their records after treatment ends.
2. Records may be requested for investigations or audits even after treatment ends.
3. Clinicians can protect client confidentiality by destroying records once the mandated record keeping period has ended.

Storage of records

For paper records, ensure the following is in place (HIPAA, 2013):

- Records are housed in a secure, private area.
- Access to records is granted only to those who need it.
- Records are securely destroyed after an identified timeframe.

For all electronic records (meaning records stored directly on a computer hard drive or other cloud-based system) make sure to have the following in place (HIPAA, 2013):

- Secure internet connection (e.g. never use public Wi-Fi)
- Encrypted files
- Password-protected access (both for hardware and logging in to software)

Cloud-based electronic health records (EHRs) may offer more security than a program available on a computer (such as typing progress notes in a Word document and saving directly to the computer). When saving directly to a computer, that computer must be encrypted and secured at all times. The clinician only has access to records if they have access to that computer.

ELECTRONIC HEALTH RECORDS (EHRS) IN VARIOUS SETTINGS

Electronic, cloud-based record keeping has quickly become the standard for mental health records. While certain settings, such as hospitals, are now required (in the U.S.) to use electronic record keeping, individual practitioners and smaller practices have options. Let's first define the various options within the world of electronic record keeping, and then review options based on the clinical setting.

Top Tip

An electronic record isn't perfect, but it's likely more secure than any protection you can provide on your own.

Personally, I know a clinician whose computer was stolen. And yes, they kept all their client notes on the computer hard drive. I also know a clinician who had records destroyed in an office flood, and a clinician whose office was broken into and the perpetrators opened locked file cabinets with client files. Lastly, I know a clinician whose office burned to the ground in a fire. However, that clinician used an electronic health record so this had no impact on their record keeping at all.

Electronic Health Record (EHR)

HealthIT.gov describes an EHR "as a digital version of a patient's paper chart. EHRs are real-time, patient-centered records that make information available instantly and securely to authorized users. While an EHR does contain the medical and treatment histories of patients, an EHR system is built to go beyond standard clinical data collected in a provider's office and can be inclusive of a broader view of a patient's care… One of the key features of an EHR is that health information can be created and managed by authorized providers in a digital format capable of being shared with other providers across more than one health care organization."

In other words, EHRs provide anyone treating the client (with some restrictions), and the client themselves, access to all the client's data and documentation. These systems streamline access and put all documentation, billing, and other administrative aspects all into one system.

EHRs are common in these settings: Hospitals, mental health agencies (private and public), integrated care settings, large group practices.

Electronic Medical Record (EMR)

This is the original version of the EHR. As medical practices integrated technology more, they initially used this term to describe formalized online records systems (Garrett & Seidman, 2011). EHR appears to be the more formally recognized term at this point.

Practice Management System (PMS)

These smaller but still very robust software systems help "healthcare practices with billing and administrative tasks. It can be used to schedule appointments, track patient records, and process insurance claims. A PMS can also help to streamline office procedures and improve communication between staff members" (Practice Management System, n.d.). Practice management systems are common in these settings: Group practices, individual or solo practitioner private practices.

What differentiates a PMS from an EHR is that practice management systems are usually meant for use within one organization. A PMS is used to communicate between the client and the clinician (e.g. signing intake documents), and sometimes among a smaller treatment team (e.g. a group practice supervisor, the clinician, and a medical biller). However, a PMS does not usually communicate with other groups or professionals *outside* of the internal organization.

There are many excellent EHR options for mental health clinicians, although none will ever be the "perfect solution." The decision about which EHR to use will likely come down to personal preference but here is a list of things to consider when shopping for an EHR:

- *Client portal:* A client portal makes electronic communication, signatures, and information sharing a secure and easy process for both clinicians and clients. It is essential that an EHR provide means for all your communication and document review with clients. The exceptions are telephone and potentially online meetings.
- *Individual or group practice:* If there are multiple clinicians in the practice you want the scheduling system to easily reflect this, offering options for booking rooms and potentially having multiple locations. Other considerations include supervisory review and co-signatures, access levels for various roles, and detailed reporting.
- *Projected growth and goals:* Even if you don't currently have clinicians working with or under you, is that something you strive to achieve? Plan ahead so you won't have to switch EHRs down the line.
- *Pricing:* While most EHRs offer a huge value considering the level of service and security they provide, there are various price points. For example, some charge based on access to certain features while others charge based on the number of active clients.
- *Payments and insurance billing:* Offering secure credit card payments simplifies billing for most clients. If you work with insurance then make sure the EHR can send electronic claims simply and also provide super bills to clients when needed.
- *Usability:* Lastly, consider the aesthetic and usability of the EHR. Is it easy for you to navigate after a five minute walk through? Could you easily describe to clients how to message you or sign a document? You will spend a lot of time using your EHR and you

want clients to have a positive user experience (Onyeaka et al., 2022), so this point is very important. Choose one that feels comfortable to you.

A QUICK REVIEW OF HIPAA

HIPAA stands for the Health Insurance Portability and Accountability Act. HIPAA is a federal requirement in the United States (HIPAA, 2013) but individual states may (and often do) have stricter guidelines. This book is not inclusive of most of HIPAA but as it relates to documentation let's review some basics of what mental health professionals need to consider.

The Centers for Disease Control and Prevention (2024) describe HIPAA as "a federal law that required the creation of national standards to protect sensitive patient health information from being disclosed without the patient's consent or knowledge."

The portion of HIPAA that most applies to documentation in mental health is called the "The Privacy Rule." Again, the Centers for Disease Control and Prevention offer an excellent summary: The Privacy Rule standards address the use and disclosure of individuals' health information (known as protected health information or PHI) by entities subject to the Privacy Rule. These individuals and organizations are called "covered entities."

The Privacy Rule also contains standards for individuals' rights to understand and control how their health information is used. A major goal of the Privacy Rule is to make sure that individuals' health information is properly protected while allowing the flow of health information needed to provide and promote high-quality healthcare, and to protect the public's health and well-being. The Privacy Rule permits important uses of information while protecting the privacy of people who seek care and healing.

Wondering whether or not you're a HIPAA covered entity? There is some nuance to this, but in general you are a HIPAA covered entity if you bill to a third party payor (e.g. insurance companies) electronically (HIPAA Omnibus Rule, 2013). Once you do this *one time,* you are a HIPAA covered entity. *For your entire mental health career.*

Although there is no tracking of covered entity status and no "lookup tool," it is very rare that a clinician has no covered electronic transactions related to providing services. For this reason, I recommend you assume you are a HIPAA covered entity and act accordingly. This may seem frustrating, especially considering many clinicians unknowingly become a HIPAA covered entity when they participate in an internship that bills on their behalf. However, consider that even if you were not a covered entity, the standards of HIPAA are often considered the minimum standard of care for mental health professionals.

HIPAA deals with two issues that relate to every mental health professional: 1) Access to records and 2) Coordination of care among healthcare professionals. These are clearly two clinical issues and things that are important to discuss with all clients. We will discuss coordinating care in Chapter 11.

CLIENT ACCESS TO RECORDS

Discuss with all clients their ability to access records and your responsibility to keep records private (regardless of whether or not you are considered a HIPAA covered entity). An important part of informed consent is clients understanding they have access to their records, how long it may take you to provide that access, and circumstances in which access may be limited.

Keep in mind that it is critical to identify *who* you consider a client and how that relates to your record-keeping. For example, do you consider a couple to be the "client" when treating them for couples therapy? If so, do you keep separate files/records for each individual in a couple, or keep one "client couple" file?

There are ramifications, both positive and negative, for each option (Matthews, 2020). Make a decision and be consistent, informing clients of this process and what that may mean for their situation (e.g. if one member of a couple wants to access records later on but the other member declines).

Related to both HIPAA and client's access to records, all covered entity clinicians in the United States should provide clients with a *Notice of Privacy Practices*. This form is colloquially called "The HIPAA Form" in many therapist circles. Clients are not required to sign the form itself, but the clinician does need to seek signature confirmation that the form was provided to the client. See the example in Chapter 5 of this book or in the Online Resources at **QAPrep.com/SFD-Resources**.

One requirement of any Notice of Privacy Practices form is to include contact information for the "Privacy Officer." There must be a Privacy Officer for every mental health practice, even if that includes only one solo practitioner. This person does not have to be a mental health clinician. Large organizations may designate an attorney or operations staff member for this role, since the primary purpose is managing client access to records. The key is to identify *someone* as the Privacy Officer and to keep this information up to date.

CULTURAL CONSIDERATIONS FOR DOCUMENTATION

Culture is commonly discussed in relation to clinical practice but not as often in relation to documentation. However, integrating culture into documentation provides a way to more quickly establish rapport with clients and to keep all aspects of their personhood at the forefront of care.

I describe culture as looking at the various components that relate to a person physically, socially, and spiritually; and considering how those components interact with the world and contribute to identity. The CLAS standards (Office of Minority Health, 2000) provide the following definition of how culture impacts healthcare:

> Culture defines how health care information is received, how rights and protections are exercised, what is considered to be a health problem, how symptoms and concerns about the problem are expressed, who should provide treatment for the problem, and what type of treatment should be given. In sum, because health care is a cultural construct, arising from beliefs about the nature of disease and the human body, cultural issues are actually central in the delivery of health services treatment and preventive interventions.

There is much to consider here so let's get practical and identify how culture works together with documentation. Here are some potential cultural considerations:

- Gender and gender identity
- Race
- Ethnicity
- Religion
- Language
- Sexual orientation
- Nationality
- Immigration status
- Disability

Consider the language used in your clinical forms. Is it gender-specific? Is it neutral and inviting? Does it prompt clients to provide their own interpretations or select from a variety of options when that may be helpful? Sometimes very slight shifts in language can make information much more accessible.

Also consider the following questions related to your general practice, regardless of the clinical setting:

- Is there anything unique to your work because of your own culture?
- Is there anything unique to your work because of the culture of your clients?
- Have you adjusted any services you provide based on the cultural needs of your clients?

It may also help to consider subculture populations in order to personalize language. For example, if you work with military personnel then asking about rank is important for understanding some of the client's roles and responsibilities. Or if you work with couples who identify as part of the kink community you can include more detailed questions about sexual practices.

In this way the documentation keeps you alert to cultural considerations and how this may impact treatment. Forms and documentation policies actually prompt you as the clinician to note important aspects of the client, and the documentation process shows that you value your client's culture.

DOCUMENTATION IN YOUR OWN STYLE

There are many barriers to completely customizing your documentation, but it is still possible to identify a style of writing. My experience working with hundreds of therapists in a variety of settings is that identifying what impacts your personal documentation style saves both time and effort for the lifetime of your career.

Below are some considerations for identifying what style of documentation works best for you. There is no "one right way" to document. The best way is usually whatever benefits the client in the simplest and easiest way for the clinician to complete.

Your skill and comfort level with English and writing
If you struggle with writing, that may also apply to notes. Similarly, if you are wordy and process while writing or if you obsessively edit your writing, that may also apply to notes. Know this about yourself and accept it now as part of your documentation process.

When you are able to create your own custom templates, keep these factors in mind so that you make documentation easier with personalized parameters. See Chapter 10 for more specific guidance on how to use templates to help with writing.

Your personal beliefs about the client/therapist dynamic

Even using the word "client" or "therapist" in documentation is a personal choice. Some clinicians use "patient" instead and others use the client's name. These options are all correct and are largely formed by your own beliefs about the psychotherapy dynamic. Own your style, while recognizing it is one of many "right" options.

Your clinical training and clinical specialties

Some clinicians are specifically taught never to document while the client is present and others incorporate client feedback or detailed tracking from the onset of therapy. This will have a huge impact on what you choose to document, along with how much you document and whether or not you involve the client in that process.

Your conceptualization of client needs and DSM diagnostic criteria

DSM diagnoses are helpful for quickly describing clusters of symptoms, but not all clinicians choose to diagnose their clients. Furthermore, not everyone in therapy meets criteria for a diagnosis. However, clients generally do seek therapy when they are feeling unwell or have a problem to work out with professional guidance.

An important role of documentation is describing both the negative and positive aspects of clinical work. It is helpful to determine how you will document problems, symptoms, behavior, progress, and DSM diagnosis. Consider how you discuss these things with clients and use that as the framework for how to document.

Your willingness (or need) to accept insurance

Related to the consideration above, when you work with insurance companies you are accepting that certain documentation standards apply. Specifically, all documentation for clients using insurance (in the United States) must support a DSM diagnosis.

There are many clinicians who choose not to work with insurance companies for this reason, and that is a valid choice. Weigh the options for your circumstances and clinical beliefs to determine whether or not this will be an important factor in your documentation style.

Clinician Spotlight: James

James was excited to begin working in a group practice after working at an agency for the last two years. He would have clients with less intensity, more flexible hours, and he was sure he would have less paperwork.

While these things were all true, James quickly found the lack of direction with documentation was anxiety provoking. No one was checking in with him about what was completed. There was no initial training and no examples of how to write progress notes in a private practice setting.

He found himself falling into a pattern of getting over a month behind in notes, then frantically catching up over the weekend or by staying up late at night. This was a very different stress from the stress of detailed agency paperwork and strict deadlines. The "freedom" to do paperwork his way was actually distressing!

When James discussed this with his new boss, they explained that they wanted to offer flexibility for clinicians and that "it doesn't really matter as long as you get your notes done."

James joined the Paperwork Catch Up Group for direction on what to put in his progress notes and how to stop the cycle of avoidance. Although James did have to use the note template and EHR determined by his boss, he was able to identify his own writing style and choose phrases he commonly uses to create cheat sheets for his notes and treatment plans.

Within a few weeks, James was spending far less time and mental effort writing progress notes. He was able to adapt the group practice templates to his own style so that writing felt both natural and meaningful to the clinical work. He then felt confident enough to discuss with his new boss the need for more frequent accountability and deadlines. Within a few months, James had all the systems in place to be successful within the group practice and enjoy his time more freely.

WORKING WITHIN THE CONTEXT OF AN ORGANIZATION

Early in clinical experience there are two common parameters for documentation style: 1) Agency or clinic policies, and 2) Supervisor preferences. Both of these parameters are largely out of your control. However, it is still possible to use many of the strategies identified in this book.

Here is the key to using this book to simplify documentation when you have no control over documentation requirements: Consider each of the templates in this book as cheat sheets with categories.

For example, a supervisor might say they do not like bullet points in documentation and want you to use full sentences. All of the checkbox sections in any template provided can be easily formatted into full sentences. Browse through the available options and create sentences, or even starter phrases, that feel most relevant to your work.

Another common example is the requirement to use a SOAP note format. This is my least favorite progress note template because the sections (Subjective, Objective, Assessment, and Plan) are ambiguous and there is little consensus among experts on what specific information goes in each section. However, if you are required to use this template, or any other specific progress note template, there are options.

Review the Progress Note Narrative Starter Phrases in Chapter 10 to see recommendations for what topics relate to each section of a SOAP note. This is the beginning of your personalized SOAP Note Cheat Sheet. If you'd like more examples to have ready for use, also review the options in the Potential Progress Note Components. Add these options to the relevant sections within the SOAP template so you have phrases ready for any progress note scenario. Ideally, you'll be able to write using bullet points and make this process very simple.

Does this process take a bit longer to set up? Yes. Does it still save hours of time and mental effort? Also yes.

Top Tip

Access the bonus content and resources at QAPrep.com/SFD-Resources for a video walk through of how to create personalized cheat sheets that work with commonly used progress note templates. There is also a Progress Note Example: Narrative in Chapter 10 that correlates to many agency and organizational standards for progress notes.

Working within the confines of outside parameters makes documentation both more simple and more complicated. While you may not have flexibility to write the way you like or use your own templates, ideally, you will also receive more guidance on how to document.

When necessary, ask for support with documentation examples and direct feedback. Share this book with a supervisor to see how they would rate the example templates and files. Share this book with colleagues and work together to create cheat sheets that use language consistent with your organization. Documentation may feel complicated, but the power to simplify the process is always within grasp. Do the work up front and reap the benefits of stress free documentation for the entirety of your career.

Quick Read Chapter Summary

- Documentation requirements vary greatly among settings, and often, these requirements have evolved from compliance plans relating to poor audit results, or even from myths or odd supervisor preferences.

- Ethics guidelines for documentation are purposely vague in order to apply to multiple settings and provide flexibility for clinicians.

- Use the framework of ethical guidelines, state laws, and HIPAA to create practice policies that apply to the way you work and to your client population.

- Electronic Health Records (EHRs) provide increased ease and security for clinicians, but may require adaptation and adjustment.

- HIPAA is a federal regulation that provides guidance on client privacy and security of records, as well as client access to records.

- Clients generally have the right to access their mental health records, both legally and ethically.

- It is possible to adapt documentation to your own style, even if you work within the confines of organizational requirements. Create cheat sheets and starter phrases when unable to create your own templates and forms.

- Considering culture in documentation ensures you use language that represents your clients and provides them options to see themselves represented and understood as part of the intake process.

NOTES

Chapter 3

Insurance AND Medical Necessity

IN THIS CHAPTER

Types of Mental Health Insurance Coverage 43
What is Medical Necessity?.. 45
Using the Clinical Loop of Documentation 46
Discussing Insurance With Clients (Even if You're Private Pay) 49
Mental Health Services Covered by Insurance 51
Why Couples Therapy is Different for Insurance Clients 52
Dealing With Insurance Audits 55
Audit Red Flags 57
Quick Read Chapter Summary... 59

> To heal is to touch with love that which we previously touched with fear.
>
> - Stephen Levine

Documentation for insurance companies sometimes

requires more work but more importantly, it requires you to understand the purpose behind insurance and how insurance companies think. **Even if you are not contracted with insurance, it is important to understand concepts such as medical necessity so that you can fully explain this to your clients** (Griswold, 2022; Pope et al., 2021).

Before reviewing medical necessity, the most important thing to know about insurance, it is important to understand the different types of insurance coverage available to many clients. Insurance coverage is complicated within all of healthcare, and confuses many clients as well as clinicians. A basic understanding of insurance options (regardless of the clinician's involvement with each option) is part of providing informed consent and being a responsible clinician.

TYPES OF MENTAL HEALTH INSURANCE COVERAGE

There are many types of insurance coverage for mental health services, including the focus of this book - outpatient psychotherapy. These various types of insurance treat coverage of services and documentation of services differently, although they all do follow the basic principles of medical necessity reviewed earlier.

Below is a very broad overview of the various types of insurance coverage clients may use when accessing psychotherapy services:

- **Government insurance** plans include Medicare (federal coverage) and Medicaid (federal and state coverage). These plans are monitored regionally so while the overarching documentation requirements are the same, interpretation of those requirements can differ among states, counties, and individual auditors.
- **Commercial insurance** includes private companies such as Aetna, Blue Cross Blue Shield, and United Healthcare. These companies have similar but slightly different requirements for documentation and medical necessity. For example, while most plans cover the most common mental health diagnoses, some plans may cover more diagnoses than others. Clinicians are considered either in-network or out-of-network by most commercial insurance companies.
    - *In-network* means that the clinician is contracted with that insurance company. The clinician agrees to see clients with that insurance plan for a specified rate.
    - *Out-of-network* means the clinician is *not* contracted with that insurance company. Some clients are able to see clinicians who are out-of-network and still have services covered at a partial or even full rate, but this is less common.
- **Employee Assistance Programs (EAPs)** are provided as an employment benefit by many large companies. EAPs often have fewer documentation requirements, and may not require a mental health diagnosis, but usually limit the number of sessions and expect the clinician to refer the client for issues requiring long-term care.
- There are other funding sources for psychotherapy that include things like employee wellness programs, victims of crime funds, and other government or privately funded initiatives. These will have a wide array of documentation requirements, from reporting only dates of sessions to providing summary reports.

Some clients qualify for more than one insurance plan, which can both increase their access to care and sometimes complicate documentation and billing. In addition to insurance coverage, some clients also have additional funds they can use for psychotherapy through a Flexible Spending Account (FSA) or Health Savings Account (HSA).

For clients who use out-of-network insurance coverage, the clinician provides a "superbill." A superbill is a summary of treatment, like a billing statement or receipt, and provided monthly or weekly. This is submitted to the insurance company directly by the clinician or given to the client so they can submit for their own reimbursement. Many electronic health records will automatically send these to clients.

WHAT IS MEDICAL NECESSITY?

The most important documentation concept related to insurance is that of *medical necessity*. Medical necessity is important because it determines whether or not you will receive reimbursement for providing a service, and determines approval of services (even if *you* are not contracted with insurance and *your client* is seeking reimbursement).

Each insurance company has their own definition, but usually medical necessity includes the following three main components:

1. **Diagnosis** - this is a literal, current DSM diagnosis and it is required for all insurance companies. Some DSM diagnoses, including Z codes, are not approved by many insurance companies so make sure you are aware of any limitations in your contract with the insurance company and that you communicate this limitation with your clients.
2. **Impairment** - this relates to the diagnosis, meaning that the diagnosis causes the client to be impaired in some way. Here are four general life areas that easily determine if the client is impaired by their diagnosis: social functioning (including family relationships), employment (or school for children), health, and daily living.
3. **Treatment Intervention** - this is what you as the clinician will do to treat the identified diagnosis and impairment.

In the initial intake session your goal is to identify a diagnosis and how that diagnosis impairs the client's functioning. Then you create a treatment plan to alleviate the impairment(s) and symptoms, and document this in ongoing therapy sessions. After the intake assessment your documentation goal shifts into consistently showing two things: Progress *and* impairment.

There is an art to documenting medical necessity for mental health services because the goal is to simultaneously portray that:

1. This client needs psychotherapy to address their impairments *so insurance should keep paying for it*, and
2. Psychotherapy is working to alleviate the client's impairments (or maintain recent improvements) *so insurance should keep paying for it*.

The phrase "the golden thread of documentation" is often used to describe this art of interweaving various components within each piece of documentation in the client's file. However, I prefer a different phrase to describe how this practice realistically plays out over time - the clinical loop of documentation (Los Angeles County DMH Program Support Bureau Quality Assurance Division, 2010).

USING THE CLINICAL LOOP OF DOCUMENTATION

While it is important to connect all the pieces of a client's file together, documentation is not a linear process from intake to discharge. The clinician is constantly tying all these pieces together, reassessing, adjusting treatment plans, and documenting progress along the way. That is why I prefer "the clinical loop of documentation" to describe how to document medical necessity throughout treatment.

THE CLINICAL LOOP OF DOCUMENTATION

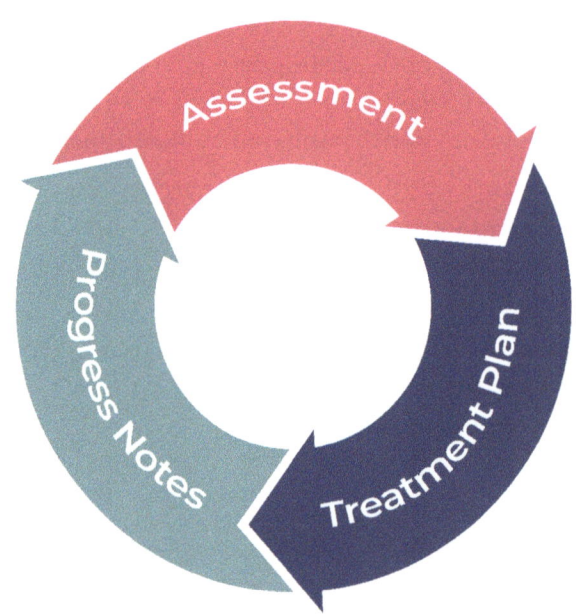

Each of the sections within the Clinical Loop of Documentation is important enough to warrant their own chapters, but we will review how these sections work together briefly.

During the initial intake *Assessment* it is critical to gather plenty of data that supports a DSM diagnosis. This will serve as the foundational evidence to show insurance that your client needs mental health services.

Your other important goals during an intake assessment are to build rapport with a new client and better understand the problem they are hoping therapy will solve. Balancing all of these can be a tricky process for even experienced clinicians.

An easy to remember acronym that helps with gathering relevant information during any assessment is FIDO, which stands for:

- **F**requency of symptoms/problem
- **I**ntensity of symptoms/problem
- **D**uration of symptoms/problem
- **O**nset of symptoms/problem

Asking questions related to these four areas ensures that you will gather the best information to support a diagnosis, even when symptoms may apply to multiple diagnoses.

Frequency = the difference between ADHD versus no diagnosis
Intensity = the difference in descriptive levels of a depressive disorder
Duration = the difference between mania and hypomania
Onset = the difference between Acute Stress Disorder and PTSD

FIDO also creates an excellent foundation for *Treatment Planning*, the next portion of the Clinical Loop of Documentation. Insurance companies want to see that you have thought through the therapeutic process and have a realistic plan for how to treat the client.

Use details related to **F**requency and **I**ntensity to provide clear measures and descriptions for treatment goals. This will help your client better evaluate their progress in an objective manner throughout treatment. This will also inform which therapeutic modalities and interventions you choose to highlight in the treatment plan.

Progress Notes then show the ongoing story of how the clinician and client work together in psychotherapy to achieve the client's treatment goals. Therapy is not a linear process and progress notes should reflect this common push and pull of two steps forward, one step back.

The Clinical Loop of Documentation emphasizes the need for documentation to adjust to changes in your client's needs and treatment. Always make the documentation suit the clinical work, rather than the other way around.

Do	Don't
Document small, incremental progress.	Under- or over-represent client progress.
Document lack of progress.	Ignore when a client is not progressing.

Do	Don't
Adjust treatment goals when they no longer apply.	Adjust notes to fit treatment goals that no longer apply.
Assess and adjust the diagnosis when symptoms change.	Keep outdated diagnoses that no longer describe the client.

Clinician Spotlight: Mary

Mary booked a consultation with me after receiving an audit notice. She was being audited by a private insurance company for all her current clients, which stood out to me as highly unusual.

When we met and reviewed her files it became apparent that she was diagnosing every single client with Adjustment Disorder and then never updating this diagnosis, regardless of how long she was providing treatment (which was often for many months or years). She had been doing this for over 10 years of private practice.

Mary valued her client's privacy and did not believe a diagnosis was relevant to whether or not someone should be able to access psychotherapy. She was trained to look beyond a diagnosis and consider the person holistically.

When insurance pays for psychotherapy they do have the right to audit client files, and insurance ALWAYS has medical necessity criteria to determine whether or not therapy is needed. This is an agreement that clients make with their insurance companies and an agreement that therapists make with insurance companies when they decide to contract with them.

Unfortunately, the insurance company determined that many of Mary's clients did not meet medical necessity criteria and she was required to pay back tens of thousands of dollars to the insurance company.

I recommended two simple things for Mary to avoid this situation in the future: 1) That she always revise a diagnosis of Adjustment Disorder after six months of treatment. 2) That she create a more structured intake process so she can better diagnose clients early on and avoid Adjustment Disorder, if possible. Thankfully, these were changes she was able to implement immediately.

DISCUSSING INSURANCE WITH CLIENTS (EVEN IF YOU'RE PRIVATE PAY)

Clinicians often feel pressured to balance 1) the ethics of accurate documentation with 2) advocating for clients to receive mental health care, regardless of their presentation or diagnosis.

Insurance does not pay for things such as "personal growth" or "improved self-esteem" on their own. While clients using insurance to pay for therapy might vary greatly in severity of symptoms, they all must meet criteria for a mental health diagnosis in order for an insurance company to pay for psychotherapy. And according to the *Diagnostic and statistical manual of mental disorders* [DSM-5] (2013), and thus, also to insurance companies, people meet criteria for a diagnosis when the related symptoms impair their life in some way.

This aspect of medical necessity is critical to discuss with clients as soon as possible (Pope et al., 2021).

Top Tip

This statement from the Medicare and Mental Health Coverage pamphlet (2024) sums up what any insurance company is looking for: "Although a provider may consider a service or test good medical practice, we don't pay for services without patient symptoms, complaints, or specific documentation."

In short, insurance only pays when a clinician is treating a client with DSM diagnosis related symptoms that are negatively impacting the client's life in a tangible way.

Inform clients of the following specific items when they decide to use insurance to pay for therapy (whether you contract with their insurance or the client submits a superbill for reimbursement):

- *Limits to confidentiality* - When insurance pays for psychotherapy, they expect access to records so they can audit for things like quality of care and potential fraud. While many clinicians are never audited, it is always a possibility.
- *Payment and approval of services* - Insurance companies sometimes require pre-authorization for mental health services. While good documentation helps, insurance may decide to restrict mental health treatment based on audit results or other criteria. They may deny claims and therefore, payment might be significantly delayed. All of these

are important to consider when creating policies. It is important to inform clients of the potential drawbacks related to this, such as denial of treatment and what you expect regarding payment for no shows.

- *Required mental health diagnosis* - A DSM mental health diagnosis is required by insurance companies as part of medical necessity. However, a diagnosis alone does not mean psychotherapy will be approved. And not all diagnoses are considered treatable via psychotherapy, therefore, some clients may meet criteria for a diagnosis *and* show significant impairment, but insurance does not approve services.

The key takeaway regarding informed consent is that clients 1) should be informed that they will have a recorded mental health diagnosis, and 2) insurance can request mental health records at any time and may choose to make a determination about continued services based on those records.

Explain to clients that insurance requires a mental health diagnosis and ask if they have questions about what that means and how it could potentially impact them in the future. Offer to discuss the diagnosis with them and explain that they are able to view their mental health records at any time.

The reality is being assigned a mental health diagnosis can have negative consequences for some people. It is important to explain this as part of the informed consent process so your client is aware of their options. While this conversation can feel intimidating to many clinicians, it is likely to increase rapport with clients (Thom & Farrell, 2017) and improve communication with them overall.

Considering all of the above, it is understandable that some clients with coverage may actually choose not to use their insurance. In particular, clients with high profile jobs, security clearances, and those with weapons requirements may prefer to pay for psychotherapy privately and avoid the necessity of a diagnosis.

Caution: When clients who have insurance coverage choose *not* to use their insurance, the clinician may still have limitations from the insurance company!

For example, a clinician who is contracted with an insurance company agrees to offer psychotherapy for all people with that insurance at a specific rate identified in their contract with the insurance company. Even if a client chooses not to use their insurance, the clinician is still required to honor the contracted insurance rate for that client, as long as they have that insurance. If the clinician charged their full rate and the client later chose to use insurance and/

or if the client asked their insurance company about this, the clinician would be required to pay back any fees above the contracted insurance company rate.

MENTAL HEALTH SERVICES COVERED BY INSURANCE

A common misconception is that insurance requires Cognitive-Behavioral Therapy. However, insurance is more concerned with medical necessity and client progress (Griswold, 2022) than with micromanaging therapeutic modalities or interventions that clearly fall within the field of psychotherapy. More commonly, insurance will outline the specific *types* of psychotherapy services they cover and provide a list of approved diagnoses.

Medicare is federal insurance coverage and provides a standard that many insurance companies follow. As of 2024, Medicare covers the following services relevant to a majority of mental health clinicians (this is not an exhaustive list):

- Alcohol misuse screening and counseling for adults who use alcohol but aren't dependent; if you detect misuse, we cover up to 4 brief face-to-face counseling sessions per year if patient is competent and alert during counseling
- Biofeedback therapy, where patients learn non-drug treatments to control bodily responses like heart rate and muscle tension
- Diagnostic psychological and neuropsychological tests
- Electroconvulsive therapy (ECT) treating depression and other mental illness using electric current to the head
- Family psychotherapy with or without patient present, as medically reasonable and necessary, with patient treatment as the primary purpose
- Hypnotherapy
- Individual and group psychotherapy; individual therapy with 1 or more therapists or more than 1 individual in therapy session with 1 or more therapists
- Interactive psychotherapy
- Interactive telecommunications system, including interactive, real-time, 2-way audio-only technology to diagnose, evaluate, or treat certain mental health or Substance Use Disorders (SUDs) using telehealth services if patient is in their home
- Marriage and family therapist (MFT) services (also available through telehealth)
- Mental health counselor (MHC) services (also available through an acceptable telehealth mental health disorder service site)
- Psychoanalysis that treats mental disorders by investigating the interaction of conscious and unconscious elements

- Psychiatric evaluation that systematically evaluates a psychiatric disorder's causes, symptoms, and course and consequences
- Screening, Brief Intervention, and Referral to Treatment (SBIRT) services that are early interventions for individuals with non-dependent substance use to help them prevent more extensive or specialized treatment
- SUD treatment in a patient's home (now an acceptable telehealth substance use treatment or a co-occurring mental health disorder service site)

The list above highlights how inclusive mental health coverage can be under an insurance plan. Some of the phrases are not easily recognizable but these usually correlate to a specific billing code. For example, "Family psychotherapy with or without patient present" both describes the type of service and the associate billing code (90847). Notice there is no description of "couples therapy" because this is included within the definition of "Family psychotherapy." See more detail on this commonly confused service in the next section.

Medicare relaxed telehealth requirements during the COVID-19 pandemic but will reinstate some in person meeting requirements starting January 2025. However, documentation can play an important role in explaining when this may not be clinically appropriate. While these requirements could change, as of this writing Medicare requires the following: "Exceptions to the in-person visit requirement require a clear justification documented in the patient's medical record."

Each insurance company provides their own guidelines on medical necessity, covered services, telehealth protocol, billing codes, and covered mental health diagnoses. While they are all similar, they are not all the same. It is critical to know the specific guidelines for each insurance a clinician chooses to contract with.

WHY COUPLES THERAPY IS DIFFERENT FOR INSURANCE CLIENTS

As mentioned above, there is no insurance billing code for "couples therapy." Insurance defines all such treatment as "family psychotherapy," which is counterintuitive to many clinicians. "Family psychotherapy" includes any psychotherapy in which family members, regardless of the number of people or the relationship (e.g. parent and child; siblings; spouses) are involved.

However, clinicians need to think about this "family psychotherapy" very differently from how they were typically trained to think about couples or family psychotherapy.

Many clinicians view the couple (or in the case of family psychotherapy, the whole family) as the client. This view informs treatment planning, interventions, modality, and also has significant legal and ethical impact. But notice the full description used by Medicare in the section above (which applies to all insurance companies): "Family psychotherapy with or without patient present, as medically reasonable and necessary, <u>with patient treatment as the primary purpose</u>."

Insurance services are always billed for *one person*. Mental health diagnosis is a primary focus of medical necessity, and DSM diagnoses are assigned to *one person*. So while family psychotherapy, including with a couple, is covered by insurance, it is covered in order to treat an individual's mental health symptoms and impairment.

There is nuance regarding treatment and it is sometimes easy to incorporate a couples therapy type of "family psychotherapy" within medical necessity criteria. For example, an individual may have a mental health disorder that is negatively impacting their marriage. This person could seek individual psychotherapy to address this issue, but couples psychotherapy may provide even more benefit. Provided medical necessity criteria is met, insurance would cover both services. The key point is that in *both* circumstances, the "client" is still the individual.

This creates confusion for both clinicians and clients, particularly around issues of confidentiality and record keeping. It is critical to determine very clear policies around couples psychotherapy and insurance. Review these as part of the informed consent process in the beginning of treatment in order to avoid messy ethical situations and disgruntled clients.

Identify the following as soon as possible any time couples psychotherapy is billed to insurance (Griswold, 2022):

- Which person in the couple is the "identified patient" for insurance
- The diagnosis of the "identified patient" and relevant treatment goals
- Your treatment view of who is the client (e.g. you are billing insurance for one individual but view the couple as the client)
- Who has legal right to clinical records
- How you manage communication with one or both partners outside of sessions

In my experience, there are as many policy differences as there are clinicians. While there is clear guidance from insurance regarding medical necessity, there is no "one right way" to approach the issue of seeing couples and billing insurance for one individual. The best approach is transparency and clear (written and signed) agreements.

Clinician Spotlight: Annie

In reviewing real complaints made against psychologists to the California Board of Psychology, there is a case that highlights how important it is to clarify roles when providing couples psychotherapy. While this information is available publicly, the clinician will be referred to as "Annie" and the two clients referred to as "Sarah" and "Sam," in order to respect privacy.

Annie began seeing Sarah for individual psychotherapy and billed Sarah's insurance, Medicare. Sarah completed assessment measures during the intake session, such as the GAD-7, and signed all intake forms. She reported issues with her marriage as a primary concern.

In all following sessions over the next two months, Sarah brought her husband, Sam. Annie kept minimal progress notes but documented as if both Sarah and Sam were in couples psychotherapy. Relational dynamics were the main focus of each session. However, Annie billed Medicare for individual psychotherapy each time.

Sarah and Sam had a disagreement and Sarah left with their children. Sam was distraught and Annie provided an emergency session with him. During this session, Sam asked for a copy of his records. Annie refused this request and Sam later made a formal complaint to the Board of Psychology.

In the Board's report, it was unclear to the Board, as well as to Sarah and Sam, if Annie was providing individual or couples psychotherapy. In follow up interviews, Annie communicated viewing the treatment as couples psychotherapy. However, she never reviewed consent or policies with Sam, never discussed with Sarah the process of shifting into couples psychotherapy, and billed Medicare for individual psychotherapy the entire time.

Unfortunately, Annie was found in violation of multiple ethics codes. The key issue was lack of clarity around multiple relationships and informed consent. Using insurance further complicated this issue and created more confusion based on the billing codes used.

Regardless of the clinician's actions, Sarah and Sam may have experienced conflict, and Annie may have received a complaint to the Board. However, it is unlikely the issues would have escalated so quickly if Annie had been more clear about the therapeutic

> relationship from the beginning. And it would have been easier for her to problem solve with the couple once conflict did escalate.

DEALING WITH INSURANCE AUDITS

The most scary part of dealing with insurance for most clinicians is the potential for an audit. However, audits don't have to be scary and can actually be a great learning experience. They are also somewhat predictable, which means that clinicians can plan ahead for success.

Audits, treatment reviews, and administrative reviews are all different ways that insurance companies review quality, monitor policy member needs, address concerns, and prevent fraud (yes, some clinicians really do commit fraud!). There are various ways insurance companies do this, including 1) Phone calls with Care or Case Managers (who are usually licensed mental health professionals), 2) Requests for records, and 3) Requests for a treatment summary.

The purpose of these requests varies and sometimes has little to do with the clinician or even with the client's specific treatment. Here are some common reasons insurance companies reach out for audits and/or reviews:

- Monitoring to make sure high needs clients are receiving appropriate treatment, using that treatment, and not receiving anything unnecessary.
- Authorization of treatment (or continuation of a prior authorization).
- Clinical appropriateness of treatment and whether or not documentation was completed correctly, based on the insurance plan's standards.
- Review of billing, coding practices, and dates of treatment.
- Data collection for overall member needs and statistics.
- Prevention and correction of potential fraud, waste, or abuse.

When interacting with insurance representatives, always keep the focus on how the client is being helped, keeping in mind that this help may *also* be in the best interest of the insurance company. For example, it is far cheaper for an insurance company to pay for outpatient psychotherapy twice a week than for a client to discontinue services, decompensate, and then require two weeks of expensive inpatient care. Use any opportunity to highlight such potential examples, especially if the client has a history of needing more intensive care.

Be prepared whenever calling the company, having your provider number and any client identifying information readily available. Review the request from the insurance company and then ask for confirmation of what they need. It is not uncommon for the initial request to include any and all documentation, but what they actually want is a simple summary.

If you go into an audit treating it as a learning experience, it most often is and the auditors involved are usually more than willing to help you learn. During and after an audit, ask questions of the auditor and let them know you are curious about their findings. Auditors are usually willing to share feedback with you in the moment and will explain what they are looking for or what they feel is missing. They may even offer specific suggestions about things you can adjust immediately. Auditors are clinicians, just like you, and they typically enjoy talking with other clinicians about the case and teaching about insurance requirements for documentation.

Top Tip

Out-of-network clinicians who provide superbills can be audited, too! Any time a client chooses to use insurance as payment for psychotherapy, they open up their records to be audited by the insurance company. The major differences for the out-of-network clinician is that 1) an audit is treated like any other records request, requiring client consent and authorization before sending records, etc., and 2) the clinician is not responsible for paying money back to the insurance company if the company deems services as not medically necessary. Refer to Chapter 4 for more information on informed consent and what to include in your policies related to insurance, even if you are out-of-network.

Regarding calls related to client care and/or authorizations for treatment, focus on the right combination of progress and ongoing need for treatment. Outline a potential timeframe in which some improvement will occur for the client. Insurance companies are not looking for vague descriptions or open ended treatment plans, and appreciate a direct assessment, as well as potential barriers. Case managers are typically familiar with the needs related to many mental health disorders and understand that clients often need many years of treatment.

One way to prepare for audits ahead of time is by reviewing client files with a simple and objective review tool. Do this before any contact with the insurance company, but also on at least an annual basis. This will help to maintain quality documentation and catch any potential mistakes before they become a problem (Benjamin, 2008). This is a task any clinician can do at any time, regardless of their clinical setting.

Keep the review simple and focused on client care/clinical quality. Incorporate any relevant insurance standards, if necessary. Then schedule a time once a year to review client files using the review tool. Review just 2-3 client files every three months, review all client files at a certain time of year, or just do one per month. Either way, this regular review won't take a lot of time but it will provide peace of mind.

There is further guidance on conducting your own quality reviews and a template for an objective review tool in the website resources available at **QAPrep.com/SFD-Resources.**

AUDIT RED FLAGS

Despite their scary reputation, audits do not have to be a burden for most individual clinicians. They are somewhat rare for clinicians in private practice and in larger agency settings, audits are usually handled by management or the quality assurance team. Audits are somewhat easy to predict, and are more likely to come up when working with clients more intensively. This is why the first step with any request from an insurance company is identifying *why this client and why now*.

Audits are typically triggered by 1) high or increased expenses for the insurance company, 2) quality review mandates for insurance companies, and/or 3) suspicions of fraud, waste, or abuse. However, an audit does *not* mean the clinician has done anything wrong. It simply means the insurance company is prompted to confirm that quality care is happening.

Here are some common reasons for audits related to psychotherapy services in practice:

- Providing psychotherapy to a client more than once a week
- Billing for more than one psychotherapy service in a single day
- Diagnosing all clients in the practice or agency with the same diagnosis
- Keeping a diagnosis of Adjustment Disorder for a client for more than six months
- Providing psychotherapy services for an extended period of time, such as for multiple years in a row

All of the above scenarios have a potentially relevant clinical reason. Unfortunately, there are clinicians who commit fraud or misuse insurance billing, and that is part of why these circumstances are more likely to trigger an audit.

Once the likely reason for the audit is identified, the clinician can take appropriate action to prepare for the audit. Become familiar with the client's symptoms and related impairments, as well as their progress to date. Identify exactly why outpatient psychotherapy treatment has helped and why it will continue to support the client.

Avoid changing diagnoses, treatment plans, and progress notes as a result of internal review. Instead, provide explanations for missing or incomplete documentation. Make note of what to improve or change moving forward. Then take a deep breath and know that you have done the best you can with the information you had at the time.

Special Note
Insurance is a large topic that could be a book on its own. In fact, it already is. Check out Barbara Griswold's book, *Navigating the Insurance Maze,* if you want a complete review of all things insurance and answers to more specific insurance-related questions, especially around billing and joining plans.

Quick Read Chapter Summary

- Third party payors include a variety of sources. Most of these require a mental health diagnosis and evidence of medical necessity to cover mental health services.

- Medical necessity includes 1) a mental health diagnosis, 2) significant impairment as a result of the mental health disorder, and 3) planned treatment that is appropriate for the disorder.

- The clinical loop of documentation explains that medical necessity is proven throughout documentation when 1) the intake assessment supports a diagnosis and identifies impairments, 2) the treatment plan identifies goals related to the diagnosis and impairments, along with appropriate interventions, and 3) progress notes document the ongoing process of psychotherapy, as outlined in the treatment plan.

- It is important to discuss with clients the potential limits of confidentiality related to using insurance to pay for psychotherapy.

- Insurance only considers clients to be individuals and as such, only covers couples or family psychotherapy in the context of treating problems related to an individual's mental health disorder.

- Audits are often easy to predict and related to more expensive services, such as billing for longer or more frequent psychotherapy sessions.

- Audits may provide a positive experience for private practice clinicians to learn from the insurance representatives, since insurance companies scale their expectations and provide teaching.

NOTES

NOTES

Chapter 4

Intake Assessment

IN THIS CHAPTER

Policies and Forms 64
What is Informed Consent for Treatment? 64
What Goes in a Client Record? 65
Connecting Policies to Forms 67
Setting the Stage for a Great Intake Interview 69
One Tip to Save Hours of Documentation Time 70
How to Ask Great Assessment Questions 71
Intakes With Minors, Couples, and Families 72
The Mental Status Exam 74
Case Conceptualization and Diagnosis Justification 75
Finalizing the Intake Assessment Process 76
Quick Read Chapter Summary 80

> *Success as a therapist is not found in doing something for the client, but rather in being someone for the client.*
>
> *- Dr. Ili Rivera Walter*

In my own anecdotal research, the most common licensing board actions against psychotherapists regarding their documentation start here with the very first session. When a licensing board reviews the client records they commonly identify:

- A lack of clarity about who is the client and who can access records,
- A lack of clarity around payment and insurance status,
- Poor documentation of the client's needs/problems for which they sought treatment and/or,
- Poor documentation of the therapist's plan for treatment.

This chapter will guide you through the key components of policies, forms, and intake assessments to help you avoid these complaints. However, there's another key element that impacts documentation from the very beginning - therapeutic rapport.

It is critical to identify that intake assessment is a *clinical process* first (Pope et al., 2021), and documentation plays a significant but supporting role in this process. Beautifully formatted forms and detailed intake notes are meaningless if a client feels disconnected in the first session. We will discuss strategies for how to establish rapport while managing documentation later in this chapter, but always consider this throughout all parts of the documentation process.

POLICIES AND FORMS

Policies are the way in which an organization or private practice does business. These determine standards for treatment of clients, finances, administrative tasks and everything in between. Carefully considered policies are the backbone of every form you have clients sign.

Forms, on the other hand, are simply proof that you have reviewed policies with clients. Forms also help to remind clients of policies after time has passed or when they need a question answered outside of session. Forms do not have to be scary or complicated and they usually have no mandated format.

This chapter explains the typical forms applicable to most mental health professionals. Use this information in conjunction with the guidance in Chapter 2 to ensure necessary topics are covered in your practice forms.

WHAT IS INFORMED CONSENT FOR TREATMENT?

Informed consent is a process, *not a form*. The American Psychological Association Dictionary of Psychology (2023) describes informed consent as "a person's voluntary agreement to participate in a procedure on the basis of their understanding of its nature, its potential benefits and possible risks, and available alternatives."

The process of informed consent begins as soon as possible but continues throughout treatment (ACA, 2014). It emphasizes that clinicians respect the autonomy and personhood of all clients (Darby & Weinstock, 2018), while also recognizing that clinicians have expert knowledge and therefore, should be mindful to share pertinent information on an ongoing basis and in understandable language.

Based on all relevant professional association guidelines, informed consent must be documented for all clients (AAMFT, 2015; ACA, 2014; AMHCA, 2020; APA, 2017; NASW, 2021). Depending on your state guidelines, it may or may not need to be a signed form. Some states allow verbal informed consent, *as long as the therapist documents this in a note*.

Make sure you take the time, as soon as possible, to review the concepts below with all clients. Revisit them as needed and make sure clients understand anything they are signing.

Topics to include as part of the informed consent process:

- Clinician's credentials, experience, and scope
- Potential benefits and drawbacks of therapy/counseling, along with treatment options and alternatives
- Limits to confidentiality (limits vary by state and license type)
- Payment and scheduling/cancellation policies
- Who is the client and who has access to records (especially important for work involving couples, minors, and families)
- Involvement of any third parties, including payors (e.g. insurance)
- Telehealth related information, if applicable

The above points should serve as the baseline information for the Consent for Services form (AAMFT, 2015; ACA, 2014; AMHCA, 2020; APA, 2017; NASW, 2021) in any clinical setting. Additional items will likely need to be included in a Consent for Services document and depend on the setting, clinical specialty, and client population. See the example form in Chapter 5 or in the online course companion at **QAPrep.com/SFD-Resources**.

Top Tip

One important thing to consider with informed consent is that a signed form does not guarantee you provided your client with the information. I have seen cases in which a psychologist was reprimanded by the state Board for having a signed form but not adequately reviewing the specific aspects of informed consent with the client. Talk with clients about the key elements of informed consent, even if they have reviewed and signed forms. Documenting this conversation with the client, *along with* having a signed form, is a better way to show evidence of obtaining informed consent.

WHAT GOES IN A CLIENT RECORD?

The client file houses almost all of the documentation related to any client. The following is a list of the minimum clinical documentation *components* for a client file (keep in mind this is *not* an exhaustive list and not every component correlates to a specific form or document):

- Client demographic information

- Payment and/or insurance information
- Signed intake forms (Consent for Services, etc.)
- Client history (Biopsychosocial Intake Assessment)
- Comprehensive mental status exam (MSE)
- Diagnosis and/or presenting problem
- Treatment plan
- Progress notes
- Closing case summary
- Supervision/consultation notes
- Medication records (as applicable)
- Correspondence (with or about clients)
- Consultations with other professionals
- Summary reports (written by you or others)
- Psychological and other testing reports (written by you or others)
- Releases of information (and reasoning for the release)

Some of these items may be combined in the same form or document. For example, a comprehensive MSE may be part of the Intake Progress Note or Intake Assessment rather than a standalone form.

Some items *may* be best served when kept separate from the client's file (APA, 2017). These include items that have what I call "the gory details." They often provide a level of detail that is clinically relevant or helpful, but is not necessary for things like coordinating care or for most requests for clinical records.

However, it is important to note that state laws vary and potentially *any* documentation can either be subpoenaed or accessed by the client. Do not use the list below as a way of hiding clinical information that you never want revealed. Always assume that anything documented can potentially be accessed by others.

Potential additional documentation to keep outside of the clinical record includes the following:

- **Process notes** - These are notes you keep for yourself. They serve as a way to jot down more personal comments, reflections, countertransference, etc. These notes are *optional*. Progress notes are *not* optional. See more information on this in Chapter 8.
- **Child abuse reports or other sensitive information** - Provide a note in the client's file

about *any* divulgence of confidentiality (more on this in Chapter 11) but there is no need to keep the actual abuse report in the client record. These reports tend to be quite detailed. A common practice is to have a separate but secure folder that houses all such reports, in case they are needed.

- **Drawings and artwork** - Some client artwork is very deep and shares a lot of meaning related to traumatic or other clinical events. Poems, stories and songs could be especially descriptive and potentially misinterpreted by others. It may be best for the client to take these home so the details are not part of the legal record. However, more benign artwork may be appropriate to keep in the client's record. Likewise, some clinicians rely on keeping these details in the clinical record as part of their modality. This requires clinical judgment and protocol may shift depending on the client and situation.

- **Client summaries for discharged clients** - It is helpful to have a summary with the general file for as long as records are required to be kept, but many clinicians also like to keep a summary after it is time to destroy the full client record. However, any documentation that is maintained continues to be discoverable. A separate (and securely maintained) list of "Closed Cases" names may be a better fit if you want to maintain minimal records of all clients.

There is no "one size fits all" recommendation for determining what to include in the client record. Large organizations and agencies may have different requirements and needs than solo private practitioners. A clinician in private practice may even choose different formats based on individual client needs.

The key is always to consider *why* something is in the clinical record. Do not include it because that is what was done in another setting or because another clinician does so. Embrace the ambiguity of documentation and determine best practices that fit the setting and situation.

CONNECTING POLICIES TO FORMS

You will find a template Consent for Services document in Chapter 5. However, this is a form that every clinician in independent practice must personalize based on their practice policies. Likewise, clinicians working in other settings must know these policies to a level they could explain them to any client during the first session.

While there is a lot of information in the Consent for Services template provided (and in most clinician's intake forms), there are a few key policies in addition to informed consent that are the most practical to personalize, understand, and review with clients (AAMFT, 2015; ACA, 2014; AMHCA, 2020; APA, 2017; NASW, 2021).

Use the following questions to determine practice policies in conjunction with the template in Chapter 5.

Limits to confidentiality

- ☐ Are you a mandated child abuse reporter and what does that entail?
- ☐ Are you required to report other circumstances, such as elder abuse?
- ☐ What are your required mandates for violence, threats, and intent to self-harm?
- ☐ For couples, families, adolescents, and children - What information (if any) is kept individually confidential and what are the potential limitations for this?
- ☐ For couples, families, adolescents, and children - Who is considered the client and who can access records?

Payment

- ☐ Who is paying (the client, insurance, a guardian/parent, a couple)?
- ☐ When is payment due/charged?
- ☐ What type of payment options do you offer?
- ☐ Will you use a collections agency for unpaid balances, if necessary?

Cancellations

- ☐ How much notice do you require for canceling an appointment?
- ☐ What fee do you charge if someone cancels late?
- ☐ How many cancellations do you accept before closing a client's file?

Communication outside of session

- ☐ What is your preferred method for clients to contact you about scheduling?
- ☐ What is your preferred method for clients to contact you about clinical issues?
- ☐ What should clients do in an emergency?
- ☐ Within what timeframe can clients expect a reply from you?
- ☐ Who would contact your clients if something happened to you?
- ☐ For couples, families, adolescents, and children - How do you manage one person contacting you outside of session?

Insurance

- ☐ With what insurance companies are you contracted?
- ☐ Who checks for the client's insurance eligibility?

- ☐ Who checks for the client's deductible? Who tracks this over time?
- ☐ What happens if the client loses their insurance coverage?
- ☐ Do you offer a superbill for clients to potentially seek reimbursement?

SETTING THE STAGE FOR A GREAT INTAKE INTERVIEW

In this section the phrase "intake assessment" references the first sessions (usually 1-4) when a clinician informs the client of the psychotherapy process, determines their needs and appropriateness for psychotherapy, gathers historical data, creates goals, and potentially identifies a diagnosis.

Many clients want to jump right in and share their story but the clinician has to manage building rapport with completing legal and ethical obligations related to paperwork. It can be helpful to remember that although the intake session is a different type of session from other psychotherapy sessions, it is still part of the overall treatment process (Miller et al., 2020). Connecting with the client is the main priority, even above documentation.

Here are some tips for creating a flow for the paperwork and clinical conversation to work in tandem so you can establish a connection while still completing the legal and ethical components of intake documentation:

- *Focus on the relationship.* The most important thing to do in the first session is to connect. Informed consent is part of the intake process because you are explaining potential limitations and offering to answer questions about the therapeutic process. Keep everything focused on the relationship.

- *Be transparent.* Explain *why* you may need to do certain things (e.g. obtain signatures or talk about diagnosis for insurance) so the client knows they are important.

- *Let the client lead the topics.* You might have a goal of what topics to review, such as family history and presenting problems, but if the client wants to start with something specific, that is important (Muecke, 2024). And the perfect place to start.

- *Go out of order.* Having a structured biopsychosocial intake form is helpful for staying on track (especially when starting out), but knowing the structure gives you the flexibility to go off script. Let the topics flow naturally based on the discussion rather than following forms. Better yet, follow the strategy identified in the next section of this chapter so you can completely avoid filling out any forms during the intake session.

- *Accept the bare minimum.* Focus on the critical aspects of confidentiality, consent, and why the client is seeking help. Any other documentation can be completed in future sessions.

You may be thinking, "*Okay, that sounds pleasant, but I have to collect enough information to assign a diagnosis for insurance.*" This is where following the recommendation in the next section is critical. It allows time for all of the above to happen in a way that focuses on the client's needs.

ONE TIP TO SAVE HOURS OF DOCUMENTATION TIME

The best way to save time on intake assessments is to have clients complete all the intake paperwork *before* the first session. Of course you will still want to ask some questions from your forms in person (e.g. questions about suicidality). Prior to the session, quickly browse what clients have already completed and know the most important topics to highlight when you are in the session together.

Become very familiar with the intake forms you use. This will save time and provide the setting to be present with the client while simultaneously completing documentation. Review key points from the intake and consent forms with every client, make sure everything is signed and move on.

If the client was unable to complete all of the intake assessment (including the biopsychosocial history form), then complete all the assessment information *in session*. Access the form (on your computer or on paper) to write as much as possible before the client leaves so you don't leave a pile of paperwork for yourself. Use as many quotes and bullet points as possible to write information while you are with the client.

My experience is that clients are very understanding of this strategy as long as I communicated what I was doing. For example, I may say "*Hold on juuuuust a second, I want to make sure I write that down.*" Or something like "*This is really important to you and I want to make sure I have that written here.*"

Involve clients by asking them what words they would use to describe something or asking them to draw or outline something to better clarify. I have never had a client become upset when I explained that I was simply trying to understand them more clearly and write their story.

Top Tip

One error I see a lot of clinicians make is having irrelevant information in their assessment form. For example, they might have detailed questions about school even though they do not see children and rarely see adults who are in school. Perhaps they copied from a supervisor or from an online resource and never personalized the document to their practice. If you have chosen a question because you think the information is valuable, ensure clients are completing it. And if not, remove it from the form! There is no need to waste everyone's time. Then, if a section is incomplete, you know to go back over it rather than ignore it.

HOW TO ASK GREAT ASSESSMENT QUESTIONS

An intake session is more than intake assessment and informed consent - it is the first psychotherapy session and the first chance to establish trust. Staying curious about the client's needs and desire for therapy will keep you both engaged while making it easier to get the necessary intake information you need.

Chow (2018) suggests that the intake session can have great emotional impact for clients, sometimes in a negative way. When questions are out of alignment with the level of familiarity and trust established, they can be experienced as invasive rather than healing. Chow suggests using questions "as a way to relate" (p.29) rather than to elicit responses merely about historical data, and to be patient about collecting information.

Quick tips for asking questions

1. **Start with the why.** One easy, and also very important, place to start the psychotherapy process is the reason for the client coming in to see you. Complete a thorough assessment of their needs and goals with a focus on how you will be able to help, always prioritizing connection and trust.

2. **Use open-ended questions** rather than those that elicit a "yes" or "no" response. If you accidentally ask a yes/no question, simply follow up with something like *"Tell me more about that"* or *"Would you mind explaining…"* Use the opportunity to learn more detail, gather more data or get a better understanding of your client.

3. **Avoid vague terms for certain questions.** If you want a specific answer, ask a specific question. Remember that your definition of something may not match a client's

definition. For example, I would consider anything like a misdemeanor or felony to be a "legal history" but I've had clients respond *"no"* to *"Do you have any legal history?"* and then answer "yes" to whether or not they had any misdemeanors or felonies. Know when you want to be specific.

4. **Avoid psychobabble when talking with clients** (Zuckerman, 2019). Many therapists describe their treatment modality in clinical terms that wouldn't make sense to most clients. Use language the client uses and encourage them to describe their experience in detail so you understand.

Yes, there are many topics to cover in the initial intake assessment. Leaving certain areas of the assessment incomplete is fine when the focus remains on connection and establishing therapeutic rapport. For agency settings or when insurance is involved, document the reason why certain areas are not yet complete, along with a preliminary diagnosis justified with the information at present.

INTAKES WITH MINORS, COUPLES, AND FAMILIES

Specific and important issues related to informed consent and intake assessment arise working with groups of people or with those who are legally unable to consent to their own treatment. The ethical principles related to these scenarios are fairly consistent but two things create endless exceptions and scenarios: State laws pertaining to specific professional licensees and nuanced situations in clinical practice.

Intake assessment tips when multiple people are involved

In general, more people involved means planning for more time to accomplish the same task. For example, when seeing a couple for psychotherapy it is common to meet with the couple together as well as meet with each individual separately for an intake session. This tends to be less common for family psychotherapy, although the length of the intake session may be extended, or the intake session may require multiple appointments in order to provide time for everyone's input.

When seeing a child or adolescent for psychotherapy, the parent (or guardian) is usually involved in the intake session. The parent is often the one paying for and/or initiating treatment, along with providing transportation and a critical role in follow up. Age is usually a major factor in how involved a parent is during the intake session, but it is common practice to meet separately with the child or adolescent for at least some time. For younger children, most of the intake session will likely include the parent whereas for older adolescents, parents might only be involved for paperwork and informed consent.

Including additional people (collaterals) in the intake session can often be helpful and culturally relevant, even when planning for individual psychotherapy. Be clear on who is the client and consider the relevance and safety of including others such as siblings, grandparents, or a spouse.

Top Tip

One clear way to distinguish "who is the client" is by having *only* the client sign intake paperwork. While this may not always be possible for children or adolescents (although it does apply in certain cases based on state laws), it is key when conducting an intake session with an adult where collaterals are present. If someone is not considered a client, they should NOT sign things such as informed consent or consent for services documents (except in the case of minors).

Informed consent with couples and families

It is critically important to be clear on who is considered the client when working with couples and families. While this may seem obvious to many clinicians, many clients do not understand the nuance and may not consider how it can impact their situation later. Here are the main considerations to review with families or couples (AAMFT, 2015; ACA, 2014; AMHCA, 2020; APA, 2017; NASW, 2021):

- Outline if records are maintained separately or jointly and who has access to records,
- Identify the potential limits to confidentiality and inability to protect information when releasing records,
- Explain the need for an individual mental health diagnosis related to insurance requirements (see Chapter 3 for specifics on this), and
- Review how communication outside of session is handled.

Informed consent with minors and guardians

While many of the above considerations also apply to working with children and adolescents, the legal aspect with minors is more nuanced. State laws vary widely regarding the age of consent, ranging from 12-18 years of age when someone can consent to their own mental health treatment. To confuse matters further, some states *allow* consent at a certain age, while others *mandate* consent at a certain age.

Know the laws related to minors and consent for all states in which you practice. If you are unaware of the specific state law, 1) never assume that anyone under the age of 18 (in the United States) is able to consent for treatment, and 2) simultaneously never assume that a minor's parent or guardian has the right to access the minor's records.

Outside of specific state laws, here are the main ethical considerations when working with minors (AAMFT, 2015; ACA, 2014; AMHCA, 2020; APA, 2017; Homeyer & Bennet, 2023; NASW, 2021):

- Identify the potential *required* limits to confidentiality,
- Identify situations in which it may be necessary to reveal content discussed in or out of sessions and the process for doing so,
- Explain who has the right to access to records,
- Explain any potential harm of submitting a mental health diagnosis to insurance for billing requirements (for example, some diagnoses may disqualify people from being accepted in the military), and
- Review how communication outside of session is handled for all parties involved.

Reference the two forms for treating minors in Chapter 5. The "Consent to Treat a Minor" form is used when minors are not able to legally consent to their own mental health services. This provides a way to include the minor as part of the informed consent process, while also clarifying roles and methods of communication. The "Minor Consent to Treatment" is used when a minor is legally considered underage, but is also legally able to consent to their own treatment.

THE MENTAL STATUS EXAM

No assessment training would be complete without a look at the mental status exam (MSE). This is an age appropriate assessment and brief, current view of the client's status. While you likely don't need to include a full MSE with every weekly progress note, it is important to complete it as part of the initial assessment session.

For each section, write just one sentence or phrase that explains the client's current state. See the example client files in the back of this book or in the online resource at **QAPrep.com/ SFD-Resources**.

Every full MSE includes the following:

- Orientation
- Appearance
- Mood and Affect
- Attention
- Concentration and Memory
- Intellectual Functioning
- Insight and Judgment
- Thought Content
- Thought Process and Perceptions
- Risk assessment

Remember that the MSE is always looking at the *current* state, so some components may change weekly (or even daily), while others remain constant throughout treatment. For weekly progress notes, most clinicians in a private practice setting only need to focus on the aspects of the MSE that do adjust on a weekly basis. This typically includes Mood, Affect, and Behavior. Otherwise, update the MSE when you notice a significant change, or when you make changes to the treatment plan.

CASE CONCEPTUALIZATION AND DIAGNOSIS JUSTIFICATION

There are both logistical and clinical aspects in the intake assessment process. Documentation should *always* follow the clinical priorities and case conceptualization, even when considering diagnosis and medical necessity. This is important to remember since the paperwork involved with intakes can easily become the focus. Always keep the client's needs as the first priority, with the documentation serving those needs in a supportive role.

Intake assessments often take longer than other typical psychotherapy sessions. Plan for this and use additional time to reflect on the client's needs as they presented them, any contributing factors to consider, and how you are able to help the client in the process of achieving their goals. That said, the intake process does not require hours of documentation or work outside of session.

Use the strategies discussed elsewhere in this book to save time while still creating high quality assessments that focus on client needs:

- Have clients fill out biopsychosocial data on forms before the intake.
- Take notes directly on the client forms or intake progress note during the intake session.
- Reference the DSM-5 whenever providing a diagnosis because 1) it is easier to summarize applicable symptoms and 2) this will ensure accuracy.
- Save completion of treatment plans for when the client is in session (which may be session 2 or 3).

Diagnostic criteria are helpful for creating shared language among mental health professionals, and some clients find having a name for their experience to be cathartic. However, not every client meets criteria for a DSM-5 diagnosis. Diagnostic definitions and criteria often fail to capture all facets of a person and the many contributing factors that lead people to psychotherapy (Schwitzer & Rubin, 2015).

A diagnosis is not necessary for providing psychotherapy - unless insurance is involved. This sometimes creates an ethical dilemma for clinicians: 1) Inflate symptoms to meet criteria for a diagnosis so a client can use their insurance for psychotherapy, or 2) Stay true to the diagnostic criteria and risk the client going without mental health services because insurance denies coverage.

There is no perfect solution to this dilemma, but keeping the client's goals and needs at the forefront will help with making decisions. To be clear, purposely misdiagnosing a client is fraud. Fraud is both unethical and illegal (ACA, 2014; Medicare 2024), and can have very real, negative consequences (for both clinicians and clients). However, clients in a variety of situations often do meet criteria for a diagnosis when a thorough intake interview was completed.

Use information from the client's paperwork, the intake interview, and the Diagnostic Symptoms Cheat Sheet and Diagnosis Justification Form in Chapter 5 to formulate a rock solid diagnosis. Document these within the intake progress note and, when in doubt, seek consultation or support from a supervisor.

FINALIZING THE INTAKE ASSESSMENT PROCESS

Common discussion about the intake process leads to confusion around two major documents: The intake *assessment* and the intake *progress note*. Many people use these terms interchangeably but these documents are distinct. Understanding this difference is key to conducting a simplified but thorough intake.

Intake assessment

This is the biopsychosocial form that includes historical data about the client and typically includes information about the following:

- Reason for seeking treatment
- Current living situation
- Family history
- History of mental health treatment
- Physical health history
- Educational history
- Vocational history
- History of substance use and legal problems
- Other personal information such as hobbies, strengths, religious affiliation, language(s) spoken, etc.

While this document can be very helpful for collecting data that informs treatment and establishes a diagnosis, it is very likely that much of the information is not relevant to the current situation for which the client is seeking treatment. Earlier in this chapter, I recommended having the client complete this form prior to the first session for this very reason. Collect data outside the session and use the intake session to focus on what is most important to the client.

Intake progress note

The intake progress note is a record of what transpired in that first intake session. This progress note is different and more detailed than most progress notes completed in ongoing psychotherapy, largely because of the requirements related to informed consent (discussed earlier in this chapter). Ethical guidelines require the clinician to show (e.g. document) they reviewed specific aspects of informed consent. Documenting that process requires more than client signatures on forms.

The intake progress note is also a helpful place to review information gained about the presenting problem that may not be included in the larger intake assessment (biopsychosocial) form. Use this progress note as a way to summarize key points not otherwise captured in the previously completed intake paperwork.

Review the Intake Progress Note Template in Chapter 5 for an example of specific items to include that are not included in most ongoing session progress notes. These items include:

- Limits to confidentiality, potential benefits and drawbacks of treatment,
- Practice policies, especially fees and cancellations,
- A description or list of any other relevant forms or policies,
- Results of any assessment measures given before or during the intake session,
- Who attended the session and, for couples or families, identification of who is the client,
- Access to records and potential limitations in the case of multiple people in treatment,
- Reason for seeking treatment and goals for psychotherapy,
- Description of how the client's life is negatively impacted and/or what they would like to change,
- Brief MSE,
- Risk assessment,
- (If applicable) Diagnostic impressions or justification for diagnosis,
- (If applicable) Justification for medical necessity,
- Recommendations for treatment and/or explanation that the assessment process will continue in the next session.

Looking at this list may feel overwhelming but many of these items are written the same for every intake session. Reference the Intake Progress Note Template in Chapter 5 to see how simple such a detailed progress note can actually be.

Clinician Spotlight: Steve

Steve booked a consultation with me because he was behind in his notes and drowning in paperwork to the point that he felt he could no longer take on new clients, despite needing to do so financially. Quickly in our consultation I discovered that he was spending hours on the intake assessment and treatment planning process. We focused here since I knew we could solve this problem and immediately save him multiple hours on paperwork.

Steve's intake process included having clients complete an intake questionnaire, and then Steve would complete a full intake assessment (biopsychosocial) form, most of which he was writing after the session was over. Then he would also write an intake assessment progress note and treatment plan for the client. He was spending about fours on paperwork outside of initial intake sessions. Since he often didn't get these completed for a few weeks, he would also wait to write the progress notes for subsequent sessions, creating a large backlog of paperwork. No wonder he was nervous about taking on even two more clients!

We reviewed all of Steve's intake assessment documents and found that he was often writing things in three separate locations. For example, the mental health history portion of his biopsychosocial was also in the client questionnaire and intake progress note. He also included diagnosis and symptoms in the biopsychosocial, the intake progress note, and the treatment plan.

I taught Steve my rule of "never write anything twice" and identified all the places where he could simply reference the information listed in another form. By removing the duplication of information we cut his paperwork time in half. To further reduce his documentation time, I suggested combining the client questionnaire with the biopsychosocial intake assessment form, eliminating the need to complete the form he was spending the most time on.

Combined with the strategy of writing most of the intake and treatment plan related notes in session with the client, Steve was able to reduce his time to about 25 minutes outside of the intake. He was less overwhelmed by the whole process which led to him completing most of the paperwork on the same day, and allowed him to feel comfortable taking on more clients.

Quick Read Chapter Summary

- *Policies* are ways of practicing psychotherapy, and *forms* are the documentation of those policies for others to see.

- Informed consent is a process that begins with the first psychotherapy session and continues throughout treatment.

- Client records include multiple components that do not always correlate to specific forms.

- One way to save time while improving documentation is to have clients complete intake assessment paperwork (forms and the biopsychosocial questionnaire) before the first session.

- Focus intake assessments on making a connection with the client more than on gathering data.

- It is critical to review roles and to identify who is considered the client when working with couples, families, and minors.

- A full mental status exam (MSE) is an important part of any intake assessment, but only a brief MSE is necessary for every session thereafter.

- A diagnosis is not necessary for psychotherapy, but may be necessary for third party payors and may be appropriate and/or helpful based on the client's presentation and need.

- The intake progress note summarizes everything that happened in the first session, including completion of the intake assessment with biopsychosocial information.

NOTES

Chapter 5

Intake Assessment Forms

IN THIS CHAPTER

Guidance on Using Templates	83
Client Intake Form: Adult	85
Client Intake Form: Child or Adolescent	93
Progress Note Template: Intake Assessment	103
Problems Questionnaire	106
Diagnostic Symptoms Cheat Sheet	107
Diagnosis Justification Form	109
Consent for Audio / Video Recording	110
Consent for Services	111
Consent for Telehealth	119
Consent to Treat a Minor	121
Minor Consent to Treatment	122
Agreement to Confidentiality in Group Therapy	123
Notice of Privacy Practices (USA Specific)	124

> *The art of being wise is the art of knowing what to overlook.*
>
> *- William James*

GUIDANCE ON USING TEMPLATES

The following pages include a variety of templates intended for the intake assessment process. The goal of all these templates is a combination of professional and legal requirements with client-friendliness, creating the foundation for establishing client rapport.

Some templates apply only in some scenarios, such as the consent form templates focused on telehealth or audio/video recording. Other templates are meant for use with a specific population, such as minors. If you have questions about whether or not you need to use a specific form, reference the related topic in Chapter 4.

Modify and adapt these templates to your own needs. Some are meant for use with clients, such as the Problems Questionnaire, while others are provided as a resource to you as the clinician, such as the Diagnosis Justification Form.

 Look for this icon to identify forms or templates meant for use with clients.

For students and clinicians working in a setting with prescribed forms:
Focus more on the information in Chapter 4 to help you improve your assessment skills and understand the overall principles related to all intakes. However, the Problems Questionnaire, Diagnostic Symptoms Cheat Sheet, and Diagnostic Justification Form may be helpful to add to your documentation and case conceptualization process.

For clinicians in a private practice setting with flexibility to choose their own template format:
Use all the forms that apply to your practice! Check out the video instructions at **QAPrep.com/SFD-Resources** for help with adapting the forms to your specific policies and needs.

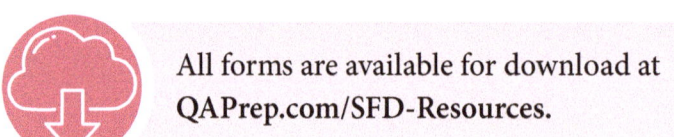
All forms are available for download at QAPrep.com/SFD-Resources.

Client Intake Form: Adult

Client Intake Form: Adult

Answering the following questions will help me get to know you. Provide as much detail as you feel comfortable sharing. Please note that all information in this form is kept confidential per the Consent for Services.

Contact Information

Name:(First) _____ (Last) _____

Preferred Name (if applicable): _____

Birth Date: _____   Age: _____

If seeking couples therapy, please add information about partner:

Name:(First) _____ (Last) _____

Birth Date: _____   Age: _____

Home Address:

_____

_____

Email Address: _____

Phone Number: _____ Type: _____

  Is it okay to leave a voice message at this number? ☐ Yes ☐ No

  Is it okay to text this number? ☐ Yes ☐ No

Alternate Number: _____ Type: _____

  Is it okay to leave a voice message at this number? ☐ Yes ☐ No

  Is it okay to text this number? ☐ Yes ☐ No

How did you hear about me?

_____

Client Intake Form: Adult (Continued)

Emergency Contact Information
Please note, I will only contact this person in the event of an emergency and will always try to inform you if I do so.

Name: _____

Phone Number: _____

Relationship to Emergency Contact: _____

About You

Preferred Language(s): _____

Hobbies/Interests:
_____

Reason for starting therapy:
_____
_____

Goals you want to accomplish in therapy:
_____
_____

How do you currently cope with stress (*examples: watching TV, talking to friends, drinking*)?
_____

Do you have any religious or spiritual practices that are important to you?

☐ No   ☐ Yes (please describe below):

_____

Client Intake Form: Adult (Continued)

Current Living Situation

Who currently lives in your home (*names and relationship*)?

_____
_____

Currently in a significant romantic relationship?

☐ No ☐ Yes (please list name and relationship type):
_____

Significant prior relationship (divorced, widowed, etc.)?

☐ No ☐ Yes (please describe below):
_____

Names of children and ages (if applicable):

_____
_____

Are you the primary caretaker for any adults?

☐ No ☐ Yes (please describe below):
_____

Do you have any pets?

☐ No ☐ Yes (please list name and type, e.g. dog, cat, etc.):
_____

How would you describe your current living situation (e.g. calm, chaotic, loving, etc.)?

_____
_____

Client Intake Form: Adult (Continued)

Family of Origin

Please describe your closest family relationships:

_____

_____

Please describe any family relationships that are distant or in conflict:

_____

_____

Select any family mental health history (parents, siblings, etc.):

- ☐ ADHD
- ☐ Alcohol abuse
- ☐ Anxiety
- ☐ Bipolar disorder
- ☐ Depression
- ☐ Drug abuse
- ☐ Eating disorder
- ☐ OCD
- ☐ Personality disorder
- ☐ PTSD
- ☐ Schizophrenia
- ☐ Suicide attempt
- ☐ Completed suicide
- ☐ Other: _____

Select any history of trauma experienced by your family or origin:

- ☐ Alcohol abuse
- ☐ Community violence
- ☐ Death of a close family member
- ☐ Divorce/separation
- ☐ Domestic violence
- ☐ Family in prison/jail
- ☐ Family separation
- ☐ Frequent hospitalizations
- ☐ Food scarcity
- ☐ Health problems
- ☐ Home insecurity
- ☐ Immigration
- ☐ Military service
- ☐ Physical violence
- ☐ Poverty
- ☐ Pregnancy loss
- ☐ Racism
- ☐ Sexual abuse
- ☐ Substance use
- ☐ Unstable relationships
- ☐ War
- ☐ Other: _____

Client Intake Form: Adult (Continued)

Employment/Education History

Profession: _____

Current Employer: _____

Employment concerns (if applicable):

_____
_____

Highest Degree Obtained: _____

Current level in school (if applicable): _____

Educational concerns (if applicable):

_____
_____

Mental Health Treatment History

Have you been in therapy before?   ☐ No   ☐ Yes

Previous therapist(s) name(s):

_____

Reasons for previous therapy:

_____
_____

What did you like or dislike about your previous experience in therapy?

_____
_____

Client Intake Form: Adult (Continued)

Please select any personal history of trauma (if comfortable disclosing):

- ☐ Bullying
- ☐ Child abuse or neglect
- ☐ Community violence
- ☐ Death of a close family member
- ☐ Discrimination
- ☐ Divorce/separation of parents
- ☐ Domestic violence
- ☐ Family instability
- ☐ Frequent hospitalizations
- ☐ Food scarcity
- ☐ Health problems
- ☐ Home insecurity
- ☐ Immigration
- ☐ Military service
- ☐ Parent in prison/jail
- ☐ Poverty
- ☐ Pregnancy loss
- ☐ Racism
- ☐ Sexual abuse
- ☐ Substance use
- ☐ Unstable relationships
- ☐ Victim of crime
- ☐ War time experiences
- ☐ Other: _____

Medical History

Primary Care Physician (name and phone number):

_____

Date of most recent physical exam:_____

Please list any current medications taken on a regular basis:

_____

_____

Please list any *current* medical problems (thyroid disorder, chronic pain, etc.):

_____

_____

Please list any significant medical history (cancer, accidents, surgeries, etc.):

_____

_____

Client Intake Form: Adult (Continued)

Please list any accommodations needed (wheelchair access, etc.):

_____

Substance Use History

Please check any substances previously or currently used. If current, please select the frequency of use:

Alcohol	☐ Prior	☐ Daily	☐ Weekly	☐ Monthly
Barbiturates	☐ Prior	☐ Daily	☐ Weekly	☐ Monthly
Benzodiazepines	☐ Prior	☐ Daily	☐ Weekly	☐ Monthly
Caffeine	☐ Prior	☐ Daily	☐ Weekly	☐ Monthly
Cigarettes	☐ Prior	☐ Daily	☐ Weekly	☐ Monthly
Cocaine	☐ Prior	☐ Daily	☐ Weekly	☐ Monthly
Ecstasy	☐ Prior	☐ Daily	☐ Weekly	☐ Monthly
Heroin	☐ Prior	☐ Daily	☐ Weekly	☐ Monthly
Marijuana	☐ Prior	☐ Daily	☐ Weekly	☐ Monthly
Methamphetamine	☐ Prior	☐ Daily	☐ Weekly	☐ Monthly
Opiates	☐ Prior	☐ Daily	☐ Weekly	☐ Monthly
PCP	☐ Prior	☐ Daily	☐ Weekly	☐ Monthly
Other: _____	☐ Prior	☐ Daily	☐ Weekly	☐ Monthly

Describe any concerns or goals related to substance use:

_____

_____

Are you currently in a substance use program or support group?

☐ No   ☐ Yes (please describe below):

_____

Legal History

Are you currently involved with any court proceedings?

☐ No   ☐ Yes (please describe below):

_____

_____

Client Intake Form: Adult (Continued)

Have you ever been arrested? ☐ No ☐ Yes

Have you ever been convicted of a misdemeanor or felony? ☐ No ☐ Yes

If yes to either above, please describe charges and outcome:

_____
_____

Do you currently have an assigned probation officer *and/or* social worker for any reason?

☐ No   ☐ Yes (please list name and phone number of worker and reason for working with them):

Contact Info:_____

Reason for working with probation officer or social worker:

_____
_____

Please list *any* other information not listed on this form that you feel is important for working with you:

_____
_____

_____
Your Signature   **Date**

_____
Spouse Signature (if applicable)   **Date**

Client Intake Form: Child or Adolescent

Client Intake Form: Child or Adolescent

Answering the following questions will help me get to know your child. Provide as much detail as you feel comfortable sharing. Please note that all information in this form is kept confidential per the Consent for Services.

Client Information

Name:(First) _____ (Last) _____

Preferred Name (if applicable): _____

Birth Date: _____ Age: _____

Home Address:

_____

Email Address: _____
☐ Check here if your child does not have their own email address.

Phone Number: _____ Type: _____
☐ Check here if your child does not have their own phone number.

Child currently lives with (check all that apply):

☐ Mother   ☐ Sibling(s)   ☐ Family friend
☐ Father   ☐ Grandparent(s)   ☐ Non-relative foster home
☐ Adoptive parent   ☐ Aunt or Uncle   ☐ Other: _____

Parent Information and Involvement

Parent or Legal Guardian 1

Name:(First) _____ (Last) _____

Preferred Name (if applicable): _____

Relationship to Client: _____

Birth Date: _____ Age: _____

Preferred Language(s): _____

Client Intake Form: Child or Adolescent (Continued)

Home Address (if different from client):

_____

Email Address: _____

Phone Number: _____ Type: _____
   Is it okay to leave a voice message at this number? ☐ Yes ☐ No
   Is it okay to text this number? ☐ Yes ☐ No

Alternate Number: _____ Type: _____
   Is it okay to leave a voice message at this number? ☐ Yes ☐ No
   Is it okay to text this number? ☐ Yes ☐ No

Please check all the ways this parent might be involved with therapy:

- ☐ Drop off and pick up for appointments
- ☐ Attending therapy appointments
- ☐ Attending parent consultations
- ☐ Available via phone
- ☐ Available via email
- ☐ Unavailable to be involved with therapy

Parent or Legal Guardian 2

Name: (First) _____ (Last) _____

Preferred Name (if applicable): _____

Relationship to Client: _____

Birth Date: _____ Age: _____

Preferred Language(s): _____

Home Address (if different from client):

_____

Email Address: _____

Client Intake Form: Child or Adolescent (Continued)

Phone Number: _____ Type: _____

    Is it okay to leave a voice message at this number? ☐ Yes ☐ No

    Is it okay to text this number? ☐ Yes ☐ No

Alternate Number: _____ Type: _____

    Is it okay to leave a voice message at this number? ☐ Yes ☐ No

    Is it okay to text this number? ☐ Yes ☐ No

Please check all the ways this parent might be involved with therapy:

☐ Drop off and pick up for appointments
☐ Attending therapy appointments
☐ Attending parent consultations
☐ Available via phone
☐ Available via email
☐ Unavailable to be involved with therapy

Parenting and Custody

Child's biological or adoptive parents are currently:

☐ Married
☐ Never married
☐ Living separately (but not legally separated)
☐ Legally separated
☐ Divorced
☐ One or both parents have passed away

If parents are married and currently living in the same home, skip the following questions and move on to "How did you hear about me?"

If parents are *not* currently married *or* living in the same home, please describe the current custody arrangement:

_____

Is this arrangement official via legal documentation?

    ☐ No   ☐ Yes (Please note that I will need a copy of the legal document.)

Do both parents have rights to make medical decisions?

    ☐ No (please describe below):   ☐ Yes

_____

Client Intake Form: Child or Adolescent (Continued)

In an average month, how much time does each parent spend with the child on a *weekly* basis?

Parent 1: _____   Parent 2: _____

How would you describe the relationship between the child and each parent?

Parent 1:
_____

Parent 2:
_____

Are there other adults living in either home who are involved with parenting duties (e.g. step-parents, grandparents, etc.)?

☐ No   ☐ Yes (please describe below):
_____

As best you can, please describe the current visitation schedule. For example, identify if weekdays are always with one parent or rotate, etc.

Weekdays:
_____

Weekends:
_____

Is there anything else I should know about the parenting schedule or custody arrangement?
_____

How did you hear about me?
_____

About Your Child

Language(s) spoken at home: _____

Client Intake Form: Child or Adolescent (Continued)

Child's Preferred Language: _____

Hobbies and Interests:

_____

Reason for starting therapy:

_____

Changes you would like your child to experience as a result of therapy:

_____

How does your child currently cope with stress (*examples: isolates in their room, temper tantrums, asks you for help, etc.*)?

_____

What are your child's strengths?

_____

Home Life

List names and ages of any siblings:

_____

How would you describe the quality of your child's relationships with their siblings (if applicable)?

_____

List any chores or responsibilities your child has at home, along with any struggles:

_____

Are there any religious or spiritual practices that are important in your home?

☐ No   ☐ Yes (please describe below):

_____

Client Intake Form: Child or Adolescent (Continued)

Do you have any pets?

☐ No   ☐ Yes (please list name and type, e.g. dog, cat, etc.):
_____

How would you describe your child's current living situation (e.g. calm, chaotic, loving, etc.)?

_____

Family History and Involvement

Select any family mental health history (parents, siblings, etc.):

☐ ADHD
☐ Alcohol abuse
☐ Anxiety
☐ Bipolar disorder
☐ Depression
☐ Drug abuse
☐ Eating disorder

☐ OCD
☐ Personality disorder
☐ PTSD
☐ Schizophrenia
☐ Suicide attempt
☐ Completed suicide
☐ Other: _____

Select any history of trauma experienced by the child's family or origin:

☐ Alcohol abuse
☐ Community violence
☐ Death of a close family member
☐ Divorce/separation
☐ Domestic violence
☐ Family in prison/jail
☐ Family separation
☐ Frequent hospitalizations
☐ Food scarcity
☐ Health problems
☐ Home insecurity

☐ Immigration
☐ Military service
☐ Physical violence
☐ Poverty
☐ Pregnancy loss
☐ Racism
☐ Sexual abuse
☐ Substance use
☐ Unstable relationships
☐ War
☐ Other: _____

Are extended family members (grandparents, cousins, etc.) regularly involved in the child's life?

☐ No   ☐ Yes (please describe below):
_____

Client Intake Form: Child or Adolescent (Continued)

School Life

Name of school: _____

Current or incoming grade level: _____

Teacher's name: _____

How does your child feel about school? Check all that apply or describe below:

- ☐ Enjoys learning
- ☐ Enjoys socializing
- ☐ Enjoys extracurricular activities
- ☐ Dislikes social environment
- ☐ Dislikes learning environment
- ☐ Previously liked school

Other: _____

Describe any educational concerns related to learning (if applicable):
_____

Describe any other concerns, such as problematic behaviors at school:
_____

Social Life

Describe your child's friendships and any related struggles:
_____

Describe where and how your child spends most of their time:
_____

List any current sports or extracurricular activities important to your child:
_____

Is your child dating or romantically involved with peers?

☐ No   ☐ Yes (please describe):
_____

Client Intake Form: Child or Adolescent (Continued)

Is your child sexually active?

☐ No   ☐ Yes   ☐ I don't know.

Have you discussed sex with your child, appropriate to their age and maturity?

☐ No   ☐ Yes

If you are concerned about your child's sexual activity, please describe below:

_____

Medical History

Child's Primary Care Physician (name and phone number):

_____

Date of most recent physical exam:_____

Please list any current medications taken on a regular basis:

_____

Please list any *current* medical problems (asthma, allergies, etc.):

_____

Please list any significant medical history (cancer, accidents, surgeries, etc.):

_____

Please list any accommodations needed (wheelchair access, etc.):

_____

Mental Health Treatment History

Has your child been in therapy before?   ☐ No   ☐ Yes
Previous therapist(s) name(s):

_____

Client Intake Form: Child or Adolescent (Continued)

Reasons for previous therapy:

_____

What did your child like or dislike about their previous experience in therapy?

_____

Please select any of the following that your child may have experienced:

- ☐ Bullying
- ☐ Child abuse or neglect
- ☐ Community violence
- ☐ Death of a close family member
- ☐ Discrimination
- ☐ Divorce/separation of parents
- ☐ Domestic violence
- ☐ Family instability
- ☐ Frequent hospitalizations
- ☐ Food scarcity
- ☐ Health problems
- ☐ Home insecurity
- ☐ Immigration
- ☐ Parent in prison/jail
- ☐ Poverty
- ☐ Racism
- ☐ Sexual abuse
- ☐ Substance use
- ☐ Unstable relationships
- ☐ Victim of crime
- ☐ War time experiences
- ☐ Witnessing substance use
- ☐ Other: _____

Substance Use

Does your child use any substances or drink alcohol?

☐ No   ☐ Yes   ☐ I don't know.

Have you discussed substance use with your child, appropriate to their age and maturity?

☐ No   ☐ Yes

If you are concerned about your child's substance use, please describe below:

_____

Client Intake Form: Child or Adolescent (Continued)

Please check any substances that are known to be previously or currently used by your child. If current, please select the frequency of use:

Alcohol	☐ Prior	☐ Daily	☐ Weekly	☐ Monthly
Barbiturates	☐ Prior	☐ Daily	☐ Weekly	☐ Monthly
Benzodiazepines	☐ Prior	☐ Daily	☐ Weekly	☐ Monthly
Caffeine	☐ Prior	☐ Daily	☐ Weekly	☐ Monthly
Cigarettes	☐ Prior	☐ Daily	☐ Weekly	☐ Monthly
Cocaine	☐ Prior	☐ Daily	☐ Weekly	☐ Monthly
Ecstasy	☐ Prior	☐ Daily	☐ Weekly	☐ Monthly
Heroin	☐ Prior	☐ Daily	☐ Weekly	☐ Monthly
Marijuana	☐ Prior	☐ Daily	☐ Weekly	☐ Monthly
Methamphetamine	☐ Prior	☐ Daily	☐ Weekly	☐ Monthly
Opiates	☐ Prior	☐ Daily	☐ Weekly	☐ Monthly
PCP	☐ Prior	☐ Daily	☐ Weekly	☐ Monthly
Other: _____				

Is your child currently in a substance use program or support group?

☐ No   ☐ Yes (please describe below):

_____

Does your child have any legal history?

☐ No   ☐ Yes (please describe below):

_____

Please list *any* other information not listed on this form that you feel is important for working with your child:

_____

_____

_____

Parent or Guardian Signature   **Date**

Client Signature   **Date**

Progress Note Template: Intake Assessment

Intake Progress Note

Clinician/Practice Name
License info
123 Main Street Long Beach CA
(999)888-7777
Email

Client Name:_____

Date of Session:_____ **Time:**_____ **Session Length:**_____

Type of Service: *Diagnostic Intake Session (90791)*

Attendees:
- ☐ Client
- ☐ Spouse
- ☐ Parent
- ☐ Other: _____

Reviewed with Client:
- ☐ Limits to confidentiality
- ☐ Potential benefits and drawbacks of treatment
- ☐ Intake forms and practice policies, including fees and cancellation policy
- ☐ Good faith estimate reviewed and copy provided (non-insurance clients only)
- ☐ Additional policies discussed (if applicable):
_____

Consent for Treatment:
- ☐ Obtained client's consent for treatment
- ☐ Client signed all intake documents

Assessment:
- ☐ Gathered biopsychosocial history
- ☐ Completed intake assessment form
- ☐ Other assessment tools completed (if applicable):
_____

Reason for Seeking Treatment:
_____
_____

Progress Note Template: Intake Assessment (Continued)

Diagnostic Impressions:

Problem(s) Reported by Client

- ☐ Alcohol Use
- ☐ Appetite
- ☐ Anxiety
- ☐ Attention/Concentration
- ☐ Communication
- ☐ Drug Use
- ☐ Family conflict
- ☐ Fearfulness
- ☐ Friends/Social life
- ☐ Health
- ☐ Identity
- ☐ Impulsivity
- ☐ Loneliness
- ☐ Motivation
- ☐ Organization
- ☐ Overwhelm
- ☐ Relationships (partner/spouse)
- ☐ Relationships (other)
- ☐ Sadness
- ☐ School
- ☐ Self harm/Intent to harm
- ☐ Sexuality
- ☐ Sleep
- ☐ Symptoms management
- ☐ Thinking
- ☐ Time Management
- ☐ Trauma
- ☐ Work
- ☐ Worry
- ☐ Other: _____

Impact on Daily Living

- ☐ Difficulty with relationships:
    - ☐ Coworkers
    - ☐ Family of origin
    - ☐ Friendships
    - ☐ Marriage/Partnership
- ☐ Problems negatively impacting:
    - ☐ Home
    - ☐ School
    - ☐ Work
- ☐ Self harming behaviors
- ☐ Difficulty with interactions:
    - ☐ Communicating needs and wants
    - ☐ Expressing, identifying, and/or managing emotions
    - ☐ Isolating from others
    - ☐ Understanding social cues/interactions
- ☐ Mental health negatively impacting physical health

Baseline Presentation/Prior Level of Functioning

_____

Client meets criteria for the following diagnosis:

_____

Progress Note Template: Intake Assessment (Continued)

Psychotherapy treatment is recommended and medically necessary to:

- ☐ Reduce symptoms related to mental health diagnosis
- ☐ Stabilize symptoms related to mental health diagnosis
- ☐ Manage symptoms related to chronic mental health symptoms
- ☐ Prevent de-compensation related to a mental health diagnosis
- ☐ Prevent need for a higher level of care to treat mental health diagnosis

Crisis:

- ☐ Not applicable
- ☐ Some risks/concerns (if applicable): _____
- ☐ Safety plan created *(if applicable):* _____
_____

In Session Notes (if applicable):
_____

Plan and Follow Up:

Recommendations

- ☐ Continue with the initial assessment process in the next session.
- ☐ Begin therapy and create treatment goals in the next session.
- ☐ Treatment plan and goals created (see treatment plan).
- ☐ Referrals/Resources provided (if applicable): _____
- ☐ Other recommendations for treatment (if applicable): _____

Coordination of Care With (as applicable):

- ☐ Nutritionist/Dietician
- ☐ Other therapist
- ☐ PCP/Physician
- ☐ Psychiatrist
- ☐ Teacher
- ☐ Other: _____

_____
Therapist Signature   Date

Problems Questionnaire

Check off any of the following experiences or symptoms that bother you:

- ☐ Alcohol use
- ☐ Appetite (Increased)
- ☐ Appetite (Decreased)
- ☐ Anger
- ☐ Anxiety
- ☐ Attention/Concentration
- ☐ Body image
- ☐ Boundaries
- ☐ Bullying
- ☐ Burnout
- ☐ Childhood experiences/trauma
- ☐ Chronic pain
- ☐ Communication
- ☐ Compulsions
- ☐ Dating
- ☐ Delusions
- ☐ Difficulty asking for help
- ☐ Difficulty managing emotions
- ☐ Drug use
- ☐ Eating/food
- ☐ Emotional awareness
- ☐ Emotional numbness
- ☐ Energy level
- ☐ Family conflict
- ☐ Fearfulness
- ☐ Food restriction
- ☐ Friends/Social life
- ☐ Fulfillment
- ☐ Guilt
- ☐ Hallucinations
- ☐ Health (physical)
- ☐ History of abuse
- ☐ Hoarding
- ☐ Identity
- ☐ Impulse control
- ☐ Irritability
- ☐ Loneliness
- ☐ Motivation
- ☐ Nightmares
- ☐ Obsessive thoughts
- ☐ Organization
- ☐ Overwhelm
- ☐ Panic attacks
- ☐ Paranoid thoughts
- ☐ Parenting
- ☐ Perfectionism
- ☐ Phobia
- ☐ Physical aggression
- ☐ Poor self-care
- ☐ Relationship struggles
- ☐ Ruminating thoughts
- ☐ Sadness
- ☐ School
- ☐ Self-image
- ☐ Self harm/Intent to harm
- ☐ Sensory modulation
- ☐ Sexual arousal/desire
- ☐ Sexual intimacy in relationship
- ☐ Sexuality
- ☐ Sleep (insomnia)
- ☐ Sleep (other)
- ☐ Social interactions
- ☐ Somatic concerns
- ☐ Suicidal thoughts/intent
- ☐ Symptoms management
- ☐ Thinking
- ☐ Time Management
- ☐ Trauma
- ☐ Work
- ☐ Worry

Diagnostic Symptoms Cheat Sheet

Diagnostic Symptoms Cheat Sheet

List of Common Potential Symptoms

- ☐ Alcohol use or addiction
- ☐ Avoidance of stimuli and/or memories
- ☐ Bullying
- ☐ Burnout
- ☐ Chronic pain
- ☐ Chronic significant stressors
- ☐ Compulsions
- ☐ Delusions
- ☐ Denying or avoiding problems
- ☐ Difficulty with:
  - ☐ Asking for help
  - ☐ Completing tasks
  - ☐ Following directions
  - ☐ Interpersonal communication
  - ☐ Maintaining boundaries
  - ☐ Maintaining friendships
  - ☐ Making decisions
  - ☐ Regulating emotions
  - ☐ School
  - ☐ Sense of identity
  - ☐ Social interactions
  - ☐ Work tasks
- ☐ Dissociation
- ☐ Distorted body image
- ☐ Drug use or addiction
- ☐ Emotionally detached
- ☐ Emotionally numb
- ☐ Explosive/fits of rage
- ☐ Fatigue
- ☐ Feelings of:
  - ☐ Anger
  - ☐ Anxiety
  - ☐ Emptiness
  - ☐ Fear
  - ☐ Grief
  - ☐ Guilt
  - ☐ Hopelessness
  - ☐ Irritability
  - ☐ Loneliness
  - ☐ Overwhelm
  - ☐ Rage
  - ☐ Rejection
  - ☐ Sadness
  - ☐ Worry
  - ☐ Worthlessness
- ☐ Flashbacks
- ☐ Food related:
  - ☐ Appetite decreased
  - ☐ Appetite increased
  - ☐ Binging
  - ☐ Purging
  - ☐ Restricted eating
  - ☐ Weight decreased
  - ☐ Weight increased
- ☐ Hallucinations
- ☐ Health problems (physical)
- ☐ History of:
  - ☐ Alcohol abuse
  - ☐ Drug abuse
  - ☐ Physical aggression
  - ☐ Relationship conflicts
  - ☐ Self-harm
  - ☐ Suicide attempts
  - ☐ Trauma

Diagnostic Symptoms Cheat Sheet (Continued)

- ☐ Hoarding
- ☐ Hypervigilance
- ☐ Impulsive
- ☐ Isolating or withdrawing
- ☐ Lack of:
    - ☐ Confidence
    - ☐ Empathy
    - ☐ Energy
    - ☐ Fulfillment
    - ☐ Hobbies/enjoyable activities
    - ☐ Motivation
    - ☐ Self-esteem
    - ☐ Social support
- ☐ Legal problems
- ☐ Obsessive thoughts
- ☐ Panic attacks
- ☐ Paranoid thoughts
- ☐ Perfectionism
- ☐ Phobia
- ☐ Physical aggression
- ☐ Poor
    - ☐ Attention
    - ☐ Concentration
    - ☐ Emotional regulation
    - ☐ Memory
    - ☐ Organization
    - ☐ Relationship satisfaction
    - ☐ Self-care
    - ☐ Self-image
    - ☐ Sensory modulation
    - ☐ School attendance
    - ☐ Time management
- ☐ Questioning identity/values
- ☐ Rapid speech
- ☐ Recent and significant loss
- ☐ Recent stressful life events
- ☐ Relationship conflict
- ☐ Restless/fidgety
- ☐ Ruminating thoughts
- ☐ Self harm/Intent to harm
- ☐ Sexual arousal/desire (increase or decrease)
- ☐ Sleep related:
    - ☐ Difficulty falling asleep
    - ☐ Frequent naps
    - ☐ Frequent waking
    - ☐ Increased need for sleep
    - ☐ Nightmares
    - ☐ Poor sleep quality
    - ☐ Tired despite regular sleep
- ☐ Slow movement
- ☐ Social anxiety
- ☐ Somatic complaints
- ☐ Struggles to maintain relationships
- ☐ Suicidal ideation/intent
- ☐ Traumatic experiences related to:
    - ☐ Abuse
    - ☐ Bullying
    - ☐ Childhood experiences
    - ☐ Discrimination
    - ☐ Domestic violence
    - ☐ Family of origin
    - ☐ Sexual assault
    - ☐ War/military experience
- ☐ Victim of crime

Diagnosis Justification Form

Client Name: _____ **Date of Intake:** _____

Symptoms reported by the client include:

_____

_____

Prior level of functioning:

_____

Previous DSM-5 mental health diagnosis(es) and source of information:

_____

Current medical diagnosis(es) and source of information:

_____

Current impairments to functioning (as a result of mental health symptoms):

- ☐ Difficulty with relationships:
    - ☐ Coworkers
    - ☐ Family of origin
    - ☐ Friendships
    - ☐ Marriage/Partnership
- ☐ Problems negatively impacting:
    - ☐ Home
    - ☐ School
    - ☐ Work
- ☐ Self harming behaviors
- ☐ Difficulty with interactions:
    - ☐ Communicating needs and wants
    - ☐ Expressing, identifying, and/or managing emotions
    - ☐ Isolating from others
    - ☐ Understanding social cues/interactions
- ☐ Mental health negatively impacting physical health

Client meets criteria for the following diagnosis(es):

_____

_____

Consent for Audio / Video Recording

Consent for Audio/Video Recording

I consent to allowing _____ to record sessions via audio or video means. My therapist has explained to me the potential benefits and drawbacks related to this and how it may impact my treatment.

I understand that my therapist will be recording sessions for the purpose of _____. These recordings will NOT be used for research or any other purpose without my further written consent.

I understand the laws that protect the confidentiality of my Personal Health Information apply to recordings, as do the limitations to that confidentiality discussed in the Consent for Services.

I understand that my therapist will destroy all recordings 1) in accordance with the record keeping guidelines of the State of _____ and the ethics of the profession *or* 2) once they have served their purpose, whichever is sooner.

All recordings will be destroyed in a manner which protects my confidentiality.

I have the right to withhold or withdraw this consent at any time and this will not impact my treatment in any way.

I also have the right to request we discontinue recording during any session and to request any recorded portion be destroyed or erased immediately.

I have read and understand the information provided above. I have discussed it with my therapist, and all of my questions have been answered to my satisfaction.

_____
Client Signature   **Date**

_____
Parent/Guardian Signature (if applicable)   **Date**

Consent for Services

Consent for Services

Welcome to my psychotherapy practice. This document outlines the policies and guidelines I follow. Please read through this entire document to understand the terms of service.

In your first session, we will spend some time going through *key points* highlighted below to make sure we both have an understanding of how we can work together. The below list is *not* a substitute for all policies included in the following pages. I welcome any questions in our first meeting and *any time following*.

Summary of Policies

Confidentiality: I have the utmost respect for your privacy and will keep all information about your treatment confidential unless one of the situations listed in the *Statement of Confidentiality* section (next page) occurs.

Process of Psychotherapy: Psychotherapy is not a treatment that can be predicted. However, one of the greatest predictors for "success" in psychotherapy is connection with your therapist. Therefore, you're encouraged to discuss any concerns along the way and we will work together to find the best solution for your needs.

Appointments: At the end of each session we will make sure to have the following session scheduled. All cancellations require at least 24 hour notice or you will be billed for the full session.

Communication: The most secure form of communication is by phone or voicemail. If you need to reach me outside of your session time, I encourage you to call the listed phone number. *Please let me know if you prefer to use text or email for communication regarding appointments*.

Payment: I require payment at the beginning of each session. You may pay via cash, check or credit card.

Insurance: I can provide you with a monthly statement to present to your insurance company for possible reimbursement. When using insurance to help pay for services, *please be aware they may request information about your treatment and even deny paying for services*. If you lose coverage at any time, we will discuss the best possible options for you.

Consent for Services (Continued)

Statement of Confidentiality
Trust is an important aspect of the therapeutic relationship. Your confidentiality is of utmost importance for maintaining this trust. However, there are times when I am legally and ethically required to release information about our work together.

In such circumstances I only disclose the least amount of information necessary to meet legal and ethical guidelines. If this occurs, and if it is safe for me to do so, I will inform you of any breaches of your confidentiality as soon as possible.

Below are situations in which I am required to release information to a necessary entity:
1. If you may be a danger to yourself or to another identified person or persons.
2. If there is suspicion of abuse of any child under the age of 18 (this includes the involvement of children under the age of 18 in pornography or sexually explicit materials).
3. If there is suspicion of abuse of any dependent and/or elder adult.
4. By order of a judge or at request of a subpoena.

Please also note that if you choose to use your insurance for payment or reimbursement, your insurance company will be able to access your treatment records. More information is available in the Insurance section below.

Process of Psychotherapy
Scope of Practice
I am a _____ governed by _____. My scope of practice is limited to therapeutic services and I am not a medical professional. My priority is to ensure you receive the appropriate services and this means I may need to refer you to adjunctive or other services if I feel that is necessary and/or outside my scope of practice.

Risks and benefits of psychotherapy:
I cannot guarantee that you will see improvement in your relationships or emotions as a result of working together. Therapy requires multiple things in order to be considered "successful." These include involvement from you and a comfortable connection between you and your therapist, as well as clear expectations for what may be possible as a result of the work together.

I encourage you to discuss your goals, expectations and concerns at all points during our work together. We will continuously discuss how treatment is working for you. If at any time I feel that treating you may be detrimental then I will recommend you discontinue treatment and provide you with appropriate referrals.

Consent for Services (Continued)

There are times when psychotherapy may bring up unexpected emotions or reactions to relationships. Some things we discuss may surprise you as you learn more about yourself and gain insight. It is possible that you may actually start to feel "worse" before feeling you have attained your goals. If that is the case, it's important we discuss these feelings along the way.

It is also possible that as a result of working together, you may wish to adjust how you interact with people in your life. That may mean engaging in some relationships more or disconnecting from other relationships. It is important you discuss any concerns about these things if they arise.

Course of treatment:
We will spend the first 1-4 sessions deciding if we are a good fit and determining your needs. You will identify your goals and we will revisit these goals throughout working together, as these often change over time.

Once we mutually agree that your goals for treatment have been met we will determine an appropriate timeframe for ending work together. Many clients prefer to do this slowly by reducing the number of sessions and some return periodically during stressful times later in life. Please know this process will be very transparent and we will determine what is best for you.

Medications:
Psychotherapists are not medical providers and do not provide medical advice or prescriptions for medication. However, we do coordinate care with applicable medical professionals and may ask about basic medication compliance. I will always let you know before communicating with any other professionals and request you provide their contact information. *Any changes in your medication should always be first discussed with and approved by your prescribing physician/nurse practitioner.*

Appointments
Canceled appointments:
All cancellations require 24 hour notice by phone or you will be billed for the full session. I may choose to make exceptions for extenuating circumstances.

Missed appointments:
All missed appointments (no show, no cancellation) will be billed at the agreed upon regular session rate and will be due prior to your next session.

If I do not hear from you after a missed appointment and have reason for concern, I *may* reach out to your identified emergency contact to ensure your well-being.

Consent for Services (Continued)

Late appointments:
All sessions begin at the scheduled time and last 50 minutes. If you arrive late, we will meet until 50 minutes after your scheduled session time.

Please note that multiple missed or canceled appointments and late arrivals may require us to discontinue treatment. In this circumstance, we will discuss the situation in person, online, or by phone.

Emergency Procedures
If something were to happen to me, _____ will contact you to discuss the situation and ensure you continue to receive services without significant interruption.

If you feel you are experiencing a life-threatening emergency, please call 911.

Communication
Our main form of communication outside the office will be via phone. If you are distressed and feel the need to call outside of your regular meeting time, please know that I am available Monday-Friday during typical business hours. I will return your call within one business day.

E - Mails:
Email is a popular, yet insecure form of communication. When you send an email it has the potential to be seen by many people prior to reaching its destination. For this reason, I will never discuss anything clinical with you via email and ask you to refrain from doing so, as well. I will never send you an email that contains extensive amounts of what is considered Personal Health Information (PHI). These include things such as a social security number or health insurance member ID.

Email may be appropriate for communication regarding appointments, but please be aware the above warning still applies. If you would like to use email communication, especially with an employee email, please discuss with me further.

Cell phones:
If you have a cell phone that provides alerts on your home screen, consider who may easily see notifications of our contact. This means how you enter my name in your phone as a contact and which form of communication you would like to have (email, text, etc.). You may also choose to turn off certain notifications in your settings for increased privacy.

Consent for Services (Continued)

Texting:
Texting uses similar communication as email and is also, therefore, not secure. For this reason, I will never discuss anything clinical with you via text and ask you to refrain from doing so, as well. I will never send you a text message that contains extensive amounts of what is considered Personal Health Information (PHI). These include things such as a social security number or health insurance member ID.

Texting may be appropriate for communication regarding appointments, but please be aware the above warning still applies. If you would like to use texting, please discuss with me further.

Social Media
I maintain social media accounts for promotion of my practice and education of the public. These accounts serve to offer encouragement and resources. They are not a substitute for treatment by a licensed mental health professional and nothing shared should be interpreted as a personal message.

I do not interact with clients via social media. If you choose to follow an account and reach out to me via that method, I am unlikely to reply using the social media platform. Instead, I encourage you to reach out via phone or in session.

Payment
Your fee for one 50 minute therapy session is: $_____

I accept cash, check or credit card as payment for services. All payment is due at the time of service. You may receive a receipt for your payments upon request.

If, at any time, you are having difficulty paying your fee please discuss with me as soon as possible.

_____*Please initial here to acknowledge that your credit card will be charged for each session on the date of the session, unless previously canceled within 24 hours of your scheduled session.* You also acknowledge you will update your credit card information with my office as needed.

Insurance Reimbursement
(In-network Provider)
I am an in-network provider with _____. If you choose to use this insurance but your status changes, it is your responsibility to inform me as soon as possible so we can discuss any possible changes to your payment process. If you switch to a company with whom I am not in-network we will establish the best possible treatment plan for you, which may include referring you to another in-network provider or seeking out-of-network benefits.

Consent for Services (Continued)

Important: When you choose to allow your insurance company to contribute payment to your treatment you also allow them access to your clinical records.

As part of this agreement, I am required to submit information necessary for claims, billing, authorizations, audits, reviews, and other scenarios as requested by the insurance company or their third party actors. These requests may include, but are not limited to, diagnosis, progress notes, treatment plans, and any other clinical documentation.

I will be required to provide you with a mental health diagnosis and share that diagnosis with the insurance company. I will also be required to follow a treatment plan that relates to that diagnosis. Your insurance company may choose to deny or modify your treatment, based on their medical necessity criteria.

(Not an In-Network Provider)
I am not an in-network provider for any insurance company. Some insurance companies will reimburse you for costs related to attending psychotherapy. However, what you and I determine to be clinically relevant may or may not be deemed "medically necessary" and covered by insurance. If you would like to seek reimbursement with your insurance company I will provide you with a monthly statement (superbill) of fees paid and services provided.

>> *Please note that when you choose to allow your insurance company to contribute payment to your treatment you do allow them access to your clinical records. They will also require a mental health diagnosis.* If you have questions or concerns about this, please speak with me before submitting any forms to your insurance company.

Court Policy
Please be advised that for any request to write a letter on any court related matter, I will NOT provide, in writing or in person, an *opinion*. As your therapist, I may only provide observations and feedback (fact-based information). The therapist-client relationship does not include advocating on your behalf in court matters. I will withhold any opportunity to engage in a dual relationship in this way. *At no time will I make a recommendation in regards to custody or any other court related matter.*

If a court order (subpoena) is served and is requesting that I be present in person and/or there is a request for records, I will request your consent before turning over confidential information. We will discuss exactly what has been requested by the court. *I will do my best to maintain the confidentiality of your records as releasing them may not be in your best interest. However, please be advised that there is no guarantee your records will be kept confidential, as this will be determined by the judge.* This information includes mental health history, diagnosis, treatment details, current status and any other records included in the request.

Fees:
Should I be ordered by court to write a letter to the court, the time will be billed at your regular hourly rate.

Should I be court ordered to appear in court, the fee stipulation is as follows:
- $750 per day (this includes travel to and from court)
- Regular hourly rate for preparation

I hold the right to waive these fees, depending upon circumstances and at my discretion.

I will not be on-call for court-related matters at any time. Should a case be rescheduled or if I am required to appear on more than one day, I will be paid in full for each day as it hinders my ability to be available to other clients.

All court fees must be received by cashier's check 14 days prior to the court date. If the court reschedules the hearing at any time, I must be re-issued a court order with the new court hearing date.

Should I be on vacation or otherwise unavailable, the party initiating the court order must take reasonable steps to avoid imposing undue burden or expense on a person subject to the subpoena.

Consultation Disclosure
There are times when I consult with other mental health professionals about cases. During these discussions, I will disclose as little information as possible in order to protect your confidentiality. If I feel there is an instance when consultation may require more information and may be helpful for our work together, I will talk with you beforehand about how to proceed.

I may also consult with other professionals about your case (for example, teachers or social workers). However, I will never consult with other professionals without your prior and written consent.

Collateral Involvement
It may be helpful to involve important people in your life during the psychotherapy process. If this is something that we both feel may be helpful, we will discuss how much information you may be comfortable disclosing and in what way. For all adult clients, I will never speak with any of your family members about your treatment, or even confirm whether or not you are a client, without first having your written

Consent for Services (Continued)

consent. *Exceptions include any circumstances listed above in the Statement of Confidentiality.*

Access to Medical Records
As a mental health professional, I keep records about our work together. This includes notes on sessions, meetings, phone calls and any other communication with or about you. Unless I feel it would be significantly harmful to you, you are able to access your records at any time.

I require 5 days of notice prior to allowing you to *view* your records. If you would like a copy of your records, I require 15 days of notice and will charge a fee of 0.25¢ per page, plus postage fees if you would like your copies mailed.

Oftentimes, clients request copies of records with the intent of securing a treatment summary for an outside entity. Requesting a summary of treatment instead may be in your best interest, as it protects your confidentiality. This is often preferable to giving someone access to your entire treatment record.

If that is the case, I am happy to provide such a summary, billed at your regular hourly rate. I require 10 business days to prepare your summary. If this is related to a court matter, please see the "Court Policy" above.

Governing Body
I am a _____ and governed by the _____. You may reach the Board at the contact information below:
Board Name
Address, City and State
Phone number
Website link

Agreement to Terms and Conditions
I agree to the above listed terms and conditions for services. I acknowledge that I have read and understood these terms and that my therapist has reviewed them with me, allowing for questions and discussion. *Please note that you may request a copy of this agreement.*

_____
Client Signature   **Date**

_____
Parent/Guardian Signature (if applicable)   **Date**

Consent for Telehealth Services

I consent to engaging in telehealth as part of my treatment with _____. I understand that "telehealth" includes the practice of health care delivery, diagnosis, consultation, treatment, transfer of personal health information, and education using interactive audio, video, or data communications.

I understand that I have the following rights with respect to telehealth:

- I have the right to withhold or withdraw this consent at any time. However, if I do so, this may require my therapist to provide referrals to other treatment providers, if face-to-face services are not an option based on geography and/or circumstance.
- The laws that protect the confidentiality of my personal health information also apply to telehealth, as do the limitations to that confidentiality discussed in the Consent for Services Agreement. I also understand that the dissemination of any personally identifiable images or information from the telehealth interaction will not be shared without my written consent.

I understand that there are unique risks and consequences with telehealth, despite reasonable efforts on the part of my therapist to avoid them. These potentially include:

- Transmission of my personal health information could be disrupted or distorted by technical failures.
- Transmission of my personal health information could be interrupted by unauthorized persons.
- Electronic storage of my personal health information could be accessed by unauthorized persons.

I understand I may be requested to install applications specific to treatment onto my phone, tablet or computer device. Some applications specifically interact via phone / tablet, device, etc. and have the capability to report activity, gps location, etc.

In addition, I understand that telehealth based services may not be appropriate for everyone seeking therapy. I also understand that if my therapist believes I would be better served by another form of therapeutic services (e.g. face-to-face services) I will be referred to a practitioner who can provide such services in my area.

I understand that this form is signed in addition to the Consent for Services Agreement, and that all policies and procedures within the Consent for Services Agreement also apply to telehealth services.

Consent for Telehealth (Continued)

I have read and understand the information provided above. I have discussed it with my therapist, and all of my questions have been answered to my satisfaction.

_____
Client Signature   **Date**

_____
Parent/Guardian Signature (if applicable)   **Date**

_____
Therapist Signature   **Date**

Consent to Treat a Minor

Consent to Treat a Minor

It is important to note that you, _____, are the client and not your parent or guardian. That means I will respect your privacy and keep information shared in session as confidential.

However, if I feel there is an issue that may relate to your safety, I may need to discuss that issue with your parent/guardian.

*This is in addition to and potentially outside of the issues already listed in the general **Consent for Services** form.*

There are also times when it is helpful to involve parents/guardians in various ways. This may include things like updates or discussion before or after our session, joint sessions where we all meet together, or phone calls. We will all discuss this together if any of these seem beneficial.

In most circumstances, it is not my practice to keep phone calls or other communication with parents/guardians secret from clients.

If your parent/guardian raises concerns outside of our meeting together, I will discuss with them the best way to address this with you. I encourage keeping communication as open as possible.

As noted in the section of the Consent for Services, *Medical Records and Your Right to Review Them*, I keep notes about our sessions together. In some circumstances, you have the right to determine whether or not your parents/guardians may view these records.

If there is a request to release or view any of your records I will discuss this further with yourself and your parent/guardian to determine the appropriate action.

_____
Client Signature   **Date**

_____
Parent/Guardian Signature (if applicable)   **Date**

_____
Therapist Signature   **Date**

Minor Consent to Treatment

Minor Consent for Treatment

This confirms that _____ is a minor consenting to his/her own treatment *without written consent from a parent/guardian*.

Your therapist will respect your privacy and keep your treatment and information shared in session as confidential. However, if your therapist feels there is an issue that may relate to your safety, they may need to discuss that issue with your parent/guardian.

This is in addition to and potentially outside of the issues already listed in the general **Consent for Services** *form and they will always alert you to this, if it applies.*

There are also times when it is helpful to involve parents/guardians in various ways. This may include things like updates or discussion before or after our session, joint sessions where we all meet together, or phone calls. We will all discuss this together if any of these seem beneficial over time.

As noted in the section of the Consent for Services, *Medical Records and Your Right to Review Them*, your therapist keeps notes about your sessions together. In some circumstances, you have the right to determine whether or not your parents/guardians may view these records. If there is a request to release or view any of your records your therapist will discuss this further with yourself and, if applicable, your parent/guardian to determine the appropriate action.

Please note that your therapist will document what circumstances allow you to consent to your own treatment as a minor.

_____
Client Signature   **Date**

_____
Therapist Signature   **Date**

Agreement to Confidentiality in Group Therapy

_____
Group Member Name

_____
Group Name

I give my consent to the Therapist for treatment in group psychotherapy.

I understand that any information I hear within this group that is shared by other group members is *strictly confidential*.

I understand that disclosing information shared in this group can negatively impact all group members and disclosing information about other members may result in my removal from the group.

I agree not to disclose any information about any member of the group to anyone outside of this group.

_____
Client Signature   **Date**

_____
Parent/Guardian Signature (if applicable)   **Date**

Notice of Privacy Practices (USA Specific)

Practice Name, Address, Phone Number

Notice of Privacy Practices

Your Information. Your Rights. My Responsibility.

This notice describes how personal health information (PHI) about you may be used and disclosed and how you can get access to this information. **Please review it carefully.**

Your Rights
You have the right to:

- Get a copy of your paper or electronic health record
- Correct your paper or electronic health record
- Request confidential communication
- Ask me to limit the information I share
- Get a list of those with whom I've shared your information
- Get a copy of this privacy notice
- Choose someone to act for you
- File a complaint if you believe your privacy rights have been violated

Your Choices
You have some choices in the way that I use and share information as I:

- Collaborate and consult with other professionals on your behalf
- Tell family and friends about your condition
- Provide you mental health care
- Provide disaster relief or emergency mental health treatment

Our Uses and Disclosures
I may use and share your information as I:

- Treat you
- Run my practice
- Coordinate treatment and comply with health plan requirements
- Bill for your services and/or collect overdue payments
- Comply with mandatory reporting laws
- Respond to lawsuits and legal actions

Notice of Privacy Practices (Continued)

Your Rights

When it comes to your health information, you have certain rights. This section explains your rights and some of my responsibilities to help you.

Get an electronic or paper copy of your health record

- You can ask to see or get an electronic or paper copy of your health record and other health information I have about you. Ask me how to do this.
- I will provide a copy or a summary of your health information, usually within 14 days of your request. I may charge a reasonable, cost-based fee.

Ask me to correct your health record

- You can ask me to correct health information about you that you think is incorrect or incomplete. Ask me how to do this.
- I may say "no" to your request, but will tell you why in writing within 60 days.

Request confidential communications

- You can ask me to contact you in a specific way (for example, home or office phone) or to send mail to a different address.
- I will say "yes" to all reasonable requests.

Ask me to limit what I use or share

- You can ask me not to use or share certain health information for treatment, payment, or business operations. I am not required to agree to your request, and may say "no" if it would negatively affect your care or my ability to practice.
- If you pay for a service out-of-pocket in full, you can ask me not to share that information for the purpose of payment or business operations with your health insurer. I will say "yes" unless a law requires me to share that information.

Get a list of those with whom I've shared information

- You can ask for a list (accounting) of the times I've shared your health information for six years prior to the date you ask, who I shared it with, and why.
- I will include all the disclosures except for those about treatment, payment, and health care operations, and certain other disclosures (such as any you asked me to make). I'll provide one accounting a year for free but will charge a reasonable, cost-based fee if you ask for another one within 12 months.

Notice of Privacy Practices (Continued)

Get a copy of this privacy notice

You can ask for a paper copy of this notice at any time, even if you have agreed to receive the notice electronically. I will provide you with a paper copy promptly.

Choose someone to act for you

- If you have given someone medical power of attorney or if someone is your legal guardian, that person can exercise your rights and make choices about your health information.
- I will make sure the person has this authority and can act for you before I take any action.

File a complaint if you feel your rights are violated

- You can complain if you feel I have violated your rights by contacting me using the information on page 1.
- You can file a complaint with the U.S. Department of Health and Human Services Office for Civil Rights by sending a letter to 200 Independence Avenue, S.W., Washington, D.C. 20201, calling 1-877-696-6775, or visiting **www.hhs.gov/ocr/privacy/hipaa/complaints/.**
- I will not retaliate against you for filing a complaint.

Your Choices

For certain health information, you can tell me your choices about what I share.
If you have a clear preference for how I share your information in the situations described below, talk to me. Tell me what you want me to do, and I will follow your instructions.

In these cases, you have both the right and choice to tell me to:

- Share information with your family, close friends, or others involved in your care
- Share information in a disaster relief or emergency situation

If you are not able to tell me your preference, for example if you are unconscious, I may go ahead and share your information if I believe it is in your best interest.

In these cases I never share your information unless you give me written permission:

- Requests from family, friends, or others
- Requests for copies of your records (unless accompanied by a subpoena)
- Most sharing of psychotherapy notes

Notice of Privacy Practices (Continued)

Our Uses and Disclosures

How do I typically use or share your health information?
I typically use or share your health information in the following ways.

Treat you

Although it is not my practice to do so without first informing you, I can use your health information and share it with other professionals for consultation.

Example: I may consult with another therapist about whether or not a particular treatment may be helpful, considering your diagnosis and history.

Although it is not my practice to do so without first informing you, I can use your health information and share it with other healthcare professionals who are treating you.

Example: I may ask your psychiatrist or primary care doctor about your overall health condition.

Run my business

I can use and share your health information to run my practice, improve your care, and contact you when necessary.

Example: I use health information about you to manage your treatment outcomes and monitor trends within my practice.

Example: I use health information about you to justify services in the event of an audit.

Bill for your services

I can use and share your health information to bill and get payment from health plans or other entities.

Example: I give information about you, such as a diagnosis, to your health insurance plan so it will pay for your services.

Example: I can give information about you, such as your address, to a collection agency if you acquire an outstanding balance.

Notice of Privacy Practices (Continued)

How else can I use or share your health information?
I am allowed or required to share your information in other ways – usually in ways that contribute to the public good, such as mandatory reporting for potential child abuse. I have to meet many conditions in the law before I can share your information for these purposes. For more information please reference the *Consent for Services* document.

Help with public health and safety issues

I can share health information about you for certain situations such as:

- Reporting suspected child abuse or neglect
- Preventing or reducing a serious threat to an identified person's health or safety

Comply with the law

I will share information about you if state or federal laws require it, including with the Department of Health and Human Services if it wants to see that I am complying with federal privacy law.

Respond to lawsuits and legal actions

Although it is not my practice to do so without first discussing the situation with you, I can share health information about you in response to a subpoena or if required to do so by a judge.

My Responsibilities

- I am required by law to maintain the privacy and security of your protected health information.
- I will let you know promptly if a breach occurs that may have compromised the privacy or security of your information.
- I must follow the duties and privacy practices described in this notice and give you a copy of it.
- I will not use or share your information other than as described here unless you tell me I can in writing. If you tell me so, you may change your mind at any time. Let me know in writing if you change your mind.

For more information see:
www.hhs.gov/ocr/privacy/hipaa/understanding/consumers/noticepp.html.

Notice of Privacy Practices (Continued)

Changes to the Terms of this Notice

I can change the terms of this notice, and the changes will apply to all information I have about you. The new notice will be available upon request, in my office, and on my website.

This notice was last updated on _____.

This form was adapted using the available example from hhs.gov.

Privacy Officer Contact

If you have any questions or concerns about this notice or about your privacy while receiving services, please contact me, the Privacy Officer:

Name:

Title:

Email Address:

Phone Number:

NOTES

NOTES

Chapter 6

Treatment Planning

IN THIS CHAPTER

Treatment Planning as Client Empowerment 135
Writing Easy and Meaningful Treatment Goals 136
When to Use "SMART" Goals 138
The Most Important Thing About Treatment Plan
Interventions 140
Integrating Strengths and Supportive Factors 141
When and How to Update Treatment Plans 141
Quick Read Chapter Summary 144

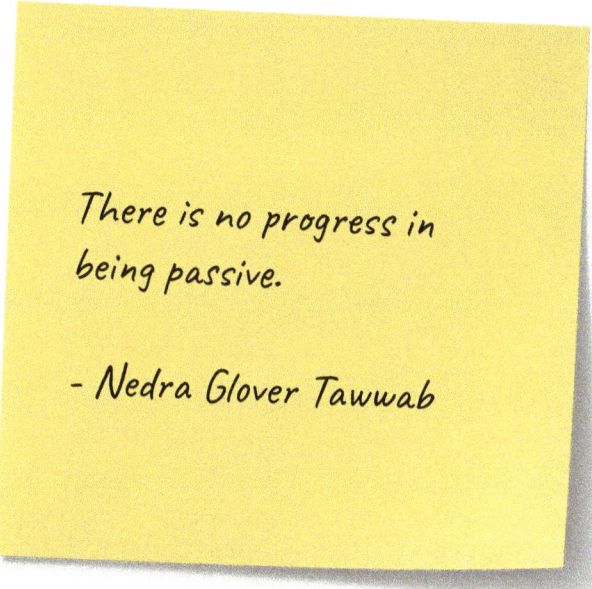

Surprisingly, most professional ethics guidelines or

codes of conduct relating to various mental health professionals do not specify the need for a treatment plan *document*. Instead, they reference treatment planning as a process (some more overtly than others), similar to informed consent (AAMFT, 2015; ACA, 2014; AMHCA, 2020; APA, 2017; NASW, 2021). This idea of treatment plans as a process, rather than a form or document to complete, provides a helpful framework for deciphering what is often conflicting feedback about what to include in a treatment plan.

Conduct a brief online search and you will find there is little consensus on how detailed treatment plans must be, or even the specifics of the content. In my consultation work I have seen therapists who write no treatment plans at all (*not* my recommendation), and those who write lengthy treatment plans with pages of goals and objectives.

You have likely heard talk about treatment plans as if they are required documentation so you might be asking these two common questions:

1. *If treatment plans are not specifically mentioned, am I ethically required to write a treatment plan?*
2. *If I do need to write a treatment plan, what should be included?*

Let's evaluate these questions from a larger perspective and use this guidance to create easy-to-follow standards for documentation.

Question 1: *If treatment plans are not specifically mentioned, am I ethically required to write a treatment plan?*

Thankfully, the five major organizations that provide ethical standards for mental health professionals (AAMFT, ACA, AMHCA, APA, and NASW) are fairly consistent in their guidelines. Here is a summary and interpretation of the guidelines:

- Ethics guidelines encourage clinicians to consider third-party agreements and comply with related requirements when clients access services (ACA, APA, NASW). The majority of insurance companies require mental health clinicians to complete a formal treatment plan. Therefore, it may be unethical to bill insurance for psychotherapy without creating a treatment plan, if the insurance identifies that as required documentation.

- Clinicians are expected to assess client needs and determine that they are able to help the client based on their experience, resources (e.g. supervision if not licensed or experienced), and the problem as presented by the client (ACA, APA, NASW). A treatment plan, in conjunction with an initial assessment, provides this information in a clear way.

- Clinicians are expected to inform clients how they can help the client, and even to present alternative options, if available (ACA, 2014; APA, 2017; APA, 2021; NASW, 2005). A simple treatment plan is an excellent way to present this information in a clear and understandable way.

- The American Counseling Association's Code of Ethics (2014, p.4) and the AMHCA Code of Ethics (2020, p.10) provide more specific guidance about counseling plans, although only ACA uses language to make completion of treatment plans appear compulsory. Both codes outline that counseling plans must be created collaboratively, and be realistic to accomplish based on the client's resources and needs at the time of creation.

Question 2: *If I do need to write a treatment plan, what should be included?*

The rest of this chapter will answer this question in detail and the examples in Chapter 7 provide further guidance. However, my overall recommendation is to write a *short and simple* treatment plan because 1) insurance companies prefer documentation that is clear and direct, and 2) clients are more involved when their treatment plan is easily accessible and understandable (Matthews, 2020; Peck et al., 2017).

Viewing the list of Potential Treatment Plan Components in Chapter 7, it may appear as though I am recommending a detailed and lengthy treatment plan. However, remember that all the templates and examples available in this book are providing options for a variety of clinicians and meant for use as a starter list to be pared down for your particular situation and common client needs. Not all components listed in Chapter 7 are described here because they are considered auxiliary.

The following sections focus on what to include in a treatment plan and how to write these components succinctly. Using these strategies clinicians can complete a high quality and insurance-appropriate treatment plan in 10 minutes or less. Most importantly though, these strategies incorporate a client-centered approach that emphasizes the true goal of treatment planning - *to create the foundation for a shared experience between clinician and client.*

The National Association of Social Workers Code of Ethics (2021) summarizes this beautifully in the description of one of their ethical principles: "Social workers engage people as partners in the helping process."

TREATMENT PLANNING AS CLIENT EMPOWERMENT

In the book *Better Results*, Miller, Hubble and Chow (2020) summarize and discuss what contributes to positive client outcomes. They share results from decades of research and hundreds of studies on what makes excellent clinicians and what constitutes effective psychotherapy.

They identify five factors that contribute to psychotherapy outcomes, along with the percent ranges for each factor:

1. **Client and Other Extratherapeutic Factors (80-87%)** - these include everything the client brings to psychotherapy. These factors are completely outside the clinician's control and oftentimes, outside even the client's control. Consider factors such as culture, family history, physical health conditions, and employment.
2. **The Alliance and Therapeutic Relationship (5-8%)** - Miller et al. note this factor includes "a wide range of relationally oriented behaviors" such as "empathy, caring, warmth, acceptance, congruence, encouragement, affirmation, and consensus building" (p. 119).
3. **The Therapist (4-9%)** - this includes factors such as personality and life experience, along with "the individual practitioners' unique ability to establish and maintain the therapeutic relationship." (p. 119).

4. **Hope and Expectancy (4%)** - this factor includes both the client and clinician's beliefs that psychotherapy will be effective. It is not focused on the *how* of psychotherapy (e.g. the specific treatment model), but does include a sense of trust in and dedication to the identified process.
5. **Structure (up to 1%)** - this small final factor is also what many clinicians focus on throughout much of their career. This factor accounts for treatment modality (e.g. EMDR, IFS, CBT, etc.).

Why is this information relevant to treatment planning and documentation? Because this is where the clinician can use documentation to *enhance* the relational aspect of the psychotherapy process, rather than detract from it.

Miller et al. note that while there is no clear evidence that one specific treatment modality within psychotherapy consistently works better than others, having a structure and focus to psychotherapy does impact effectiveness. Identifying a formal psychotherapy structure, regardless of what that is, and discussing it with the client can be a potentially a powerful way to impact hope and expectancy.

It is not enjoyable for anyone, clinician and client alike, to create a cold and boring treatment plan focused on documentation for insurance or other regulatory bodies. Use therapeutic, relational aspects throughout the treatment planning process to enhance the experience, build rapport, and establish an alliance. Focus on what is truly important to the client, and create a paper (or digital) representation of that with the treatment plan (Zuckerman, 2019).

WRITING EASY AND MEANINGFUL TREATMENT GOALS

Treatment goals don't need to be complicated to be meaningful. Simple and clear goals are not only easier to write, they are preferred by insurance companies, and more importantly, clients (Schwitzer & Rubin, 2015).

The key to keeping treatment goals simple is doing what may feel most intimidating at first - involving clients in the process. This collaborative process is more engaging for clients (APA 2021) and will help you avoid distraction. Stick to *one* goal at a time. Many therapists try to fit multiple points of focus into a single goal, creating confusion for both themselves and their clients. Let's look at an example.

> **Complicated goal:** Client will reduce symptoms of depression and anxiety by learning mindfulness strategies for coping with symptoms.

This goal is complicated because it is actually tracking *three* things: (1) depression symptoms, (2) anxiety symptoms, and (3) learning mindfulness strategies. The goal attempts to reduce two of these (depression and anxiety symptoms) and simultaneously increase another aspect (learning mindfulness strategies). It is also not clear what "learning mindfulness strategies" means and that will be difficult to track over time.

Any time you write phrases such as "so that," "by," or "in order to" in a treatment goal, you can likely delete that phrase, write a period, and end the goal instead. Don't overcomplicate things. Stick to tracking one behavior (or group of behaviors) with each goal.

We can actually make three separate, more simple goals from the one goal above.

> **Simpler goal 1:** Client will reduce depressive symptoms (depressed mood, crying, feelings of guilt, insomnia, etc.) from 7 days/week to 5 days/week.

Note: This is called a "SMART goal" and we'll discuss this specific format for writing goals in the next section.

> **Simpler goal 2:** Client will reduce anxiety symptoms (poor concentration, ruminating thoughts, worry) from 7 days/week to 5 days/week.

> **Simpler goal 3:** Client will practice mindfulness techniques (e.g. meditation, grounding, and other strategies learned in sessions) 5 days per week.

These three goals are sufficient for a treatment plan, provided they align with the client's presentation, diagnosis, and stated goals for therapy. Once you practice using this format, writing goals is quick and easy.

Separate treatment objectives are not necessary. Sources that outline differences between objectives and goals are usually referencing other prior examples in a circular manner. Furthermore, I have yet to find an insurance company that requires *both* goals *and* objectives be included in treatment plans. Including both makes the treatment plan more complicated to follow for everyone involved.

I recommend writing treatment goals that are easy for clients to understand, evaluate, and follow. These goals will also be easy for insurance companies to read and connect with medical

Top Tip

Write two goals for all clients. One goal focuses on reducing symptoms or unwanted behaviors, and the other goal focuses on increasing a coping skill.

The majority of topics discussed in session will fall into one of these two categories, making your goals applicable week by week. These two goals are broad enough to cover many topics, but still specific enough to satisfy insurance requirements.

You can even have these goals ready as an easy-to-use template. This quickens the process of creating treatment goals with clients and takes the pressure off you to translate a client's stated goal into complicated clinical language.

WHEN TO USE "SMART" GOALS

The previous examples of "Simpler goals" used a common format called "SMART," which is popular in many fields and not specific to mental health. This acronym stands for:

Specific
Measurable
Attainable
Realistic
Timebound

The idea with writing SMART goals is that a goal is very easy to track over time. It is clear what needs to happen for the goal to be achieved, and when to check in about the goal.

Most insurance companies prefer goals written in SMART format because it makes therapy a more objective process. While some therapists may balk at this requirement, personally, I believe writing SMART goals actually helps with therapeutic rapport and clinician confidence. Clients benefit from this clarity and from developing goals collaboratively with the clinician (van Rijt et al., 2021; Schwitzer & Rubin; Miller et al.; APA 2021).
Let's look at some examples of generic goals and make them "SMART" in order to meet most insurance criteria.

Example 1

Generic goal: Client will reduce PTSD symptoms.

SMART goal: Client will reduce PTSD symptoms (e.g. nightmares, avoidance of specific stimuli, hypervigilance, etc.) from 5 times a day to 2 times a day.

In this example, the details in parenthesis make the goal more *specific* and adding the number of times symptoms occur in a day makes the goal *measurable*. The *time* to achieve the goal is listed elsewhere in the treatment plan and clinical judgment determines the goal is *attainable* and *realistic*.

Example 2

Generic goal: Client will increase management of ADHD behaviors.

SMART goal: Client will use ADHD management tools (behavior tracking, mindfulness strategies, etc.) at least twice per day.

In this example, the goal becomes *specific* when the tools are identified in parenthesis. The goal is *measurable* once we identify how often the tools will be used. This goal is likely *attainable* and *realistic* based on a general presentation of ADHD and the *timebound* portion is covered by the overall timeframe for the treatment plan.

Top Tip

When it feels difficult to create a goal, try shifting the goal in the opposite direction.

For example, I had difficulty creating the above goal related to ADHD. When struggling to easily write a goal, a better strategy is to create a goal focused on the opposite behavior. In the example above that would mean reducing behaviors, such as "Client will reduce ADHD behaviors (e.g. interrupting others, stopping tasks before completion, etc) from 7 days/week to 5 days/week."

While SMART goals can initially feel complicated and restrictive, they actually make goal writing more simple. Follow a basic formula and stick with observable and objective behaviors your client has presented to you. Make sure everything connects to the diagnosis and/or presenting problem (Griswold, 2022).

Remember, the majority of clients are coming to see you because they want to change something about their life (Miller et al.). They are in distress and want to see change. Your job is to guide them through that change. Regardless of the modality you use, having an objective way to measure that change over time is extremely helpful (Homeyer & Bennet, 2023; Schwitzer & Rubin).

THE MOST IMPORTANT THING ABOUT TREATMENT PLAN INTERVENTIONS

The interventions in psychotherapy treatment plans are meant to be broad and apply to treatment overall. Therefore, it is not necessary to list out *every* potential intervention. Identify the modality (or modalities) of treatment and give a snapshot of the types of interventions within that modality (Gehart, 2016). Describe an overview of the planned psychotherapy treatment, rather than specific details. Progress notes will fill in further details and more specific interventions ongoing.

Remember, this section focuses on *your* actions as the clinician (Homeyer & Bennet). Use checkboxes or bullet points and phrases, rather than full sentences, to describe the types of things you do in therapy.

Top Tip

This is an excellent section to create a checkbox section or reference list of common interventions and modalities of treatment you provide. Many clients will come in with similar problems and while your treatment is individualized, your broad interventions and conceptualizations are not likely to change dramatically. Select what is relevant to your common clients to create a quick reference sheet or checkbox list for yourself.

Reference the Planned Therapeutic Interventions list in the next chapter for examples of what to include. Select which modalities and interventions apply to the work you do with clients and modify them as needed.

Don't overthink this section. Keep it simple and clear. It should only take about 30 seconds to

Don't overthink this section. Keep it simple and clear. It should only take about 30 seconds to complete this for each client's treatment plan, unless the client has questions about this part of the process.

INTEGRATING STRENGTHS AND SUPPORTIVE FACTORS

An important component of treatment planning, both in practice and in documentation, is considering your client's strengths and supportive factors. This places a positive focus on psychotherapy and acknowledges your client comes to the table with their own resources. This also provides a more complete case conceptualization as part of the treatment planning process (Homeyer & Bennet, Schwitzer & Rubin).

Strengths and supportive factors can include things such as:

- Skills the client has already learned through experience or education
- Inherent factors such as intelligence, creativity or perseverance
- Evidence of functioning such as stable work or involvement in school
- History of success with psychotherapy/seeking treatment
- Pet ownership
- Interests in hobbies or involvement in community groups
- Other social or family support

Including this list as part of the treatment plan shows your client that you recognize positive aspects of their personality simultaneously with their needs. You will notice that all of the above are also things to consider when evaluating protective factors for clients who may self-harm (Houston, 2017).

While you will find a list of potential strengths and supportive factors in the next chapter, this is a section where you can leave space to include quotes from your client. Ask them directly about their strengths and their support system/coping methods and then include what they plan to use. This makes for a very personalized and very easy to complete treatment plan!

WHEN AND HOW TO UPDATE TREATMENT PLANS

One of the most common questions I get about treatment plans is *"How often do I need to update a treatment plan?"* As usual, the answer to that question is *"It depends."*

Some insurance companies do require frequent updates at specific intervals. For example, most state Medicaid programs require goals to be evaluated every three months and treatment plans to be renewed annually. If you contract with Medicare or Medicaid in the United States, make sure to follow the regional format.

Keep this in mind when creating treatment goals since it may have a significant impact on making goals *attainable* and *realistic* within your identified timeframe. Write goals that can likely be completed within 3-6 months. That way you may continue a goal after the first check-in, but you are showing progress over longer periods of time and able to update the goals thereafter.

If you are working with private insurance companies who do not have guidelines for treatment goal time frames, or if you do not contract with insurance at all, it is still helpful to identify a clear timeline. A year-long treatment plan with quarterly check-ins provides plenty of time for therapeutic interventions and themes to play out, while still encouraging the clinician and client to evaluate effectiveness over time. It also reminds you to celebrate wins and recognize progress that may be more difficult to see on a weekly basis.

Clinician Spotlight: Tara

Tara used to spend hours completing treatment plans. She would typically write them without the client at some point after intake, using their discussion from the intake session to inform goals. Treatment plans felt tedious and it seemed their only purpose was security in case of an insurance audit.

After a consultation session with me, Tara realized she had not updated any treatment goals or plans in months. This task felt daunting until we created a plan for her to discuss treatment goals in her upcoming sessions with clients.

She was able to update all of her client treatment plans within two weeks and with almost no documentation work outside of client sessions. These sessions were clinically rich and she was surprised at some of the insights her clients presented. Making this one change in her documentation practice saved her hours of administrative work and created a positive experience with clients.

Reviewing treatment plans or specific goals does not have to be a daunting or time-consuming process. Simply mention to your client that it has been a certain number of months and you'd like to check in with them about the goals you created a while ago. Have a clinically focused discussion based on your personal style and seek honest feedback about how your client thinks treatment is going.

Come prepared with your own evaluation of how treatment is going and recognize the growth your client has made. You might use this time to address past therapeutic ruptures or even make suggestions about things you would like to do differently to improve as the clinician. You may also notice that certain themes of recent sessions are not reflected in the treatment plan and suggest a goal is revised or added.

Altogether this conversation can easily happen in conjunction with updating the treatment plan in 5-15 minutes, depending on the client. Keep the paperwork part of things short and sweet. Focus on the clinical process and your client's experience of therapy to date. When done well, reviewing treatment goals and treatment plans is not only quick, it is a valuable clinical discussion that also enriches the psychotherapy process (Baldwin, et al., 2021).

Quick Read Chapter Summary

- The treatment plan is a broad overview of what you and the client plan to achieve in psychotherapy.

- Treatment plans serve as a way to honor client autonomy and agency in the therapy process.

- Treatment plans are easiest *and* most relevant when completed with client input.

- Two goals are enough to cover the majority of treatment in most outpatient psychotherapy settings, provided these two goals cover 1) reducing symptoms and 2) increasing a coping skill.

- SMART goals are specific, measurable, attainable, realistic, and timebound. Insurance sometimes requires goals written in SMART format.

- Including strengths and supportive factors, along with needs for progress, ensures treatment plans capture a more complete picture of the client.

NOTES

Chapter 7

Treatment Plan Templates

IN THIS CHAPTER

Guidance on Using Templates 147
Potential Treatment Plan Components 149
Treatment Plan Example: Insurance 156
Treatment Plan Example: Simple 161
Treatment Plan Example: Narrative 165
Treatment Plan Example: Child 167
Treatment Plan Example: Couples 171

The greatest glory in living lies not in never falling, but in rising every time we fall.

- Nelson Mandela

GUIDANCE ON USING TEMPLATES

The following pages include options for various components to include in a treatment plan template. The lists within the Potential Treatment Plan Components are meant to be extensive and include a variety of items so clinicians can choose what best applies to their situation and for their clients. I strongly recommend reviewing the lists, then paring them down based on preference and need, rather than referencing the full list every time you write a treatment plan.

 All treatment plans are meant for use with clients but the Potential Treatment Plan Components in this chapter is provided as a resource for creating a treatment plan template. Therefore, it is the only form in this chapter without the icon to the left showing that it is meant for use with clients.

For students and clinicians working in a setting with prescribed forms:

Use the Treatment Plan Components lists as a reference when completing treatment plans with the template you are required to complete. For example, review the list of Treatment goals and have it handy when discussing goals with clients and when completing documentation. Choose 10-15 goals that best apply to your clients so you are not overwhelmed by the list every time.

If you are required to use a narrative style, use the Components lists as starter phrases. See the *Treatment Plan Example: Narrative* for how to adapt the checkbox format to a narrative format.

For clinicians in a private practice setting with flexibility to choose their own template format:

Option 1: Review the two Treatment Plan Templates provided. The Insurance plan includes medical necessity components and the Simple plan does not. You may be able to use these templates as is! However, I still recommend you then review the list of Treatment Plan Components and add in (or subtract) anything that better relates to your work with clients.

Option 2: Review the lists of Treatment Plan Components and identify 1) Which components apply to your practice that you want to include in a treatment plan template, and 2) Put the lists together to create your personalized treatment plan template.

The list of Components is long and can feel intimidating, but support is available so you will not be overwhelmed. Check out the video instructions at **QAPrep.com/SFD-Resources** for help with adapting the templates to your preferences.

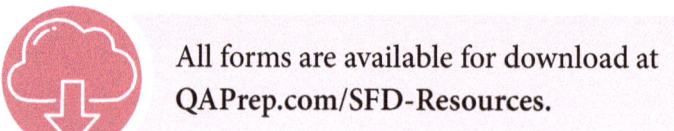

All forms are available for download at QAPrep.com/SFD-Resources.

Potential Treatment Plan Components

Problems/Symptoms (check all that apply):

- ☐ Addiction
- ☐ Alcohol use
- ☐ Appetite (Increased)
- ☐ Appetite (Decreased)
- ☐ Anger
- ☐ Anxiety
- ☐ Attention/Concentration
- ☐ Body image
- ☐ Boundaries
- ☐ Bullying
- ☐ Burnout
- ☐ Childhood experiences/trauma
- ☐ Chronic pain
- ☐ Communication
- ☐ Compulsions
- ☐ Dating
- ☐ Delusions
- ☐ Difficulty asking for help
- ☐ Drug use
- ☐ Eating/food
- ☐ Emotional awareness
- ☐ Emotional regulation
- ☐ Energy level
- ☐ Expressing anger
- ☐ Family conflict
- ☐ Fearfulness
- ☐ Food restriction
- ☐ Friends/Social life
- ☐ Fulfillment
- ☐ Guilt
- ☐ Hallucinations
- ☐ Health (physical)
- ☐ History of abuse
- ☐ Hoarding
- ☐ Identity
- ☐ Impulse control
- ☐ Loneliness
- ☐ Motivation
- ☐ Nightmares
- ☐ Obsessive thoughts
- ☐ Organization
- ☐ Overwhelm
- ☐ Panic attacks
- ☐ Paranoid thoughts
- ☐ Parenting
- ☐ Perfectionism
- ☐ Phobia
- ☐ Physical aggression
- ☐ Poor self-care
- ☐ Relationship struggles
- ☐ Ruminating thoughts
- ☐ Sadness
- ☐ School
- ☐ Self-image
- ☐ Self harm/Intent to harm
- ☐ Sensory modulation
- ☐ Sexual arousal/desire
- ☐ Sexual intimacy in relationship
- ☐ Sexuality
- ☐ Sleep (insomnia)
- ☐ Sleep (other)
- ☐ Social interactions
- ☐ Somatic concerns
- ☐ Suicidal ideation/intent
- ☐ Symptoms management
- ☐ Thinking
- ☐ Time Management
- ☐ Trauma (acute)
- ☐ Trauma (chronic)
- ☐ Work
- ☐ Worry

Potential Treatment Plan Components (Continued)

Treatment Goals (2-3 goals per treatment plan):

☐ Client will **reduce** symptoms of:
_____
from ____ to ____ times a day/days a week/days a month.

☐ Client will reduce anger outbursts (insert 2-3 examples) from ____ to ____ times a day/days a week/days a month.

☐ Client will reduce anxiety symptoms (insert 2-3 examples) from ____ to ____ times a day/days a week/days a month.

☐ Client will reduce autonomic arousal from non-threatening stimuli (insert 2-3 examples) from ____ to ____ times a day/days a week/days a month.

☐ Client will reduce depressive symptoms (insert 2-3 examples) from ____ to ____ times a day/days a week/days a month.

☐ Client will reduce negative self-statements (insert 2-3 examples) from ____ to ____ days a week/days a month.

☐ Client will reduce PTSD symptoms (insert 2-3 examples) from ____ to ____ times a day/days a week/days a month.

☐ Client will reduce perfectionism thoughts/behaviors (insert 2-3 examples) from ____ to ____ days a week/days a month.

☐ Client will reduce poor sleep (insert 2-3 examples) from ____ to ____ days a week/days a month.

☐ Client will reduce repetitive behaviors (insert 2-3 examples) from ____ to ____ days a week/days a month.

☐ Client will reduce suicidal ideation/thoughts/actions (insert example) from ____ to ____ times a day/days a week/days a month.

☐ Client will reduce symptoms of grief (insert 2-3 examples) from ____ to ____ times a day/days a week/days a month.

☐ Client will reduce using substances as coping skills from ____ to ____ times a day/days a week/days a month.

☐ Client will **increase** using coping skills such as:
_____
from ____ to ____ times a day/days a week/days a month.

☐ Client will increase asking for support (insert 2-3 examples) from ____ to ____ times a day/days a week/days a month.

☐ Client will increase completion of daily living tasks (insert 2-3 examples) from ____ to ____ times a day/days a week/days a month.

☐ Client will increase engagement in positive activities (insert 2-3 examples) from ____ to ____ times a day/days a week/days a month.

Potential Treatment Plan Components (Continued)

- ☐ Client will increase frustration tolerance (insert 2-3 examples) from ____ to ____ times a day/days a week/days a month.
- ☐ Client will increase regulating emotions (insert 2-3 examples) from ____ to ____ times a day/days a week/days a month.
- ☐ Client will increase socializing with others (insert 2-3 examples) from ____ to ____ times a day/days a week/days a month.
- ☐ Client will increase use of assertive communication skills (insert 2-3 examples) from ____ to ____ times a day/days a week/days a month.
- ☐ Client will increase use of relapse prevention skills (insert 2-3 examples) from ____ to ____ times a day/days a week/days a month.
- ☐ Client will increase use of relaxation skills (insert 2-3 examples) from ____ to ____ times a day/days a week/days a month.
- ☐ Client will increase use of resourcing skills (insert 2-3 examples) from ____ to ____ times a day/days a week/days a month.
- ☐ Client will increase use of self-care strategies (insert 2-3 examples) from ____ to ____ days a week/days a month.
- ☐ Client will increase use of sleep hygiene skills (insert 2-3 examples) from ____ to ____ days a week/days a month.
- ☐ Client will increase using conflict resolution skills (insert 2-3 examples) from ____ to ____ times a day/days a week/days a month.v
- ☐ Client will practice using coping skills such as:
  _____
  from ____ to ____ times a day/days a week/days a month.

- ☐ Client's stated long-term goal:
  _____

- ☐ Other goal:
  _____
  _____

Potential Treatment Plan Components (Continued)

Progress at _____ months:
- ☐ Made progress in the following areas: _____
- ☐ Continues to experience impairment in: _____
- ☐ Met goal as written. Will continue with other goals in treatment plan.
- ☐ Met goal as written. Will continue treatment focus with a revised goal.
- ☐ Met goal as written and treatment is concluded.
- ☐ Made some progress toward goal but goal is not met. It is clinically beneficial to continue as written.
- ☐ Did not make progress toward goal. New goal created to better address needs.
- ☐ Did not make progress toward goal but it is clinically beneficial to continue as written.

Medical Necessity:
Psychotherapy treatment is recommended and medically necessary to:
- ☐ Reduce symptoms related to mental health diagnosis
- ☐ Stabilize symptoms related to mental health diagnosis
- ☐ Manage symptoms related to chronic mental health symptoms
- ☐ Prevent de-compensation related to a mental health diagnosis
- ☐ Prevent need for a higher level of care to treat mental health diagnosis

Extended session times (53+ minutes) are recommended and medically necessary to:
- ☐ Allow adequate time for processing traumatic events and assisting the client with emotional regulation prior to leaving sessions.
- ☐ Allow adequate time for discussion, problem-solving, and practicing coping skills due to the client's current lack of social support.
- ☐ Allow adequate time for all individuals in the session to meaningfully participate.
- ☐ Address the complexity of the client's presenting problems and adequately problem-solve solutions in sessions.
- ☐ Address the severity of the client's symptoms and prevent the need for further escalation of care.
- ☐ Accommodate the client's need for frequent redirection and refocusing.
- ☐ Accommodate the client's need for extended discussion and extra time to process information from sessions.

Potential Treatment Plan Components (Continued)

Client Participation(choose 1-3):

- ☐ Communicate with spouse/partner/family
- ☐ Complete rating scales
- ☐ Journaling
- ☐ Practice skills learned in session
- ☐ Reflect on therapy sessions
- ☐ Review progress made
- ☐ Seek support when needed
- ☐ Share concerns, thoughts, feelings about therapy
- ☐ Track and monitor symptoms
- ☐ Other: _____

Strengths/Resources (check all that apply):

- ☐ Comfortable expressing feelings and emotions
- ☐ Community support/involvement
- ☐ Engages in hobbies/interests
- ☐ History of positive interactions with other providers/treatment
- ☐ Motivated for therapy
- ☐ Pet owner
- ☐ Spiritual or religious beliefs
- ☐ Strong support system
- ☐ Other: _____

Potential Barriers (if applicable):

- ☐ Financial difficulties
- ☐ History of psychiatric hospitalizations
- ☐ Interaction with legal system
- ☐ Lack of social support
- ☐ Limited access to healthcare
- ☐ Physical health concerns
- ☐ Transportation
- ☐ Unstable living situation
- ☐ Other: _____

Potential Treatment Plan Components (Continued)

Planned Therapeutic Interventions (choose 3-6):

Therapeutic interventions based on:
- ☐ Acceptance and Commitment Therapy (ACT)
- ☐ Attachment theory
- ☐ Biofeedback
- ☐ Brainspotting
- ☐ Cognitive Behavioral Therapy (CBT)
- ☐ Dialectical-Behavior Therapy (DBT)
- ☐ Eye Movement Desensitization & Reprocessing (EMDR)
- ☐ Emotional Freedom Technique (Tapping)
- ☐ Emotionally Focused Therapy (EFT for couples)
- ☐ Exposure and response prevention
- ☐ Gottman Method couples therapy
- ☐ Hypnosis
- ☐ Internal Family Systems (IFS)
- ☐ Mindfulness Based Stress Reduction (MBSR)
- ☐ Music therapy
- ☐ Play therapy
- ☐ Polyvagal theory
- ☐ Sand tray therapy
- ☐ Solution-Focused Brief Therapy
- ☐ Somatic therapy

Other treatment interventions:
- ☐ Art projects
- ☐ Creative expression
- ☐ Genogram/exploring family history
- ☐ Gratitude work
- ☐ Grief work
- ☐ Guided imagery
- ☐ Identify impact of history and traumatic experiences
- ☐ Movement
- ☐ Psychoeducation
- ☐ Role play

Practice and teach skills for:
- ☐ Autonomic regulation
- ☐ Anger management
- ☐ Building and using a support system
- ☐ Communication
- ☐ Cognitive restructuring
- ☐ Conflict resolution
- ☐ Coregulation
- ☐ Decision clarification
- ☐ Distress tolerance
- ☐ Emotional regulation
- ☐ Empathy and attunement
- ☐ Expressing emotions
- ☐ Frustration tolerance
- ☐ Interrupting negative patterns
- ☐ Making transitions
- ☐ Managing boundaries
- ☐ Mindfulness
- ☐ Organization/time management
- ☐ Problem-solving
- ☐ Recognizing and communicating needs and wants
- ☐ Recognizing and reacting to triggers
- ☐ Recognizing and responding to social cues
- ☐ Reducing impulsivity
- ☐ Reinforcing positive thoughts/behaviors
- ☐ Self-care
- ☐ Sensory regulation
- ☐ Sleep hygiene/routine
- ☐ Stress management

Assess and monitor symptoms of: _____

Potential Treatment Plan Components (Continued)

Frequency of Treatment:	*Modality of Treatment:*
☐ Weekly ☐ 2x/week ☐ Every other week ☐ Monthly ☐ Other: _____	☐ Individual therapy ☐ Couples therapy ☐ Family therapy ☐ Group therapy ☐ Other: _____

Expected time to achieve goals or next review of treatment plan:

☐ 3 months ☐ 6 months ☐ 9 months ☐ 12 months

Tracking and assessment measures (check any that apply):

☐ Beck Depression Inventory
☐ Client self-report
☐ Clinical ratings scale: _____
☐ Clinician observation
☐ GAD-7
☐ Observer/collateral report
☐ Outcome Rating Scale (ORS)
☐ PHQ-9
☐ Other: _____

Coordination of Care with (if applicable):

☐ Nutritionist/Dietician
☐ Other therapist
☐ Parent/Guardian
☐ Partner/Spouse
☐ PCP/Physician
☐ Psychiatrist
☐ Teacher
☐ Client declines
☐ Not applicable
☐ Other: _____

Treatment Plan Example: Insurance

Psychotherapy Treatment Plan (Insurance)

Client Name: Elsa Agnarrsdottir   **Date:** 08/31/2024

Problems/Symptoms:

- ☐ Alcohol Use
- ☐ Appetite (increased)
- ☐ Attention
- ☑ Childhood experiences
- ☐ Communication
- ☐ Concentration
- ☐ Dating
- ☐ Drug Use
- ☑ Energy
- ☐ Family conflict
- ☑ Fearfulness
- ☑ Friends/Social life
- ☑ Fulfillment
- ☐ Health
- ☑ Identity
- ☑ Loneliness
- ☐ Motivation
- ☐ Organization
- ☑ Overwhelm
- ☐ Parenting
- ☐ Relationships (partner/spouse)
- ☑ Relationships (other)
- ☐ Sadness
- ☐ School
- ☐ Self harm/Intent to harm
- ☑ Self-image
- ☐ Sexuality
- ☐ Sleep
- ☐ Thinking
- ☐ Time Management
- ☑ Trauma
- ☐ Work
- ☑ Worry
- ☐ Other: _____

Treatment Goals:

Goal #1
Client will reduce anxiety symptoms (anxious mood, insomnia, restlessness, fatigue, etc.) from 5 times a day to 2 times a day.

Progress at _____ months:
- ☐ Made progress in the following areas: _____
- ☐ Continues to experience impairment in: _____
- ☐ Met goal as written. Will continue with other goals in treatment plan.
- ☐ Met goal as written. Will continue treatment focus with a revised goal.
- ☐ Met goal as written and treatment is concluded.
- ☐ Made some progress toward goal but goal is not met. It is clinically beneficial to continue as written.
- ☐ Did not make progress toward goal. New goal created to better address needs.
- ☐ Did not make progress toward goal but it is clinically beneficial to continue as written.

Treatment Plan Example: Insurance (Continued)

Goal #2
Client will increase use of relaxation skills (deep breathing, grounding, taking a pause, etc.) from 0 times a day to 2 times a day.

Progress at _____ months:
- ☐ Made progress in the following areas: _____
- ☐ Continues to experience impairment in: _____
- ☐ Met goal as written. Will continue with other goals in treatment plan.
- ☐ Met goal as written. Will continue treatment focus with a revised goal.
- ☐ Met goal as written and treatment is concluded.
- ☐ Made some progress toward goal but goal is not met. It is clinically beneficial to continue as written.
- ☐ Did not make progress toward goal. New goal created to better address needs.
- ☐ Did not make progress toward goal but it is clinically beneficial to continue as written.

Medical Necessity:
Psychotherapy treatment is recommended and medically necessary to:
- ☒ Reduce symptoms related to mental health diagnosis
- ☐ Stabilize symptoms related to mental health diagnosis
- ☐ Manage symptoms related to chronic mental health symptoms
- ☐ Prevent de-compensation related to a mental health diagnosis
- ☐ Prevent need for a higher level of care to treat mental health diagnosis

Extended session times (53+ minutes) are recommended and medically necessary to:
- ☒ Allow adequate time for processing traumatic events and assisting the client with emotional regulation prior to leaving sessions.
- ☒ Allow adequate time for discussion, problem-solving, and practicing coping skills due to the client's current lack of social support.
- ☐ Allow adequate time for all individuals in the session to meaningfully participate.
- ☒ Address the complexity of the client's presenting problems and adequately problem-solve solutions in sessions.
- ☐ Address the severity of the client's symptoms and prevent the need for further escalation of care.
- ☐ Accommodate the client's need for frequent redirection and refocusing.

Treatment Plan Example: Insurance (Continued)

☐ Accommodate the client's need for extended discussion and extra time to process information from sessions.

Client Participation (choose 1-3):

☑ Communicate with spouse/partner/family
☐ Complete rating scales
☑ Journaling
☑ Practice skills learned in session
☑ Reflect on therapy sessions

☑ Review progress made
☑ Seek support when needed
☑ Share concerns, thoughts, feelings about therapy
☑ Track and monitor symptoms

Strengths/Resources (check all that apply):

☐ Comfortable expressing feelings and emotions
☐ Community support/involvement
☐ Engages in hobbies/interests
☐ History of positive interactions with other providers/treatment

☑ Motivated for therapy
☑ Pet owner
☐ Spiritual or religious beliefs
☑ Strong support system
☐ Other: _____

Potential Barriers (if applicable):

☐ Financial difficulties
☐ History of psychiatric hospitalizations
☐ Interaction with legal system
☐ Lack of social support

☐ Limited access to healthcare
☐ Physical health concerns
☐ Transportation
☐ Unstable living situation
☑ Other: High stress work

Frequency and Modality:

Frequency of Treatment:	Modality of Treatment:
☑ Weekly ☐ 2x/week ☐ Every other week ☐ Monthly ☐ Other: _____	☐ Individual therapy ☐ Couples therapy ☐ Family therapy ☐ Group therapy ☐ Other: _____

Treatment Plan Example: Insurance (Continued)

Planned Therapeutic Interventions:

Assess and monitor symptoms of:
_____

Therapeutic interventions based on:
- ☐ Acceptance and Commitment Therapy (ACT)
- ☐ Biofeedback
- ☐ Brainspotting
- ☐ Cognitive Behavioral Therapy (CBT)
- ☐ Dialectical-Behavior Therapy (DBT)
- ☐ Eye Movement Desensitization & Reprocessing (EMDR)
- ☐ Exposure and response prevention
- ☐ Hypnosis
- ☐ Internal Family Systems (IFS)
- ☐ Mindfulness Based Stress Reduction (MBSR)
- ☐ Solution-Focused Brief Therapy
- ☐ Somatic therapy

Other treatment interventions:
- ☐ Art projects
- ☐ Creative expression
- ☑ Genogram/exploring family history
- ☑ Gratitude work
- ☑ Grief work
- ☑ Guided imagery
- ☐ Identify impact of history and traumatic experiences
- ☐ Movement
- ☑ Psychoeducation
- ☐ Role play

Practice and teach skills for:
- ☑ Autonomic regulation
- ☐ Anger management
- ☑ Building and using a support system
- ☐ Communication
- ☐ Cognitive restructuring
- ☐ Conflict resolution
- ☐ Coregulation
- ☐ Decision clarification
- ☐ Distress tolerance
- ☑ Emotional regulation
- ☐ Empathy and attunement
- ☑ Expressing emotions
- ☑ Frustration tolerance
- ☑ Interrupting negative patterns
- ☐ Making transitions
- ☐ Managing boundaries
- ☑ Mindfulness
- ☐ Organization/time management
- ☐ Problem-solving
- ☑ Recognizing and communicating needs and wants
- ☑ Recognizing and reacting to triggers
- ☐ Recognizing and responding to social cues
- ☐ Reducing impulsivity
- ☑ Reinforcing positive thoughts/behaviors
- ☐ Self-care
- ☑ Sensory regulation
- ☐ Sleep hygiene/routine
- ☑ Stress management

Treatment Plan Example: Insurance (Continued)

Expected time to achieve goals or next review of treatment plan:

☐ 3 months ☑ 6 months ☐ 9 months ☐ 12 months

Tracking and assessment measures (check any that apply):

☐ Beck Depression Inventory
☐ Client self-report
☐ Clinical ratings scale:
　_____
☐ Clinician observation

☑ GAD-7
☐ Observer/collateral report
☐ Outcome Rating Scale (ORS)
☐ PHQ-9
☐ Other: _____

Coordination of Care with (if applicable):

☐ Nutritionist/Dietician
☐ Other therapist
☐ Parent/Guardian
☐ Partner/Spouse
☐ PCP/Physician

☐ Psychiatrist
☐ Teacher
☐ Client declines
☑ Not applicable
☐ Other: _____

Elsa Agnarrsdottir　　　　　　　　　　　　　　　　　　08/31/2024

Client Signature　　　　　　　　　　　　　　　　　　**Date**

Awesome Therapist　　　　　　　　　　　　　　　　　08/31/2024

Therapist Signature　　　　　　　　　　　　　　　　**Date**

Treatment Plan Example: Simple

Psychotherapy Treatment Plan

Client Name: Moana Waialiki **Date:** 08/06/2024

Problems/Symptoms (check all that apply):

- ☐ Alcohol Use
- ☐ Appetite (increased)
- ☐ Attention
- ☐ Childhood experiences
- ☐ Communication
- ☐ Concentration
- ☐ Dating
- ☐ Drug Use
- ☐ Energy
- ☐ Family conflict
- ☐ Fearfulness
- ☑ Friends/Social life
- ☐ Fulfillment
- ☐ Health
- ☑ Identity
- ☑ Loneliness
- ☐ Motivation
- ☐ Organization
- ☐ Overwhelm
- ☐ Parenting
- ☐ Relationships (partner/spouse)
- ☐ Relationships (other)
- ☐ Sadness
- ☐ School
- ☐ Self harm/Intent to harm
- ☑ Self-image
- ☐ Sexuality
- ☐ Sleep
- ☐ Thinking
- ☐ Time Management
- ☐ Trauma
- ☐ Work
- ☐ Worry
- ☐ Other: _____

Treatment Goals:

Goal #1
Client will reduce negative self-statements from 5 days a week to 1 day a week.

Progress at _____ months:
- ☐ Met goal as written. Will continue with other goals in treatment plan.
- ☐ Met goal as written. Will continue treatment focus with a revised goal.
- ☐ Met goal as written and treatment is concluded.
- ☐ Made some progress toward goal but goal is not met. It is clinically beneficial to continue as written.
- ☐ Did not make progress toward goal. New goal created to better address needs.
- ☐ Did not make progress toward goal but it is clinically beneficial to continue as written.

Treatment Plan Example: Simple (Continued)

Goal #2
Client will increase asking for support from friends and family from 0 times a week to 3 times a week.

Progress at _____ months:
- ☐ Met goal as written. Will continue with other goals in treatment plan.
- ☐ Met goal as written. Will continue treatment focus with a revised goal.
- ☐ Met goal as written and treatment is concluded.
- ☐ Made some progress toward goal but goal is not met. It is clinically beneficial to continue as written.
- ☐ Did not make progress toward goal. New goal created to better address needs.
- ☐ Did not make progress toward goal but it is clinically beneficial to continue as written.

Client Participation:
- ☑ Communicate with spouse/partner/family
- ☐ Complete rating scales
- ☑ Journaling
- ☑ Practice skills learned in session
- ☑ Reflect on therapy sessions
- ☐ Review progress made
- ☑ Seek support when needed
- ☐ Share concerns, thoughts, feelings about therapy
- ☐ Track and monitor symptoms

Strengths/Resources:
- ☐ Comfortable expressing feelings and emotions
- ☑ Community support/involvement
- ☑ Engages in hobbies/interests
- ☐ History of positive interactions with other providers/treatment
- ☑ Motivated for therapy
- ☑ Pet owner
- ☑ Spiritual or religious beliefs
- ☐ Strong support system
- ☐ Other: _____

Treatment Plan Example: Simple (Continued)

Planned Therapeutic Interventions (choose 3-6):

Assess and monitor symptoms of:
- ☐ ADHD
- ☐ Adjustment Disorder
- ☐ Anxiety
- ☐ Bipolar Disorder
- ☐ Depression
- ☐ OCD
- ☐ Stress
- ☐ Trauma

Other treatment interventions:
- ☐ Art projects
- ☐ Creative expression
- ☑ Genogram/exploring family history
- ☑ Gratitude work
- ☐ Grief work
- ☐ Guided imagery
- ☑ Identify impact of history and traumatic experiences
- ☑ Movement
- ☐ Psychoeducation
- ☐ Role play

Practice and teach skills for:
- ☐ Autonomic regulation
- ☐ Anger management
- ☑ Building and using a support system
- ☐ Communication
- ☐ Cognitive restructuring
- ☐ Conflict resolution
- ☐ Coregulation
- ☐ Decision clarification
- ☑ Distress tolerance
- ☐ Emotional regulation
- ☐ Empathy and attunement
- ☑ Expressing emotions
- ☐ Frustration tolerance
- ☑ Interrupting negative patterns
- ☐ Making transitions
- ☑ Managing boundaries
- ☐ Mindfulness
- ☐ Organization/time management
- ☐ Problem-solving
- ☑ Recognizing and communicating needs and wants
- ☐ Recognizing and reacting to triggers
- ☐ Recognizing and responding to social cues
- ☐ Reducing impulsivity
- ☑ Reinforcing positive thoughts/behaviors
- ☑ Self-care
- ☐ Sensory regulation
- ☐ Sleep hygiene/routine
- ☐ Stress management

Treatment Plan Example: Simple (Continued)

Expected time to achieve goals or next review of treatment plan:

☐ 3 months ☑ 6 months ☐ 9 months ☐ 12 months

Tracking and assessment measures (check any that apply):

☐ Beck Depression Inventory
☑ Client self-report
☐ Clinical ratings scale: _____
☑ Clinician observation

☐ GAD-7
☐ Observer/collateral report
☑ Outcome Rating Scale (ORS)
☐ PHQ-9
☐ Other: _____

Coordination of Care with (if applicable):

☐ Nutritionist/Dietician
☐ Other therapist
☐ Parent/Guardian
☐ Partner/Spouse
☐ PCP/Physician

☐ Psychiatrist
☐ Teacher
☐ Client declines
☑ Not applicable
☐ Other: _____

Moana Waialiki   08/06/2024
_____
Client Signature   **Date**

Awesome Therapist   08/06/2024
_____
Therapist Signature   **Date**

Treatment Plan Example: Narrative

Psychotherapy Treatment Plan: Narrative

Client Name: Pocahontas Powhatan **Date:** 02/02/2024

Problems/Symptoms:
Client reports ongoing symptoms related to trauma, such as difficulty regulating emotions, avoiding places that remind her of past traumatic events, recurring nightmares, insomnia, easily startled, hypervigilant and worried about her children to the point of not being able to focus on other tasks when they are away.

Medical Necessity:
Psychotherapy treatment is recommended and medically necessary to reduce symptoms related to a mental health diagnosis.

Extended session times (53+ minutes) are recommended and medically necessary to allow adequate time for processing traumatic events and assisting the client with emotional regulation prior to leaving sessions, and address the severity of the client's symptoms and prevent the need for further escalation of care.

Treatment Goals:
Expected time to achieve goals or next review of treatment plan:
1 year with check-ins every 6 months

Goal #1
Client will reduce autonomic arousal from non-threatening stimuli (sounds outside, phone calls from family, etc.) from 7 days a week to 3 days a week.

Progress at 6 months: 08/02/2024
Made some progress toward goal but goal is not met. Client experiences autonomic arousal from non-threatening stimuli daily but does report a reduction in the number of times daily. It is clinically beneficial to continue the goal as written.

Goal #2
Client will increase use of resourcing skills (positive memories and supports, grounding, etc.) from 0 times a day to 2 times a day.

Progress at 6 months: 08/02/2024
Met goal as written. Will continue treatment focus with a revised goal.

Revised Goal #2:
Client will increase use of resourcing skills (additional relaxation skills, using support system, etc.) from 2 times a day to 4 times a day.

Treatment Plan Example: Narrative (Continued)

Client Participation:
The client will communicate with her spouse about support needs. She will practice skills learned in session, reflect on sessions, and review progress made in therapy. The client will seek additional support when needed by communicating with the therapist. She will monitor and track symptoms to discuss progress in therapy.

Strengths/Resources:
The client is comfortable expressing feelings and emotions and has support from her spouse, family, friends, and community members. She is motivated for therapy and has strong spiritual beliefs that she uses as a resource.

Potential Barriers:
No significant barriers to treatment are immediately apparent.

Planned Therapeutic Interventions:
Therapist will assess and monitor symptoms of PTSD.
Therapist will use EMDR to assist with symptoms of trauma and anxiety.
Therapist will teach and practice with client skills for autonomic regulation, emotional regulation, recognizing and interrupting negative or maladaptive patterns, mindfulness, and reinforcing positive thoughts and behaviors.

Frequency and Modality:
The client will attend individual therapy once a week.
Couples therapy sessions may be included as needed to assist with resourcing.

Tracking and assessment measures:
Client self-report, Clinician observation, and PHQ-9

Coordination of Care:
Client agrees to coordination of care with spouse through couples therapy sessions as needed, and to progress reports for the referring physician.

Pocahontas Powhatan   02/02/2024
___
Client Signature   **Date**

Awesome Therapist   02/02/2024
___
Therapist Signature   **Date**

Treatment Plan Example: Child

Psychotherapy Treatment Plan (Child)

Client Name: Wendy Darling   **Date:** 06/01/2024

Problems/Symptoms:

- ☐ Anger
- ☑ Anxiety
- ☑ Attention/concentration
- ☐ Appetite
- ☐ Communication
- ☐ Compulsions
- ☐ Emotional regulation
- ☐ Energy
- ☐ Family conflict
- ☐ Fearfulness
- ☐ Friends/Social life
- ☐ Health
- ☐ History of abuse
- ☐ Identity
- ☐ Impulse control
- ☐ Loneliness
- ☑ Nightmares
- ☐ Organization
- ☐ Overwhelm
- ☐ Panic attacks
- ☐ Phobia
- ☐ Physical aggression
- ☐ Relationships
- ☑ Ruminating thoughts
- ☐ Sadness
- ☐ School
- ☐ Self harm/Intent to harm
- ☐ Self-image
- ☐ Sleep
- ☐ Social interactions
- ☑ Somatic concerns
- ☑ Trauma
- ☑ Worry
- ☐ Other: _____

Treatment Goals:

Goal #1
Client will reduce anxiety symptoms (worry, insomnia, nightmares, ruminating thoughts) from 7 days a week to 5 days a week.

Progress at _____ months:
- ☐ Made progress in the following areas: _____
- ☐ Continues to experience impairment in: _____
- ☐ Met goal as written. Will continue with other goals in treatment plan.
- ☐ Met goal as written. Will continue treatment focus with a revised goal.
- ☐ Met goal as written and treatment is concluded.
- ☐ Made some progress toward goal but goal is not met. It is clinically beneficial to continue as written.
- ☐ Did not make progress toward goal. New goal created to better address needs.
- ☐ Did not make progress toward goal but it is clinically beneficial to continue as written.

Treatment Plan Example: Child (Continued)

Goal #2
Client will increase regulating emotions (anxious thoughts) from 0 times a day to 2 times a day.

Progress at _____ months:
- ☐ Made progress in the following areas: _____
- ☐ Continues to experience impairment in: _____
- ☐ Met goal as written. Will continue with other goals in treatment plan.
- ☐ Met goal as written. Will continue treatment focus with a revised goal.
- ☐ Met goal as written and treatment is concluded.
- ☐ Made some progress toward goal but goal is not met. It is clinically beneficial to continue as written.
- ☐ Did not make progress toward goal. New goal created to better address needs.
- ☐ Did not make progress toward goal but it is clinically beneficial to continue as written.

Medical Necessity:
Psychotherapy treatment is recommended and medically necessary to:
- ☑ Reduce symptoms related to mental health diagnosis
- ☐ Stabilize symptoms related to mental health diagnosis
- ☐ Manage symptoms related to chronic mental health symptoms
- ☐ Prevent de-compensation related to a mental health diagnosis
- ☐ Prevent need for a higher level of care to treat mental health diagnosis

Extended session times (53+ minutes) are recommended and medically necessary to:
- ☑ Allow adequate time for processing traumatic events and assisting the client with emotional regulation prior to leaving sessions.
- ☑ Allow adequate time for reviewing and practicing coping skills taught in sessions.
- ☑ Allow adequate time for all individuals in the session to meaningfully participate.
- ☐ Address the complexity of the client's presenting problems and adequately problem-solve solutions in sessions.
- ☑ Address the severity of the client's symptoms and prevent the need for further escalation of care.
- ☐ Accommodate the client's need for frequent redirection and refocusing.

Treatment Plan Example: Child (Continued)

Client Participation:

- ☑ Ask for help when needed
- ☑ Communicate with family
- ☑ Communicate with therapist
- ☑ Practice skills learned in session
- ☑ Report on symptoms
- ☑ Review progress in sessions
- ☑ Share concerns, thoughts, feelings about therapy

Strengths/Resources:

- ☑ Communicates well
- ☑ Community support and involvement
- ☐ Engages in hobbies/interests
- ☑ Expresses feelings/emotions
- ☑ Good insight and reflection
- ☐ History of positive interactions with other providers/treatment
- ☑ Strong support system
- ☐ Other: _____

Potential Barriers:

- ☐ Financial difficulties
- ☐ History of psychiatric hospitalizations
- ☐ Interaction with legal system
- ☐ Lack of social support
- ☐ Limited access to healthcare
- ☐ Physical health concerns
- ☐ Transportation
- ☐ Unstable living situation
- ☑ Other: None reported

Frequency and Modality:

Frequency of Treatment:	Modality of Treatment:
☑ Weekly ☐ 2x/week ☐ Every other week ☐ Monthly ☐ Other: _____	☑ Individual therapy ☑ Family therapy ☐ Group therapy ☐ Other: _____

Expected time to achieve goals or next review of treatment plan:

☑ 3 months   ☐ 6 months   ☐ 9 months   ☐ 12 months

Tracking and assessment measures:

- ☑ Client self-report
- ☐ Clinical ratings scale: _____
- ☑ Clinician observation
- ☑ Collateral report
- ☐ Other: _____

Treatment Plan Example: Child (Continued)

Planned Therapeutic Interventions:

Assess and monitor symptoms of:
Anxiety

Therapeutic interventions based on:
EMDR, Mindfulness, Play therapy

Other treatment interventions:
- ☑ Art projects
- ☑ Creative expression
- ☐ Gratitude work
- ☐ Grief work
- ☑ Guided imagery
- ☑ Movement
- ☐ Psychoeducation
- ☑ Role play

Practice and teach skills for:
- ☐ Anger management
- ☐ Asking for help/support
- ☐ Cognitive restructuring
- ☐ Conflict resolution
- ☐ Distress tolerance
- ☑ Emotional regulation
- ☐ Empathy and attunement
- ☐ Expressing emotions
- ☐ Frustration tolerance
- ☐ Making transitions
- ☑ Mindfulness
- ☑ Positive thoughts and behaviors
- ☐ Problem-solving
- ☑ Recognizing and reacting to triggers
- ☐ Recognizing and responding to social cues
- ☐ Reducing impulsivity
- ☑ Sensory regulation
- ☑ Sleep hygiene/routine
- ☑ Stress management

Coordination of Care with:
- ☐ Nutritionist/Dietician
- ☐ Other therapist
- ☑ Parent/Guardian
- ☐ PCP/Physician
- ☐ Psychiatrist
- ☑ Teacher
- ☐ Not applicable
- ☐ Other: _____

Wendy Darling   06/01/2024
_____
Client Signature   **Date**

Awesome Therapist   06/01/2024
_____
Therapist Signature   **Date**

Psychotherapy Treatment Plan (Couples)

Client Names: Aladdin Cassim and Jasmine bint Hamed Bobolonius
Date: 07/18/2024

Problems/Symptoms:

- ☐ Alcohol Use
- ☑ Boundaries
- ☑ Childhood experiences
- ☐ Chronic pain
- ☐ Communication
- ☑ Difficulty asking for help
- ☐ Drug Use
- ☐ Expressing emotions
- ☐ Extended family
- ☐ Family conflict
- ☐ Fearfulness
- ☐ Friends/Social life
- ☐ Fulfillment
- ☐ Health
- ☐ History of abuse
- ☐ Home management
- ☑ Identity
- ☐ Infidelity
- ☑ Loneliness
- ☐ Organization
- ☐ Overwhelm
- ☑ Parenting
- ☐ Physical aggression
- ☐ Relationships with others
- ☐ Sadness
- ☐ School
- ☐ Self harm/Intent to harm
- ☑ Sexual intimacy in relationship
- ☐ Sleep
- ☐ Social interactions
- ☐ Symptoms management
- ☐ Time Management
- ☐ Trauma
- ☐ Work
- ☐ Worry
- ☐ Other: _____

Treatment Goals:

Goal #1
Clients will increase conflict resolution skills such as listening and reframing what their partner has said during arguments.

Progress at _____ months:
- ☐ Met goal as written. Will continue with other goals in treatment plan.
- ☐ Met goal as written. Will continue treatment focus with a revised goal.
- ☐ Met goal as written and treatment is concluded.
- ☐ Made some progress toward goal but goal is not met. It is clinically beneficial to continue as written.
- ☐ Did not make progress toward goal. New goal created to better address needs.
- ☐ Did not make progress toward goal but it is clinically beneficial to continue as written.

Treatment Plan Example: Couples (Continued)

Goal #2
Clients will increase positive interactions with one another (e.g. date night, positive affirmations, etc.) from 2 times a month to 5 times a month.

Progress at _____ months:
☐ Met goal as written. Will continue with other goals in treatment plan.
☐ Met goal as written. Will continue treatment focus with a revised goal.
☐ Met goal as written and treatment is concluded.
☐ Made some progress toward goal but goal is not met. It is clinically beneficial to continue as written.
☐ Did not make progress toward goal. New goal created to better address needs.
☐ Did not make progress toward goal but it is clinically beneficial to continue as written.

Expected time to achieve goals or next review of treatment plan:
☐ 3 months   ☐ 6 months   ☐ 9 months   ☑ 12 months

Client Participation:
☑ Communicate with spouse
☐ Complete rating scales
☑ Practice skills learned in session
☑ Reflect on therapy sessions
☑ Review progress made
☑ Seek support when needed
☑ Share concerns, thoughts, feelings about therapy

Strengths/Resources:
☑ Both partners motivated
☑ Comfortable expressing feelings and emotions to one another
☐ Community support and involvement
☐ History of positive interactions with other providers/treatment
☑ Spiritual or religious beliefs
☐ Strong support system
☐ Other: _____

Treatment Plan Example: Couples (Continued)

Planned Therapeutic Interventions:

Therapeutic interventions based on:
- ☑ Attachment theory
- ☑ Emotionally Focused Therapy (EFT for couples)
- ☐ Gottman Method couples therapy
- ☐ Internal Family Systems (IFS)
- ☐ Mindfulness
- ☐ Polyvagal theory
- ☐ Sand tray therapy
- ☐ Solution-Focused Brief Therapy
- ☐ Somatic therapy

Other treatment interventions:
- ☐ Creative expression
- ☑ Genogram, exploring family history
- ☐ Gratitude work
- ☐ Grief work
- ☐ Guided imagery
- ☑ Identify impact of history and traumatic experiences
- ☐ Movement
- ☑ Psychoeducation
- ☑ Role play

Practice and teach skills for:
- ☐ Anger management
- ☑ Communication
- ☐ Cognitive restructuring
- ☑ Conflict resolution
- ☐ Coregulation
- ☐ Decision clarification
- ☐ Distress tolerance
- ☐ Emotional regulation
- ☑ Empathy and attunement
- ☑ Expressing emotions
- ☐ Frustration tolerance
- ☑ Interrupting negative patterns
- ☑ Managing boundaries
- ☐ Managing home tasks
- ☐ Mindfulness
- ☐ Organization/time management
- ☑ Problem-solving
- ☑ Recognizing and communicating needs and wants
- ☑ Recognizing and reacting to triggers
- ☐ Recognizing and responding to behavioral cues
- ☑ Reinforcing positive thoughts and behaviors
- ☑ Self-care
- ☐ Sensory regulation
- ☑ Sexual intimacy
- ☐ Sleep hygiene/routine
- ☐ Stress management

Treatment Plan Example: Couples (Continued)

Tracking and assessment measures:
- ☑ Client self-reports
- ☐ Clinical ratings scale: _____
- ☑ Clinician observation
- ☐ Outcome Rating Scale (ORS)
- ☐ Other: _____

Coordination of Care with:
- ☐ Nutritionist/Dietician
- ☐ Other therapist
- ☐ PCP/Physician
- ☐ Psychiatrist
- ☐ Clients decline
- ☑ Not applicable
- ☐ Other: _____

Aladdin Cassim   07/18/2024

Client Signature   **Date**

Jasmine bint Hamed Bobolonius   07/18/2024

Client Signature   **Date**

Awesome Therapist   07/18/2024

Therapist Signature   **Date**

NOTES

Chapter 8

Progress Notes

IN THIS CHAPTER

What Goes in a Progress Note? 177
Psychotherapy Notes Versus Progress Notes 179
Making Notes Simple and Meaningful 180
The Perfect Progress Note Template 181
Different Types of Progress Notes.. 183
Collaborative Documentation 185
Amending Progress Notes 188
Documenting Risky Situations 190
Documenting Ethical Dilemmas 194
Quick Read Chapter Summary 196

> *See if you can allow gentle self-acceptance to coexist with the active drive for self-improvement.*
>
> *- Dr. Kristin Neff*

Progress notes are the lifeblood of your documentation.

They protect you from liability and provide continuity of care for your clients. Progress notes also assist you in tracking progress and themes in treatment. Lastly, quality notes also provide justification for reimbursement by insurance (if needed).

WHAT GOES IN A PROGRESS NOTE?

Similar to treatment planning, most professional ethics codes (AAMFT, 2015; ACA, 2014; AMHCA, 2020; APA, 2017; NASW, 2021) applicable to mental health clinicians offer little guidance on the question, *"What goes in a progress note?"* These codes provide general guidance and allow for flexibility among a variety of specialties and scenarios.

While clinical examples of progress notes can vary widely and ethics codes are vague, all these sources do provide enough information to create general criteria that applies to most mental health clinicians in most scenarios.

Based on a review of the current professional association codes of ethics, various state laws, HIPAA, and common insurance requirements, each progress note should (generally) include the following:

- Client name
- If applicable, other attendees (parent, spouse, etc.)
- Date, time, and length of session
- Type of session (with applicable billing code if needed for insurance)
- Summary of the topic(s) covered in session
- Interventions provided
- Client presentation, including brief MSE and behavioral observations
- Client progress and current symptoms or impairments
- If applicable, notes on risk and resulting safety planning
- If applicable, changes to treatment goals/plan
- Notes on any other poignant items (e.g. referral made to psychiatrist)
- Any assignments/plan for the next session
- Date of the next session, or explanation for no follow up appointment
- Clinician signature and date of signature

There are other things to consider for progress notes, such as your clinical setting, treatment modality, and employer requirements. Some insurance companies also want to see the treatment goals addressed during the session in each progress note. Additionally, your electronic health record (EHR) may have other elements meant to assist clinicians with note taking.

If you prefer a different way of thinking about what to include in progress notes, consider asking yourself questions when writing notes. Here are some potential questions that cover the same topic areas but in a way that guides you to think differently:

- *What did you do during the session and why?* These are your interventions and your rationale.
- *What did the client discuss during the session?* These are your topics and themes of the session.
- *How did the client appear, seem to feel, or report they were feeling? What did they do in the session that you could observe (e.g. cry)?* This is the client presentation.
- *What seemed important to your client? What did they say was important to them about the session?* This is the client progress, and maybe a client quote.
- *What progress has your client made toward their treatment goals? Was there any insight gained or actions taken since the previous session? What did they say they struggled with since the last session?* This is the client's progress and impairments.

- *Did you make any decisions or recommendations? Did you assign homework or create a plan for you or the client to do something before the next session?* This is your plan section.

Asking yourself these questions before or during writing progress notes will help to summarize what happened and keep you focused on the most poignant things to include in the note. You can also use these questions regardless of the setting in which you work or the progress note template that you use.

PSYCHOTHERAPY NOTES VERSUS PROGRESS NOTES

What is the difference between progress notes and psychotherapy notes (more commonly called process notes)?

Progress notes are ethically required for every session (AAMFT, 2015; ACA, 2014; AMHCA, 2020; APA, 2017; NASW, 2021), although the format varies. They provide a brief summary of the session and are exactly what the majority of this chapter discusses.

Psychotherapy (or process) notes, however, are optional. They are geared toward the therapist's process of the session and are kept separate from the general client record. This is a space for the clinician to write things such as:

- Clinical impressions that feel more like "hunches,"
- Things you'd like to remind yourself about for future sessions,
- Names of client connections that don't belong in the client's formal record,
- Personal reflections or feelings about the client,
- And just about anything else related to working with that particular client.

The phrase "psychotherapy notes" comes from the HIPAA Privacy Rule and recognizes that psychotherapy as a profession may warrant increased confidentiality when related to other healthcare areas.

Top Tip

Psychotherapy notes are not meant to hide relevant clinical information. These notes are meant for the clinician's personal use and should never replace progress notes.

While HIPAA does provide added protection for psychotherapy notes, it is important to remember that this protection does not mean these notes are immune from subpoena or even a records request. *Any* document of any kind is open to a potential subpoena, and this topic is covered in Chapter 11.

States have the freedom to extend HIPAA regulations, which focus on client access to records, provider-to-provider access to records, and provider responsibility to protect those records from people not directly involved in the client's treatment.

In other words, clinicians commonly focus on the privacy aspect of HIPAA but fail to recognize that client access to records is always paramount. For example, HIPAA allows clinicians to deny access to psychotherapy notes (not progress notes) when requested. However, Washington state expands the client access portion of HIPAA to include *all* client records (Washington Administrative Code [WAC], 2005; WAC, 2009; WAC, 2017). This means that clinicians in Washington state cannot refuse access even to psychotherapy records.

This is one of many reasons to consider avoiding psychotherapy notes and simply focus on writing quality and objective progress notes. Keep your documentation simple and your clients informed about the fact that you take notes.

MAKING NOTES SIMPLE AND MEANINGFUL

Putting yourself in the right mindset prior to writing notes is crucial. Poor documentation happens when you're hurried or stressed. Ironically, documentation tends to take longer when you are stressed, as well.

This doesn't mean you need to meditate for an hour before writing notes but taking even two minutes to clear your head will make the entire process easier. Use this quick exercise to prepare before writing a progress note:

- First, get into a quiet space, meaning you are not rushed to complete the note.
- Second, reflect on your time spent in treatment with this client so far.
- Third, visualize your client after the session.
    1. What have they learned?
    2. What action might they take as a result?
    3. What emotions may come up for them when reflecting on the session?

Now that you are in a calmer state of mind and focused on the client's presentation, you can write the progress note more easily and objectively. You will also train yourself to associate writing notes with feelings of reflection and calm, rather than feelings of stress.

Clear and objective language is more helpful than clinically complicated language. The old marketing adage "clear is better than clever" also applies to progress notes. For example, rather than spending time figuring out how to translate a client's insight, use their direct quote.

Use commonly accepted abbreviations or short keys to save time but keep the language easily understandable. It is more important that an average person could read the progress note and understand what happened than for the note to sound like a clinical conceptualization for a graduate school project.

Top Tip

Avoid using full sentences in progress notes as much as possible. Use bullet points and short phrases to summarize information when a checkbox or dropdown format is not available. This significantly reduces the mental effort from the process of writing, allowing you to focus on the purpose of the progress note and the client.

My top strategy for easy but high quality notes is using cheat sheets, checkboxes, and dropdown menus that are personalized to your clinical work and to your common client needs. There is no need to reinvent the wheel with every individual progress note. Combine your personal writing style with common therapeutic interventions and common client responses to create a structured progress note template that is both easy to read and easy to complete.

Reference the example progress notes and starter phrases available in Chapter 10 to see examples of how to start this process.

THE PERFECT PROGRESS NOTE TEMPLATE

Using a consistent template allows clinicians to save time and provides prompts to remember key components for each progress note. Even the best of us forget things or hit a "writer's block" at times so plan ahead and make it easy to translate what happened in session into a note.

Templates also provide flexibility depending on your style and preference. In Chapter 10 you'll find potential sections of a progress note template along with examples of various templates. You can also download the Progress Note Templates using the link for the book's bonus resources: **QAPrep.com/SFD-Resources.**

When trying a new template, choose one of two different "testing" methods:

- Option one is to use the template with all clients for 2-4 weeks. This provides the opportunity to see how the template captures information over time, as well as across different client needs.
- Option two is to use the template for all clients on a certain day for a month. For example, if you want to try using the suggested checkbox template in Chapter 10, use that template for all Tuesday clients but stick with your old template on your other clinical days.

Don't be discouraged if the template doesn't resonate with you. Make notes on what you find yourself wanting to add or subtract. Add in your own clinical language or language specific to common issues your clients present. Break up the sections into different areas. Play around with it until you have something that feels like it works for you and your client's needs.

Most importantly, don't become distracted by what works for others. Some people love SOAP notes and I really dislike them (as mentioned in Chapter 2). All note templates serve the same purpose, just choose what is easiest for you, and what gets the progress notes *done*.

Clinician Spotlight: Maria

Maria was a very conscientious therapist who frequently worried about the quality of her progress notes. Because she felt progress notes were so important she tended to include a lot of information and spent extensive time rewriting sentences to make sure her notes were of excellent clinical quality.

When I met with Maria to review her progress notes, I noticed that she actually had quite a few sections in her template with checkboxes or dropdowns already. However, she was also writing a narrative for these same sections, creating duplicate work for herself.

Maria also had a few sections in her template that appeared to be copied and pasted from week to week with little or no change in the content. This was concerning to her, but she reported that a supervisor had told her to include these things in every note and so she thought they were required, even though they felt irrelevant for most client sessions.

I recommended Maria remove the sections of her template that were copied week to week since these did not add any clinical value and were not related to treatment progress or any other external documentation requirement.

I also recommended Maria remove all but one of the narrative sections from her progress note template so that she could more easily rely on the detailed and personalized checkboxes and drop down menus she had created, without feeling compelled to fill in a text field.

Instead, I recommended keeping just one text field and labeling that as "Other Notes - As Applicable" to remind her this text field was only for out of the norm situations. I also recommended that when she did need to use this field, to only write in bullet points so she could keep the writing more succinct.

Within two weeks of following this advice, Maria's time writing progress notes went down from an average of 30 minutes per note to 5 minutes per note!

DIFFERENT TYPES OF PROGRESS NOTES

There is potentially a different type of progress note for every type of service offered, such as phone contact, intake sessions, and regular psychotherapy sessions. For insurance purposes, types of progress notes usually relate to the service provided and are considered either "billable" or "non-billable." Billable services typically include interaction with the client (or collaterals) in a meaningful way and for at least a brief but extended amount of time. Services that are non-billable to insurance vary depending on individual insurance contracts, but often include many day-to-day clinician activities such as:

- Brief phone calls or texting to discuss scheduling or canceling sessions
- Brief phone calls or emails regarding basic client updates
- Writing a summary letter for clients
- Collaborating with other providers or collaterals on the client's behalf
- Responding to requests for records, consultation, or other information
- Making copies of and sending records

There are times when clinicians can charge clients for some of the above services even if the clinician is contracted with the client's insurance company. However, review your contract before charging clients to make sure this is acceptable.

Top Tip

For clinicians who do not accept insurance and who want to charge for some of the non-billable services listed, it is important to include this information as part of informed consent at the beginning of treatment. For example, many private pay clinicians charge a fee for clients who request a treatment summary letter. This is an important policy to review with clients *before* the situation happens.

Specific types of progress notes

Other, more specific types of progress notes are up to the discretion of the individual clinician. Creating multiple templates and types of progress notes can be helpful, especially when working with specific groups of people. For example, a clinician may only see adults but have four different progress note templates for 1) Intake sessions, 2) Psychotherapy sessions for college students, 3) Psychotherapy sessions focused on trauma, and 4) Generic psychotherapy sessions.

My recommendation is to have at least two progress note templates:

1. Intake progress note template
2. Generic psychotherapy progress note template

If creating a more specific progress note template helps with writing notes, then get as detailed as you like. Some other options for progress notes include:

- Child/play therapy
- Therapy with adolescents
- Parent consultation sessions
- Family therapy
- Couples therapy
- Group therapy
- Treatment planning session
- Modality specific notes, such as for EMDR or IFS
- Diagnosis or problem specific notes, such as for ADHD or Trauma

It can be helpful to create specific progress note templates when you see a few different types of clients who commonly present with similar problems/concerns. For example, if you work with couples and individuals, you will likely want to have at least an Individual Therapy Template and a Couples Therapy Template, because the context, interventions, and important things to note may be very different between these two types of services.

Specializing the types of progress notes allows you to create a more streamlined template while still keeping the template personalized to individual client needs. However, it can be easy to engage in "productive procrastination" with this task! Do not let creating and revising multiple progress note templates overtake your administrative time that could better be used on actually writing progress notes. However, if you find yourself constantly adapting a template, or wanting more specific interventions listed, it may be time to create a new specialty template to save yourself time in the long run.

COLLABORATIVE DOCUMENTATION

Collaborative documentation is the process of including your client in documentation. This includes a variety of options from minimally involved to fully collaborative:

- Minimal involvement: Remind clients of progress notes and make notes during the session.
- Partially collaborative: Take notes during sessions and ask clients for input at the end of session, writing in their response.
- Fully collaborative: Write the progress note with the client at the end of each session, asking for their feedback to your writing, as well as for what they would like to include.

This process sounds a bit scary for most clinicians at first, and many have strong, negative reactions to the thought of writing progress notes with a client. However, collaborative documentation de-mystifies documentation for clients and typically has a very high success rate, meaning that most clients actually enjoy the process. While not all clinicians are initially on board, collaborative documentation tends to create a positive and empowering experience for clients (Matthews, 2020).

Maniss and Pruit (2018) report collaborative documentation leads to "stronger therapeutic alliance, shared decision making for treatment options, and greater accuracy in documentation." Other benefits include saving time on documentation, and better explanations for clients. In fact, client access to records helps clinicians consider their wording and provide clearer examples for clients (Zanaboni et al., 2022). While collaborative documentation may not be appropriate for all clients, it is certainly worth trying out if you have struggled with falling behind in notes, or with client miscommunication issues.

How to start using collaborative documentation

Perhaps collaborative documentation sounds appealing after reading more about it, but many clinicians become stuck at implementation. Introducing this topic to clients is simple. Start with the template below and adapt it to your own way of speaking:

> *"You may remember that I write notes about each of our sessions. Today I'd like to try something new and get your feedback while I write the note. It may feel a little weird the first few times but research shows this actually improves the results for most clients and I am really interested in getting your ongoing feedback about each session. We'll try it out for the next six weeks and then see if we want to keep going."*

Depending on the therapeutic relationship already established, you may be able to start with a more simple phrase such as, *"You know that I write notes about our sessions and today I'd like to have you help with that."*

There are many potential phrases to use when ending the session and transitioning to collaborative documentation:

- *"I'd like to get your feedback on our session today."*
- *"Okay, let's sum up what we've discussed today."*
- *"Let's stop here and review what we've talked about."*
- *"What stood out to you about our session today?"*
- *"What is your biggest takeaway from today's session?"*
- *"What do you feel is most important for me to write about today's session?"*

Chow (2018) provides a framework for eliciting client feedback that can be incorporated here. One potential way to start is by priming the client with *"Today we talked about ___ and we did ___ exercise. We came up with some ideas on how to deal with ___"* (p.150).

Follow by asking for feedback about the next session. Chow (2018, p.151) uses these two approachable questions:

*"Based on today's session, what should we do **more** of?"* and
*"What should we do **less** of?"*

Using this type of framework the clinician receives invaluable feedback on the client's experience, empowers the client to include their voice within their progress notes, and accomplishes the task of starting (or even completing) a progress note.

A note about using artificial intelligence (AI) for progress notes

There is increased potential for using AI to write progress notes. Many of these options incorporate an aspect of collaborative documentation because the progress note is generated, with client consent, from a recording of the psychotherapy session. Below is an outline of how most AI progress note generators (software) create progress notes.

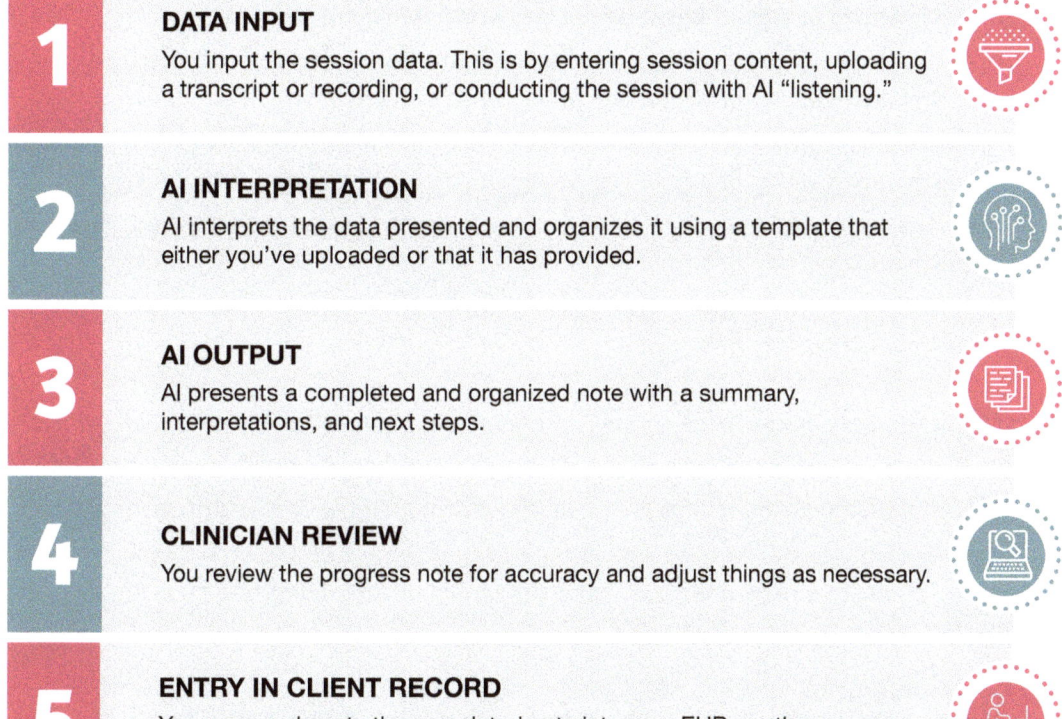

AI NOTE WRITING PROCESS

1. DATA INPUT
You input the session data. This is by entering session content, uploading a transcript or recording, or conducting the session with AI "listening."

2. AI INTERPRETATION
AI interprets the data presented and organizes it using a template that either you've uploaded or that it has provided.

3. AI OUTPUT
AI presents a completed and organized note with a summary, interpretations, and next steps.

4. CLINICIAN REVIEW
You review the progress note for accuracy and adjust things as necessary.

5. ENTRY IN CLIENT RECORD
You copy and paste the completed note into your EHR or other secure records system.

The ethical standards for using artificial intelligence to generate progress notes are still in creation for most professions. The American Counseling Association (2023) is the only national body to offer guidance on this topic as of 2024. They recommend clinicians obtain client consent before using AI with clients in any way. While this option may be exciting and stress-reducing for some clinicians, there is still much to consider when trying such a new method.

When considering whether or not AI is an effective tool for psychotherapy-related tasks, use these questions from the workshop Using Artificial Intelligence (AI) as a Mental Health Clinician: Managing risk, ethics, and clinical benefits (McCaffrey, 2024):

- ☐ I have confirmed that the AI platform is HIPAA secure and I have a BAA from the platform (for US professionals).
- ☐ I am using AI to help with time and efficiency, not because I lack confidence in my note *quality*.
- ☐ I have considered the practicality of using the AI platform in conjunction with my record keeping software/methods.
- ☐ I have reviewed with my client how AI will be used in documentation and have received their informed consent. *I have also documented this in a progress note.*
- ☐ I review all of the documentation (progress notes, forms, etc.) the AI tool creates and edit that documentation as needed.
- ☐ I make sure all documentation is personalized to my client and accurately reflects their experience.
- ☐ I track my use of AI tools to make sure it is truly saving me time on documentation.

AMENDING PROGRESS NOTES

Even if you feel fully confident in writing progress notes using all the methods identified in this book, there will inevitably be a time that you need to change something in a note *after* it is completed and signed. This is not only legal and ethical, it is also a very normal experience.

Amending a progress note does not make the clinician look "bad." In fact, it shows the clinician is conscientious and ethical (and human).

Before amending a progress note, confirm that the information you want to add or delete is truly necessary. It is tempting to focus on creating a "perfect" note but only amend a note when the information is vital. Here are some examples of when it is appropriate to amend a progress note:

- You accidentally wrote the client's partner's name in the progress note but usually just refer to them as "partner" because it is your practice to do so. You want to go in and adjust the information to simply say "partner."
- You were writing on auto pilot and forgot to include in your progress note that your client will be on vacation for two weeks. Instead you wrote "Will continue with weekly sessions" at the end so you want to correct the information.

- After a long day of client sessions, you accidentally wrote a progress note meant for Client A in Client B's file. You want to delete that note completely from Client B's file.
- After meeting with a client for a second time, you discover you were not using the correct pronouns in your documentation for the first session. You want to go back and change documentation to reflect the client's preferences.

The important consideration with amendments is that it is not a practice meant to hide information or to make slight adjustments to a progress note. The purpose of amending a note is to correct information that is misrepresented in the client's file, usually due to human error.

How to amend progress notes

Amending something handwritten or typed on paper is fairly simple. Simply cross out the information that is incorrect and add your initials and the date of amendment. Then, underneath that section or underneath whatever relevant section, add in the correct information and the reason for amendment. It can be as simple as "Amended note to add missing information." If there is not enough space to write the information in the relevant section, add the relevant information at the bottom of the note.

Once the note is corrected, sign the progress note again as you normally would, with the date of amendment. This means a handwritten or printed progress note will have two signatures and dates. The first will be the original date of creation, the second will be the date of the amendment. This creates a clear story of what happened and shows that this was an amendment, not an attempt to hide something.

Amending an electronic record is usually simple, but varies based on the EHR. Some EHRs provide an amendment option, which preserves the original progress note, and then creates an additional note underneath the first one, identified as an amendment.

This option is usually sufficient, but in the case of needing to delete information, you may need to actually delete the original progress note and re-create it instead. If you are concerned about creating a brand new progress note and signing it at a much later date than the originally written progress note, offer an explanation such as *"Progress note originally written on xx/yy/zz but included inaccurate information and required deletion due to no amendment option within the EHR."*

Some EHRs do not provide a separate amendment option and instead, allow you to erase your signature and edit the original note. In this case, clinicians are often worried about the original signature being missing. You can include the same note from the last paragraph to highlight that the note was originally created on a different day. The EHR will also have an audit record of any changes made to progress notes, so that report could always be pulled, if necessary.

DOCUMENTING RISKY SITUATIONS

There are many high risk issues that clinicians might deal with at some point in their career. These issues are beyond other ethical dilemmas because they include the added element of real or potential harm, often significant physical harm. Some broad categories of these risky situations include:

- Suicidality/Homicidality
- Child/Elder/Dependent Adult Abuse
- Domestic Violence
- Therapist Safety

When dealing with high risk issues, documentation becomes especially important. Know the laws, regulations, and professional standards in common situations. Note that these may be very different across state lines and among countries. These are not only helpful for guidance on how to proceed in a situation, they are helpful for what to reference in documentation.

Clinicians are encouraged to seek consultation and support for difficult scenarios (AAMFT, 2015; ACA, 2014; AMHCA, 2020; APA, 2017; Pope et al., 2021; NASW, 2021). For all ethical conflicts or risky situations, document consultations and any conversations with other professionals about the situation. Explain why you came to the conclusion you chose and what actions you took. Always document your rationale and clearly outline safety concerns for parties involved.

Suicidality & Homicidality

When documenting assessment of suicidality and homicidality, include client quotes whenever possible. This applies to either denial or condoning the ideation. Include what safety plans you created (Houston, 2017) along with the client's agreement to the plan.

In a progress note discussing an assessment of suicide or homicide risk, include information about resiliency factors, social support, and outline specific steps the client will take in various circumstances. Note that safety plans appear to be more effective than safety contracts (Gehart, 2016; Houston, 2017). Contracts have the client agree not to harm themself or someone else but do not go in depth regarding the alternative behaviors, triggers and actions to take.

Next, identify reasons for actions such as breaking confidentiality, or for not acting to further protect the client. Include a plan to follow-up after the fact. Identify when and how you will do so and any others who may be involved (e.g. family or friends).

> **Example 1:**
> *Client reported feeling hopeless, could not identify any social support and had an identifiable plan for suicide. Client has a history of 2 suicide attempts. Clinician called the crisis response team for further assessment and potential psychiatric hospitalization to maintain the client's safety. The response team recommended hospitalization and the client agreed for them to transport her.*
>
> **Example 2:**
> *Client reported that even when she thinks of dying she pictures her children and "just couldn't do that to them." She has never attempted suicide. Client was able to agree that she would not self-harm before the next psychotherapy session, identified two people she could talk with and agreed to call them when thoughts of self-harm appear. She also agreed to a follow up session in the office in three days.*

Also reference the Risk Assessment section of the Potential Progress Note Components in Chapter 10.

Child/Elder/Dependent Adult Abuse

Concerning abuse and reporting, clinicians are generally not required to determine whether or not actual abuse *occurred*. Instead, clinicians are required to report *suspicion of* abuse. This significantly lowers the bar for potential reporting, making it an important aspect of informed consent to review with clients as early as possible.

Document the general reason for suspecting potential abuse, but avoid documenting details of the story itself. These situations require some clinical judgment but consider that detailed reports of abuse are often not in the client's best interest (APA, 2017). They are likely unnecessary to convey the need for a report or as a benefit to the client's ongoing treatment.

> **Example:**
> *Client (age 15) reported during session that she was molested at the age of 10 by a cousin who was 14 years old at the time. She reported that "I told my mom some of it, but not the details. I think she talked to my aunt about it but that's it. It hasn't happened since then but we also don't get together with them anymore."*

These incidents can understandably create therapeutic ruptures. For this reason, I sometimes gave adult clients the option to join me in making the call and reporting the incident. While this is not always appropriate for all scenarios, there were times it made a significant impact on the results of the report and served to increase therapeutic rapport.

Document discussing the report with the client, their response, and potential follow up. Document the agency you reported to and any reference number assigned. Keep copies of any formal reports (the part with the details of the story) in a separate file. Remember to consider the client's confidentiality and the guideline to only share the minimum amount necessary (APA, 2017) in any follow-up conversations (e.g. an assigned case worker calling to ask more questions) and related documentation.

Intimate Partner Violence

Intimate partner violence (IPV) presents a slightly different dilemma because the clinician may be documenting the ongoing risk and *lack* of action on the clinician's part. IPV situations can be extremely dangerous (Sabri et al., 2022) but when only adult clients are involved, the client's right to confidentiality and autonomy usually preclude any type of reporting.

It is common that these situations last for months, or even years. Document completion of any screening or assessment tools, and ongoing discussions about safety and community resources. Specifically, identify the risks related to therapy and your role in keeping confidentiality. Focus on the safety of the client and any children involved (which may impact potential reporting based on state laws).

Documentation regarding safety planning should include the following (Sabri et al.):

- Outline any psychoeducation provided to the client regarding patterns of violence, ongoing impacts to children, and signs of increased danger.
- Identify a safety plan, including ways in which the client will respond to their partner during periods of escalation, where the client will go if they feel their life is in danger and are able to leave the location, and who they will contact during periods of violence.
- Identify specific plans for children's safety, if children are in the home, along with conversations about mandated reporting requirements.
- List resources provided, including hotlines, local shelters, handouts, etc.
- List consultations with other clinicians or professionals.

It is especially important that clinicians working in these scenarios have a network of support and reach out to colleagues for consultation when needed.

Therapist Safety

A commonly overlooked concept in discussions surrounding risk is that of clinician safety. What actions do you take when you are the one who is at risk from your client? This may include experiences such as real or perceived threats in sessions, frequent and alarming messages, and stalking.

Unfortunately, this scenario does arise in all types of clinical settings, with one report indicating there is a 35-40% chance of psychologists being at risk of assault at some point in their career (Munsey, 2008). Aggressive and violent clients also contribute to clinician burnout (Posluns & Gall, 2020). If this happens to you, reach out to other clinicians, and make sure you are not remaining silent on this issue!

Document any safety concerns from interactions with clients. Trust your gut in these scenarios - no issue is too small to mention. Documentation is the story of treatment and that includes different things for different clients. For example, a passing comment from a client about noticing the type of car you drive may be perceived or intended in very different ways:

- For a friendly client who has been looking at purchasing a new car soon, this may be harmless small talk along with genuine interest in your opinion about the car. In this scenario, you likely wouldn't document this brief conversation topic at all.
- For a client with a history of boundary violations with you and no prior discussions about or interest in cars, this might be a way for the client to reach out for connection. In this scenario, you *might* document the conversation, if it leads to a more in depth discussion and appears related to the clinical work and/or therapeutic rapport.
- For a client who has made other comments that reveal they are investigating more of your personal life (e.g. asking details about your relationships, and searched for you in an online database), this comment might be cause for concern. In this scenario, you *likely would* document the conversation, along with noting that you reviewed appropriate boundaries and explored reasons for the client's interest.

Oftentimes, clinicians ignore what are perceived to be innocent comments until something more significant happens, or until there is a pattern. As soon as any potential threat or pattern is evident, document everything leading up to that scenario that may have been missed in past progress notes. Here is a guideline for what to consider regarding documentation and potential clinician safety issues:

- Explain the statement or behavior as objectively as possible.
- Identify your perception of reasons for the behavior and why it stood out.

- Identify how this potentially impacts your safety (or possibly the safety of others).
- Explain your response to the client and boundaries established.
- Outline any patterns of behavior and prior responses by the client.
- Identify people with whom you consulted and their recommendations.
- List any necessary actions taken (e.g. restraining order).

Follow up as needed and continue to stay aware of the situation, documenting as objectively as possible. Seek consultation and support from colleagues so you do not overlook potential risks to yourself and remain comfortable managing the situation, also considering the best interest of the client.

DOCUMENTING ETHICAL DILEMMAS

An ethical dilemma is typically a situation which requires quick thinking and where no outcome is obviously positive. Ethical dilemmas are common and will happen for almost every clinician. These scenarios arise from personal experience and it is nearly impossible to predict or plan ahead for when they occur or in what manner. Some realistic examples may be interactions with intoxicated clients, receiving extravagant gifts from clients, or deciding what to do after discovering multiple roles with a client.

Pre-emptive steps to prepare for potential ethical dilemmas include:

- Know your discipline's ethical principles well.
- Join an ongoing consultation group.
- Obtain continuing education focused on ethics related to your state, discipline, population, etc.
- Consult with supervisors, mentors, and colleagues as needed or required.

Each situation is unique and may produce different results, which highlights the importance of documenting a clear rationale for your decision (Pope et al., 2021). This information may be relevant in the progress note for that session, if a session occurred, or it may be a separate note in the client's file. Be sure to include all the relevant details. These are not typically situations where you would want to invite doubt about what happened or why!

Include the following in a progress note for such scenarios, based on what is relevant to the situation:

- Any persons with whom you consulted, their relevant expertise or role, discussion points, and their recommendations

- Specific legal advice from an attorney and/or malpractice insurance
- Considerations for determining a course of action, such as ethics code, state law, employer directives, etc.
- Client factors such as safety concerns and potential benefits and drawbacks for the client and/or the therapeutic relationship
- Specific actions taken or planned for the situation
- Relevant follow-up, including with the client or with others

Ethical dilemmas are not meant to be handled alone and isolation is one factor that often leads to clinicians acting unethically (Pope et al.). Consultation is discussed more in Chapter 11, with an example progress note for consultation in Chapter 12.

Lastly, it is important to reflect on the situation. Do so as objectively as possible and include colleagues for support, if needed. This aspect does not necessarily need to be documented, but is part of ongoing professional growth. Remember that excellent clinicians are open to questioning their actions (Miller et al., 2020), admitting mistakes, and learning from them.

- In hindsight, is there anything you could have done differently to prevent this situation?
- Is it necessary to adjust any policies related to the situation?
- Should you seek further training in a clinical area related to the situation?
- Do you have the ongoing social and professional support you need related to this client or situation?

As discussed in Chapter 2, focus on the concept of beneficence. Whether or not you were able to do so in the moment, how can you work in the best interest of the client at this point in time? Regardless of this particular outcome, you are likely to use this experience for the benefit of all future clients.

Quick Read Chapter Summary

- Progress notes are both ethically and legally required, but similar to treatment plans, there are minimal requirements that are consistent outside of medical necessity criteria.

- 'Psychotherapy notes' is a term identified in HIPAA that gives special protection to notes taken by psychotherapists for their personal use (also called process notes). Psychotherapy notes do *not* replace progress notes and should not include information necessary for treatment.

- Taking a moment to review and reflect before writing progress notes can help clinicians to maintain focus and calm while documenting.

- Using a consistent progress note template, along with easy-to-use options like checkboxes or drop down menus, shifts the clinician's focus from the act of writing to pointing out the relevant clinical details.

- Documentation of risky scenarios and ethical dilemmas requires you to write more information explaining the situation and to provide a rationale for your decision and actions (or lack thereof).

- Collaborative documentation involves actively including clients in the documentation process, and research shows it offers multiple benefits for clients.

- The purpose of amending progress notes is to correct misinformation in the client record. Amending a progress note is ethical and shows respect for the accuracy of the record.

NOTES

Chapter 9

Common Problems with Progress Notes

IN THIS CHAPTER

Using the QUOTE Framework to Identify Problems and Solutions 200

Questioning Yourself While Completing Documentation 200

Understanding What to Include in Notes and When 203

Other People Who Read Progress Notes..204

Time Management in Real Practice 207

Emotionally Charged Documentation and Burnout 210

Common Struggle: How to Catch Up on Progress Notes 212

Quick Read Chapter Summary..215

> *The curious paradox is that when I accept myself just as I am, then I can change.*
>
> *- Dr. Carl Rogers*

After working in quality assurance departments for

local and state agencies, consulting for over 10 years with group and individual private practice owners, and delivering nearly 100 trainings for mental health professionals, clear and common struggles with documentation have emerged. The most common and most distressing struggles relate to progress notes.

In my experience, these struggles span across clinical settings, professional license types, and length of time working in the profession. While some clinicians struggle with documentation from the outset, others may experience struggles only after a significant life event or transition. The 2020 COVID-19 pandemic made this point especially clear.

I want to reiterate a point here: You are not a bad clinician if you struggle with documentation.

Every clinician is at risk of struggling with documentation at some point in their career. However, the reasons for clinician struggles vary greatly. Identifying the reason behind the struggle is key to identifying the solution. The QUOTE Framework on the following page was created to help clinicians (and clinical supervisors) do both.

USING THE QUOTE FRAMEWORK TO IDENTIFY PROBLEMS AND SOLUTIONS

If you have ever struggled to write progress notes, you will likely identify with at least one of the points within the QUOTE Framework. This acronym stands for the five most common struggles I see when working with clinicians on documentation:

Questioning yourself while completing documentation
Understanding what to include in notes and when
Other people who read progress notes
Time management in real practice
Emotionally charged documentation and burn out

While documentation struggles present themselves in similar ways, such as falling behind in progress notes or taking a long time to write notes, I noticed the reasons behind the struggles varied greatly. The five points in the QUOTE framework speak to the underlying issues at the heart of documentation struggles so clinicians can identify realistic solutions. These points can be reviewed out of order without impacting one another. Focus on the topic(s) that feels most relevant and continue with others as needed.

Top Tip

If you are a clinical supervisor, or in any advisory role for other clinicians, this chapter may be the most important one you read in this book. It will help you identify potential struggles with documentation that clinicians tend to avoid bringing up with supervisors, assess a clinician's needs when they present struggles, and understand how to problem-solve. *Never* assume a clinician (regardless of clinical experience or license status) has training in documentation, or that they understand what is expected of them in a particular role.

QUESTIONING YOURSELF WHILE COMPLETING DOCUMENTATION

Many clinicians do not give themselves credit for what they already know about documentation. This is true regardless of the training, experience, or competence of the clinician. Self-doubt creeps in with every progress note, often leading to extended time on documentation and ultimately, to dreading or avoiding the task altogether.

These clinicians often get stuck in patterns of:

- Editing progress notes while writing and re-writing the same thing over in multiple ways.
- Changing templates frequently and downloading multiple versions of templates in search of the "perfect" solution.
- Attending multiple documentation trainings but assuming the information does not apply to them without reviewing their specific notes, situation, etc.
- Falling behind in progress notes because so much time and energy is spent in either completing a very detailed note, or collecting more information and resources for templates.
- Waiting to sign progress notes (or never signing them) due to fear they missed a critical piece of information.

These clinicians lack *confidence* in their documentation skills. Interestingly, Miller et al. (2020, p.147) point out that "top-performing clinicians" also consistently have higher amounts of self doubt. My own experience consulting with many of these clinicians is that they tend to be extremely conscientious and may be perfectionistic. They are good clinicians who care deeply about their work and more so than training, they seek confirmation that they are "doing the right thing."

Improving confidence in documentation skills

Merely attending a training on documentation can improve confidence (Leon & Pepe, 2012), even when clinicians do not show a deficiency in skills prior to the training. For this reason, training can be helpful as a first step in improving confidence. Clinicians can use this to confirm their skills and gain additional resources.

However, no training can provide answers on how to manage every clinical situation. Focusing on principles rather than rules is more useful for a skill such as documentation. When tackling the common question, *"Am I writing too much or too little?"* the APA's Record Keeping Guidelines (2007) provide helpful considerations:

> Although there may be advantages to keeping minimal records, for example, in light of risk management concerns or concerns about unintended disclosure, there are, alternately, legitimate arguments for keeping a highly detailed record. Those may include such factors as improved opportunities for the treatment provider to identify trends or patterns in the therapeutic interaction, enhanced capacity to reconstruct the

details of treatment for litigation purposes, and more effective opportunities to use supervision and consultation. The following issues may provide a guide to assist the psychologist in wrestling with these tensions:

- The client's wishes,
- Emergency or disaster relief settings,
- Alteration or destruction of records,
- Legal/regulatory,
- Agency/setting,
- Third-party contracts.

These guidelines remind us that documentation may look different for different clients, even within the same setting and with/for the same clinician. Some strategies for embracing these overarching principles in a more pragmatic way include:

- *Curate and combine lists and resources.* Go through all the documentation resources you have, save what you love and what best applies to clients, then get rid of everything else. This includes the resources in this book. Perhaps you save the original resources but I recommend only revisiting those resources annually. Otherwise it is too easy to fall back into constant revisions that make only minor improvements, if any. Good reference sheets include medical necessity criteria, common treatment goals, and commonly used interventions.
- *Review documentation quarterly and annually.* Setting your schedule for review at these intervals allows improvement in skill and confidence to build over time rather than expecting to make great strides from a specific training, resource, or isolated change. We will discuss how to review records in Chapter 11.
- *Start or join a consultation group.* One of the best ways to stay up to date with standards, popular topics, and clinical skills in the profession is by joining (or starting) a consultation group with other mental health clinicians. Suggest the activity of writing progress notes as a group, or sharing documentation templates and discussing why each member included different components. This is a great way to casually get ideas and professional feedback.

Embrace the ambiguity of documentation standards. The lack of specific guidance from laws and ethics guidelines regarding what to include in documentation allows for flexibility. The lack of a clear standard also means licensing boards have few reference points for required elements and will focus on the bare minimum necessary. Embracing this truth, along with the knowledge that great clinicians question themselves, may be the best paradoxical intervention for clinicians seeking confidence.

> **Reflection for Action**
>
> *What pattern keeps you stuck? What questions do you ask yourself when writing progress notes? Make notes of the principles to follow and have those in front of you as a reminder that 1) there is no such thing as a perfect progress note, and 2) you already have the information you need.*

UNDERSTANDING WHAT TO INCLUDE IN NOTES AND WHEN

There are times when clinicians truly do not know what they do not know. Perhaps a supervisor has never provided clear guidance on documentation requirements and the clinician never attended a documentation training. In this case, documentation training is beneficial (Khan, et al., 2022) for both confidence and helps with motivation to complete documentation.

Many of the strategies from the **Q** section on the previous page will help, along with the resources and examples in this book, seeking help from an understanding supervisor or mentor, and documentation training (check out the free Crash Course available at *qaprep.com/crash-course* for more support). However, even with training, it can be difficult to determine what goes in a progress note, especially when working with complex clients. In these scenarios it is helpful to have some questions to quickly guide you in decision making.

Questions to ask when thinking: "Should I add this information in the progress note?"

- Is this information clinically relevant or necessary for a diagnosis?
- Is this information clinically relevant to my ongoing work with this client?
- Would this information be important for another professional to know if they needed to treat my client?
- Is the information based on fact or observation (client reported, therapist observed, etc.)?
- Would a client quote be the best representation of this information?

If the answer is yes to any of these questions, it is likely needed in the progress note. Keep in mind that noting context may be important (APA, 2007). For example, a client may have presented in a negative way that needs to be documented, but it was out of character due to something like a recent stressor, or not being on medication. This additional information provides important context so the information is not later misrepresented.

> **Reflection for Action**
>
> *When you sit down to write progress notes, what is the most confusing part? What keeps you from completing a progress note? Start with information related to those sections in Chapter 8 and create cheat sheets to help.*

OTHER PEOPLE WHO READ PROGRESS NOTES

Many clinicians are focused on progress note content in a different way- they are concerned about the consequences of others reading the notes. These clinicians tend to worry about three specific scenarios in which someone other than themselves is reading progress notes.

Beliefs about others reading progress notes

1. **Insurance audit or records review** - These clinicians are most concerned about receiving a clawback (the insurance company recouping money already paid for services rendered). They wonder whether or not their progress notes meet medical necessity and agonize over how to translate what really happened in session into a progress note that insurance would approve.

2. **Subpoena or court case** - These clinicians are concerned about nefarious attorneys requesting mental health records and using them against the client in a negative way. They envision the attorney reading client progress notes aloud in a court room to a crowd of onlookers, exposing the client's negative attributes, darkest memories, and vulnerabilities.

3. **Client request for records** - These clinicians worry that a client reading their own progress notes will create a rupture in the therapeutic relationship. They assume the client will feel judged, confused, or misrepresented. They also worry that releasing records to a client invites an opportunity for records to be exposed and cause harm.

These three scenarios share one major commonality, the motivator is FEAR. The solution to this fear is unmasking the truth about what happens in each of the above scenarios. Most clinicians have this fear instilled by well-meaning supervisors or colleagues who offer advice such as:

"Insurance companies only reimburse for CBT so make sure to turn all your interventions into CBT interventions."

"Write as little as possible so no one will know what is actually in your notes."

"Don't just give clients their records because it might make them upset. Tell them you only provide treatment summaries."

From reading this book up to this point, you already recognize that these statements are simply not true. However, these are common myths perpetuated in mental health professional circles. We will evaluate each scenario to identify the myth and the more accurate, commonly occurring situation.

Realities of others reading progress notes

Guess what? Unless this is a licensing board complaint, it is unlikely anyone is reading progress notes to evaluate your performance as a therapist. They have other motives.

1. **Insurance audit or records review** - Audits and records reviews often enter the clinician's world during the formative experiences of practicum and internship. Community mental health and large agencies are much more heavily scrutinized in audits than private practitioners or even group practices. Combine this with the stress of learning *everything* in those early clinical experiences, and many clinicians develop an almost irrational fear of audits that follows them throughout their career. Yes, clinicians need to consider medical necessity, but not at the expense of professional fulfillment and quality care. Follow the guidance in Chapter 3 and throughout this book.

2. **Subpoena or court case** - There is no option to ignore a subpoena, but it is possible to pre-empt one. If a client mentions anything court related, immediately discuss with them the potential for their attorney to request mental health records. Discuss with the client the possibility of using a summary instead, and if appropriate, review records with the client so they can see what may be requested and make a more informed decision. Responding to subpoenas is actually fairly straightforward and discussed in Chapter 11, along with further advice about managing potential records releases.

3. **Client request for records** - Clients may, and sometimes do, request a copy of their records. There is one key qualifier in that sentence- <u>their</u> records. The records are the client's property, safely stored by the clinician. HIPAA (2013) and other state laws give clients the right to access to their records, except in very rare circumstances. This is a good thing, and in alignment with ethical values surrounding client autonomy,

involvement in care, and access to records (ACA, 2014; APA, 2017; NASW, 2021). Most clients have a positive experience when reading their notes so requests for records need not be perceived as negative. Schwarz et al., 2021 notes multiple benefits reported by clients, including enhanced trust in clinicians, and in one study 94% of the participants thought access to notes was positive.

An overarching concern about others reading a client's progress notes is *"everyone will see how bad my notes are and think I'm a horrible therapist."*

Insurance companies are reading notes or reviewing records to establish medical necessity. They are focused on the client's symptoms, impairments, and progress.

Attorneys (or more often, paralegals) are reading notes as research in the case. They want to see if there is anything that can help or harm the case. An example of this is an attorney in a workman's compensation case reviewing records for frequent discussions in therapy about how work is impacting mental health symptoms.

Clients have a variety of reasons for requesting records. They may be curious about what is in their records, need records submitted to another entity, or plan to transfer care. In rare circumstances, clients request records when they are angry about something treatment related. Regardless of the reason, a collaborative approach is best for maintaining the therapeutic alliance long-term.

Tips for writing progress notes anyone might read

Psychotherapy is not restricted to treating only specific scenarios. It is an overarching practice that applies to a variety of people. Documentation is also an ongoing and broad practice. Lean in to the more vague ethical guidelines reviewed earlier in Chapter 2 and establish methods for documentation that apply to multiple scenarios.

There is no way to predict each client interaction and potential progress note formulation. However, remembering a few key principles helps, especially when there is a history of fear and retribution around writing progress notes.

- **Keep your writing objective and free of judgment.** This generally includes anything that is observable (e.g. seen, heard, etc.). For example, rather than writing that a client is "aggressive," stay focused on the observed characteristics. A better observation may be "the client was yelling loudly and cursing, with wide eyes and clenched fists." Use client quotes when writing about complicated situations and stick to the facts of the session. If you'd like to add more in-depth analysis for your own sake, consider writing separate process notes or consulting with a colleague.

- **Be consistent in your documentation practices.** Identify schedules, templates, and common practices that work for you. Then stick with them. This will make documentation less intimidating because it becomes familiar. You will create habits and standards for yourself. However, if you are constantly revamping your templates and conducting intake assessments differently each month, documentation will always feel stressful and chaotic. Stressful documentation is laborious, contributes to burnout (Johnson et al., 2018), and is more likely to be avoided and therefore incomplete, which only increases worry about records requests.

- **Discuss potential scenarios with clients.** We have already established that mental health records are the client's records but in the clinician's care for safe-keeping. Inform clients of potential reasons for requests and discuss concerns and scenarios with them. Shift to the perspective of records requests as a team activity in which you are the guide or coach for your client, and ultimately they make the decision based on the information available.

- **Always assume your client might see documentation.** When I had a private practice I had an open notes policy where clients always had access to their progress notes and I encouraged them to read the notes weekly. I did this to keep myself accountable for writing progress notes, but I also did this to face my own fear of what a client might think if they saw my notes. It was liberating. When I did receive records requests, I knew my clients were already aware of what they were getting. And this practice did prompt me to write differently. **It is much easier to stay fact-based and objective when assuming the client will read your notes, rather than hoping they never do.**

Reflection for Action

What kind of language do you use when discussing or writing about your clients? Is it language you would want someone else to use about you? Review 2-3 progress notes from this lens. If you would feel uncomfortable sharing those notes with a client, imagine the client with you the next time you write a progress note to shift your language accordingly.

TIME MANAGEMENT IN REAL PRACTICE

Time management is critical for all clinicians, regardless of comfort level with writing progress notes. However, it is not a matter of "good time management" or "poor time management." The main consideration is how your schedule fits all the varied priorities in your current life situation - family, friends, clinical work, administrative work, documentation, professional development, hobbies, volunteering, adulting tasks, etc.

Spoiler alert: It takes time to figure out what works best for your schedule, your body, your family, etc. Don't rush the process. Be kind to yourself and honest about your strengths, weaknesses, and current priorities based on your stage of life. Your needs for time and structure will shift throughout your career so you will likely need to revisit what works every few years or as circumstances change. I have actually used four of the five options listed below at different times in my career.

Below are many strategies for completing the administrative task of writing progress notes. Keep an open mind and reflect on your experience to date.

Strategy 1: Progress notes in between clients
This is really the ideal situation. See a client for 45-50 minutes, write the progress note for 5-10 minutes, see the next client, write their progress note, etc. This method rarely works well for therapists because most need to use the time in between clients for other things such as taking a break, returning voicemails or text messages, or even just grabbing some water. However, this is worth trying if you tend to get backed up on progress notes. One way to make this method easier is to combine it with collaborative documentation (discussed in Chapter 8). Another option is scheduling longer breaks every 2-3 clients to allow for administrative tasks, breaks, and sessions that go over time.

Top Tip

One caveat here: If you tend to have poor boundaries with time and often have sessions run over time, strategy #1 is not likely to work for you. You will be stressed and without the time needed to complete the task. Instead, try one of the different schedules below as you work on maintaining the session time boundary. Watch out for this one- it's a time thief for many clinicians!

Strategy 2: Progress notes at the end of each day
If you enjoy feeling a sense of completion or tend to take unfinished work home with you at the end of the day, this is a great strategy. Allow yourself 30-90 minutes (depending on the number of clients you saw) at the end of each clinical day to write all the progress notes for those sessions. The content will be fresh in your mind and you'll be able to end the day knowing everything is complete.

Strategy 3: Progress notes at the beginning of each day

This strategy works well if you tend to feel tired at the end of a clinical day and the thought of writing progress notes after seeing all your clients sounds exhausting. Here is how it works: If you saw five clients on Monday you would then schedule an hour on Tuesday morning to write the progress notes for all your Monday clients. The information is still recent and fresh in your mind, but you are able to look at things with new eyes without feeling rushed to complete the task at the end of the day.

Strategy 4: Progress notes in time blocks

If writing notes daily doesn't seem feasible with your schedule, another option is to block out chunks of time each week. Perhaps you see 20 clients each week and therefore need to write 20 progress notes weekly. If each note takes you 10 minutes, that's three hours and 20 minutes of note writing each week. Round up and schedule two hours of note writing every Tuesday and two hours every Thursday (or whatever days work best for you). If you work well in "marathon sessions" where you can focus on one task and avoid distractions for an extended time, this may be the best option for you.

Strategy 5: Progress notes on an "administrative day"

Some clinicians prefer to have one day a week that is free of clients and complete all administrative tasks on that day. The key to making this strategy successful is doing the math as in the options above. Make sure you are allowing enough hours to write *all* your progress notes, as well as complete whatever other administrative tasks are necessary.

This strategy requires discipline and focus for longer periods of time. In the example above with 20 clients per week, you are likely to spend about four hours writing progress notes in one day, *on top of* the other administrative tasks scheduled for completion. This also requires contingency planning for sick days and emergencies. If you miss that one day you will suddenly find yourself behind in progress notes a whole week. Consider carefully before trying this strategy.

As an aside, this is the one strategy that I have not tried myself, because I knew it was not likely to work well for me. However, some clinicians find this schedule works.

Other options for saving time on progress notes

- *Use dictation after sessions.* If you have always struggled with writing, this is an excellent strategy to try. Dictating a quick summary can be helpful for completing fast notes in a narrative format. Some EHRs even allow you to dictate notes within an app. This is especially helpful if you are conducting multiple teletherapy sessions and need a break to stand up or walk around the room.

- *Type during sessions instead of handwriting.* Almost everyone types faster than they handwrite. While this is not as convenient for in person sessions, this works well if you are already at the computer for teletherapy.

- *Complete notes during session.* Collaborative documentation is mentioned throughout this chapter because this strategy is a life saver for those with ongoing struggles completing progress notes. It is the fastest way to maintain notes and usually produces quality notes because the material is fresh in your mind and uses client feedback.

- *Go all in with handwritten notes.* Jot down points throughout the session and complete the progress note at a later time. Use bullet points or keywords so your final note needs very little editing. Another option is to complete the entire progress note during session using a pre-printed template. Format the template so you can easily circle options and add details in various sections as needed. Then you will likely only need 1-2 minutes to proofread the final product after the session.

- *Use a tablet during sessions.* Combine the last two strategies by using a tablet and smart pen to complete the note during session. With some EHRs, you may be able to enter the information directly in the electronic progress note with this method.

Reflection for Action

What have you found that does or doesn't work for you? What would you like to give a second (or first) try? Decide on one strategy to test, and schedule a time to start it this week.

EMOTIONALLY CHARGED DOCUMENTATION AND BURNOUT

Documentation is the final process in a psychotherapy session, and sometimes clinicians avoid progress notes as a way to avoid vicarious trauma and processing difficult content. Unfortunately, this avoidance is often a sign of clinician burnout, which has negative outcomes for both clinicians and clients.

Thankfully, the solution to this potential burnout is not avoiding clinical work. The solution is prevention through dedicated and ongoing self-care practices (Barnett & Cooper, 2009; Figley, 2002; Johnson et al., 2018). Posluns and Gall (2020) identify the following areas of self-care as important for clinicians who want to prevent burnout:

- Awareness - mindfulness, self-reflection, creative writing
- Balance - leisure activities, variety of work, non-work related passions and relationships, boundaries, breaks, time management, realistic work goals
- Flexibility - attitude of openness, adaptability, effective coping skills, realistic self-expectations, professional development, self-compassion
- Physical health - sleep hygiene, exercise, balanced diet and hydration
- Social support - family, friends, psychotherapy, supervision, consultation, mentors
- Spirituality - prayer, mindfulness, time in nature, spiritual connection, practicing gratitude, and intentionality

Along with ongoing self-care, there are strategies for making progress notes less emotionally overwhelming. Below are strategies you can use all together, or choose just one depending on what resonates with you. Make these a natural part of self-care related to the transition from session to documentation:

- *Pause before you write notes.* Check in with how you're feeling, noticing any tension or anxiety about the session or writing progress notes.
- *Shake out the stress from the session.* Physically shake off any negativity or stress that resides in your body as you prepare to write.
- *Breathe and center yourself.* Spend 30-60 seconds focused on relaxing your body and being present.
- *Practice gratitude.* Identify one thing about the client, the session, or your work for which you are thankful.
- *Remove the pressure.* A clinician in one of my groups shared that she often reduces stress about writing progress notes by saying to herself *"Just write my shitty little note."* Framing the progress note in this amusing way helped her overcome perfectionism and view the note for what it is - simply one of thousands of progress notes she'll write throughout her career.

Time management and self-care needs shift throughout life as personal and professional circumstances change. Strategies that work today may not work three years from now. Expect this, plan for it, and give yourself time to adapt throughout your career.

Reflection for Action
Which area of self-care in Posluns and Gall's list have you been neglecting? Which self-care documentation strategy seemed most appealing? Schedule a reminder to try one out during the next time you write progress notes.

COMMON STRUGGLE: HOW TO CATCH UP ON PROGRESS NOTES

Most clinicians have fallen behind in progress notes at one point or another. For some it may be a few days or weeks, and for others it turns into months and even years. Understandably, this situation creates an enormous amount of stress. One of the most stressful aspects of this experience is the shame related to falling behind in notes. The thought of catching up is daunting but the thought of asking for help and admitting to other clinicians that documentation is incomplete can be paralyzing.

Below is a detailed plan for catching up on progress notes, regardless of the number. There is also a fillable PDF version of this plan in the Bonus Resources available at **QAPrep.com/SFD-Resources**. That plan will help you count the numbers and walk you through some reflection, but you can just as easily start right here with a notes app or pen and paper.

Step 1: Keep up with current progress notes.

The first step to catching up on progress notes is counterintuitive: Write your *current* notes! Clinicians frequently make the mistake of only focusing on the old, unwritten notes and neglecting the current notes. By doing this you remain in the vicious catch up cycle.

THE CATCH UP CYCLE

Self-doubt → Extended time on paperwork → Dreading paperwork → Avoiding paperwork → Worrying about paperwork

Focus on creating a consistent schedule for progress notes, along with other documentation and administrative tasks. See the strategies in the section on Time Management in previous pages of this chapter. Stick with a schedule of regular weekly documentation for 1-2 weeks before creating a plan to catch up or working on older progress notes. This first step is difficult for many clinicians, but it is critical for breaking the cycle of falling behind in progress notes and setting yourself up for success.

Step 2: *Time your progress notes.*
Identify the amount of time it takes to write notes. Many clinicians are unsure about this and knowing your average note writing time is important for creating a realistic catch up plan.

1. Time yourself writing at least six progress notes. Do NOT time yourself writing notes for older sessions. That time is less reliable because it tends to take longer to write older notes. The goal is to know how long it takes to write progress notes when you are maintaining a good schedule and your memory is fresh.

2. Set a timer each time you start a progress note, then stop the timer when you are done and write down the time. Go to the next progress note and repeat. Do this for 6-10 notes and you will have a decent sample size.

3. Once you finish all progress notes for the day, average the time it took to complete them all. Please note: It can be easy to get down on yourself in this process if you find it takes a long time to write progress notes. *This is a time to gather information so you can problem-solve, not a time to judge yourself.*

Now you have all the information you need to create a realistic schedule for ongoing progress notes, and you have a piece of information for creating an effective catch up plan.

Step 3: *Adjust your schedule.*
Make some adjustments in your schedule *before* identifying how many notes you need to write or how much time you will spend so that you don't overwhelm yourself. Look at your schedule and consider what you can realistically commit to for about three months (understanding that the actual time may be longer or shorter). Realistic means you are still allowing time for things like dinner with family, working out, or other commitments. However, you might temporarily be willing to reduce the number of hours watching TV, decide to head to the office an hour early every day, or choose to spend a few hours on the weekend writing notes until you've caught up.

Step 4: *Know your numbers.*
Invest the time to identify how many progress notes you need to write. Writing an exact number will provide information for the most effective catch up plan. This includes everything - notes

that are not started, notes that are partially completed, intake assessments, notes on phone or email interactions, no shows, etc. If you use an EHR, this may be a simple 10 second task. If you take notes on paper, this task may take a little longer.

Next, use the number you discovered in Step 2 as your average time to complete notes. Multiply that times the number of notes you need to catch up on and that is how many minutes it will take you to catch up. Divide by 60 to get the total hours.

Example:
120 notes pending x 10 minutes per note = 1,200 minutes to get caught up
1,200 minutes / 60 = 20 hours of notes to write

What if I'm too scared to find out the number of progress notes I need to write?
If identifying a specific number feels overwhelming, there is an alternative method. Write out the names of all clients who have pending notes. Then simply choose a name from the list each time you sit down to catch up on notes.

Step 5: Schedule your catch up time.
Schedule the time in your calendar, based on the realistic adjustments you identified in Step 3. Write this time in your calendar as non-negotiable. Remember, the first priority is actually keeping up with current notes so this is *added* documentation time. Make the plan feasible so you will stick to it and keep yourself accountable, even if that only means 2 hours per month.

Step 6: Practice self-compassion.
Lastly, forgive yourself for getting behind and look forward to being caught up! Many clinicians feel guilty, frightened and get stuck in a paralyzed mode. That is not you. You will get through this because you have a clear plan and have made it realistic based on your priorities and other commitments. To add in more accountability, share with a friend, family member, or colleague that you think would be understanding. Having a community during times of stress is invaluable.

Quick Read Chapter Summary

- The QUOTE Framework helps clinicians tackle the most common problems associated with writing progress notes. Use it to identify both problems and solutions.

- **Q**uestioning yourself while completing documentation: The solution is embrace ambiguity, trust the resources you've already gathered, and know that great clinicians doubt themselves.

- **U**nderstanding what to include in notes and when: The solution is training, cheat sheets, and checklists to help with practice and confidence.

- **O**ther (important and unimportant) people who read progress notes: The solution is to focus on what is best for the client and discuss any concerns with them.

- **T**ime management in real practice: The solution is to carve out specific time for documentation that is separate from other administrative tasks, and to experiment with different times for writing notes to determine what works best for your current phase of life.

- **E**motionally charged documentation and burnout: The solution is self-care based on your current needs, whether that is reducing hours, joining a consultation group, or adjusting your schedule to better accommodate stress-reducing and non-work activities.

- All of these struggles potentially lead to clinicians falling behind in notes. An effective paperwork catch up plan requires you to know how long it takes to write notes, and to focus on writing current notes on a regular schedule before you begin the catch up process.

NOTES

NOTES

Chapter 10

Progress Note Templates

IN THIS CHAPTER

Guidance on Using Templates 219
Potential Progress Note Components 221
Progress Note Example: Simple 237
Progress Note Example: Insurance 242
Progress Note Narrative Starter Phrases 248
Progress Note Example: Narrative 251
Progress Note: Child/Play Therapy Additions 253
Progress Note Example: Child 255
Progress Note: Couples Therapy Additions 262
Progress Note Example: Couples 264
Progress Note: Group Therapy Additions 269

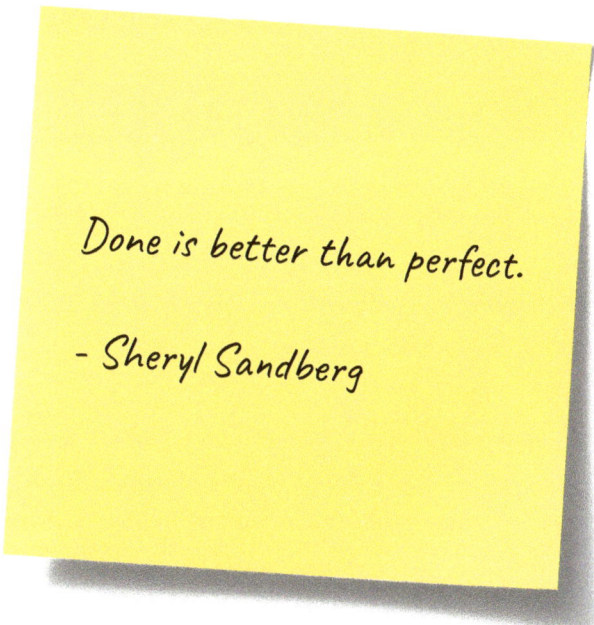

GUIDANCE ON USING TEMPLATES

The following pages include options for various components to include in a progress note template. The Potential Progress Note Components list is meant to be extensive and include a variety of items so clinicians can choose what best applies to their situation and for their clients.

I strongly recommend reviewing the lists and then paring them down based on preference and need, rather than referencing the full list every time you write a progress note or trying to include all the components in one template. To avoid feeling overwhelmed by the many options, follow the steps below based on your situation.

For students and clinicians working in a setting with prescribed forms:

Use the relevant Progress Note Components lists as a reference when completing progress notes with the template you are required to complete. For example, review the list of Interventions and have it handy when writing progress notes. Choose 15-20 interventions that best apply to your clients and create a separate cheat sheet so you are not overwhelmed by the list every time.

If you are required to use a narrative style, use the Components lists to create a cheat sheet of starter phrases instead of checkboxes. The Progress Note Narrative Starter Phrases provide examples of sentences and starter phrases you can use immediately with any progress note template. See the Progress Note Example: Narrative for how a completed progress note looks using this method.

For clinicians in a private practice setting with flexibility to choose their own template format:

Option 1: Review the two Progress Note Examples provided. The "Insurance" example includes medical necessity components and the "Simple" example does not. You may be able to use these templates as is! However, I recommend you also review the list of Potential Progress Note Components and add in (or subtract) anything that better relates to your work with clients.

Option 2: Review the lists within the Potential Progress Note Components and 1) identify which components apply to your practice and that you want to include in a progress note template, and 2) put the lists together to create your personalized progress note template.

Creating a progress note template can be especially overwhelming and time-consuming. There are many options provided in this chapter and you will not need most of them! Check out the video instructions at **QAPrep.com/SFD-Resources** for help with adapting the templates to your preferences.

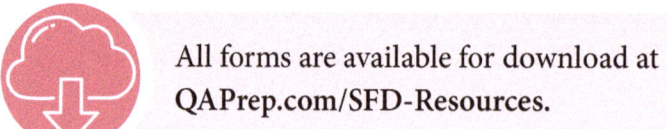
All forms are available for download at QAPrep.com/SFD-Resources.

Potential Progress Note Components

Demographic and Insurance Info:

Client name: *Session Date:*

Session Start Time: *CPT Code:*
Session Stop Time:

Extended session time required in order to (special note for 90837):
- ☐ Address the severity of the client's symptoms and prevent the need for further escalation of care.
- ☐ Allow all individuals in the session to meaningfully participate.
- ☐ Process complex trauma and then regulate emotions effectively prior to leaving session.
- ☐ Process emotions and events with frequent redirection and encouragement to stay focused.
- ☐ Problem-solve through complex concepts and adequately practice skills reviewed in session.

Session Location: *Verified Client Location for Telehealth:*
- ☐ In office   ☐ Home (address on file)
- ☐ Telehealth   ☐ Work (address on file)
- ☐ Telephone   ☐ Other:
- ☐ Other:

Statement for Telehealth:
- ☐ Client is appropriate for telehealth. Session environment, privacy risks, and emergency and disconnection protocols reviewed with client.
- ☐ Clinician used best practices for confidentiality, client safety, and security of communication.

Potential Progress Note Components (Continued)

Topics/Themes of Session:

- ☐ Alcohol Use
- ☐ Anxiety
- ☐ Attention/Concentration
- ☐ Childhood experiences
- ☐ Communication
- ☐ Cultural experiences
- ☐ Dating
- ☐ Divorce/Separation
- ☐ Eating behaviors
- ☐ Family conflict
- ☐ Fearfulness
- ☐ Friends/Social life
- ☐ Fulfillment
- ☐ Grief/Loss
- ☐ Health
- ☐ Identity
- ☐ Loneliness
- ☐ Major life changes
- ☐ Medication/side effects
- ☐ Motivation
- ☐ Organization
- ☐ Overwhelm
- ☐ Parenting
- ☐ Perinatal issues
- ☐ Relationships (partner/spouse)
- ☐ Relationships (other)
- ☐ Sadness
- ☐ School
- ☐ Self harm/Intent to harm
- ☐ Sexuality
- ☐ Sleep
- ☐ Social support
- ☐ Substance use
- ☐ Symptoms management
- ☐ Thinking
- ☐ Time Management
- ☐ Trauma
- ☐ Values/beliefs
- ☐ Work
- ☐ Worry
- ☐ Other: _____

Interventions:

- ☐ Advocated for: _____
- ☐ Assessed: _____
- ☐ Assisted client in building support system.
- ☐ Assisted client in creating:
    - ☐ List of pros and cons
    - ☐ New ways of coping
    - ☐ Priorities based on values
    - ☐ Schedule/structure
- ☐ Assisted client in identifying:
    - ☐ Alternative behaviors
    - ☐ Boundaries
    - ☐ Coping skills
    - ☐ Effects of negative coping skills
    - ☐ Familial roles

Potential Progress Note Components (Continued)

- ☐ Feelings of dysphoria
- ☐ Irrational thoughts
- ☐ Needs and wants
- ☐ Relapse prevention skills
- ☐ Sabotaging behaviors
- ☐ Ways of expressing anger
- ☐ Assisted client in labeling feelings related to:
  - ☐ Acute trauma
  - ☐ Chronic trauma
  - ☐ Cultural norms
  - ☐ Lived experience
- ☐ Assisted client with accessing: _____
- ☐ Challenged:
  - ☐ All or nothing thinking
  - ☐ Catastrophizing
  - ☐ Irrational thoughts
  - ☐ Negative self-statements
  - ☐ Rigid thoughts/beliefs
  - ☐ Stereotypes
- ☐ Clarified/Sought clarification on: _____
- ☐ Coached client on: _____
- ☐ Collaborated with client to: _____
- ☐ Completed art project to assist with:
  - ☐ Building rapport
  - ☐ Exploring/identifying emotions
  - ☐ Expressing emotions
  - ☐ Improving communication
  - ☐ Perfectionism
  - ☐ Problem-solving
- ☐ Consulted regarding:
  - ☐ Case conceptualization
  - ☐ Coordinating care
  - ☐ Differential diagnosis
  - ☐ Ethical dilemma
  - ☐ Making a referral
  - ☐ Symptom presentation
  - ☐ Treatment options
- ☐ Created a plan for: _____
- ☐ Created treatment goals with client.

Potential Progress Note Components (Continued)

- ☐ Clarified decision around: _____
- ☐ De-escalated client using:
    - ☐ Deep breathing
    - ☐ Experience of senses
    - ☐ Grounding exercise
    - ☐ Reflection of emotions/experience
    - ☐ Reflection of needs
    - ☐ Self-compassion statements
- ☐ Demonstrated:
    - ☐ Deep breathing
    - ☐ Mindfulness techniques
    - ☐ Tapping for stress management
- ☐ Developed coping strategy of: _____
- ☐ Differentiated between: _____
- ☐ Directed client to: _____
- ☐ Discussed concept of:
    - ☐ Attachment styles
    - ☐ Burnout
    - ☐ Codependency
    - ☐ Division of labor
    - ☐ Emotional regulation
    - ☐ Frustration tolerance
    - ☐ Generational trauma
    - ☐ Hyperfocus
    - ☐ Love languages
    - ☐ Non-Judgmental stance
    - ☐ Parts of self
    - ☐ Perfectionism
    - ☐ Physiological expression of symptoms
    - ☐ Resilience
    - ☐ Self-compassion
    - ☐ Self-talk
    - ☐ Trauma and trauma responses
    - ☐ Unconscious influences
- ☐ Encouraged client regarding:
    - ☐ Expressed resiliency
    - ☐ Positive attributes
    - ☐ Progress in treatment
    - ☐ Support system

Potential Progress Note Components (Continued)

- ☐ Evaluated consequences of: _____
- ☐ Examined benefits of: _____
- ☐ Explored feelings of:
  - ☐ Anger
  - ☐ Anxiety
  - ☐ Depression
  - ☐ Fear
  - ☐ Guilt
  - ☐ Hopelessness
  - ☐ Loneliness
  - ☐ Loss
  - ☐ Overwhelm
  - ☐ Worthlessness
- ☐ Explored feelings related to:
  - ☐ Body image
  - ☐ Cultural experiences
  - ☐ Family dynamics
  - ☐ Family of origin
  - ☐ Infertility
  - ☐ Parenting
  - ☐ Partner
  - ☐ People pleasing
  - ☐ Pregnancy loss
  - ☐ Relationship
  - ☐ School stress
  - ☐ Separation
  - ☐ Trauma
  - ☐ Values
  - ☐ Work stress
- ☐ Explored onset of:
  - ☐ Patterns
  - ☐ Relationship struggles
  - ☐ Stressors
  - ☐ Symptoms
  - ☐ Trauma
- ☐ Explored patterns in:
  - ☐ Communication
  - ☐ Family of origin
  - ☐ Relationships

Potential Progress Note Components (Continued)

- ☐ Stress response
- ☐ Facilitated: _____
- ☐ Gathered information regarding:
    - ☐ Biopsychosocial history
    - ☐ Current symptoms
    - ☐ Family of origin
    - ☐ Living situation
    - ☐ Social support
    - ☐ Strengths and resources
    - ☐ Substance use
    - ☐ Traumatic experiences
- ☐ Guided client in:
    - ☐ Body scan
    - ☐ Communication techniques
    - ☐ Grounding exercise
    - ☐ Identifying motivation
    - ☐ Identifying parts of self
    - ☐ Mindful acceptance
    - ☐ Mindful hypnosis
    - ☐ Positive self-talk
    - ☐ Self-compassion exercises
- ☐ Identified alternative behaviors to: _____, such as: _____
- ☐ Identified coping strategies such as: _____, to assist with: _____
- ☐ Identified triggers related to:
    - ☐ Angry outbursts
    - ☐ Dissociation
    - ☐ Emotional dysregulation
    - ☐ Feeling a loss of control
    - ☐ Past experiences
    - ☐ Sense of identity
- ☐ Implemented: _____
- ☐ Introduced game to practice:
    - ☐ Age appropriate social skills
    - ☐ Anger management skills
    - ☐ Asking for help
    - ☐ Communicating with others
    - ☐ Coregulation

Potential Progress Note Components (Continued)

- ☐ Expressing empathy
- ☐ Flexibility in interactions
- ☐ Identifying emotions
- ☐ Identifying social cues
- ☐ Planning ahead
- ☐ Regulating emotions
- ☐ Taking turns
- ☐ Introduced strategy of:
  - ☐ CBT triangle
  - ☐ Creating attainable goals
  - ☐ Gratitude journal
  - ☐ Journaling/expressive writing
  - ☐ Mapping
  - ☐ Repatterning
  - ☐ Resourcing
  - ☐ Thought stopping
  - ☐ Using a mood log to review emotions
- ☐ Involved collaterals to: _____
- ☐ Labeled feelings of: _____
- ☐ Led client in: _____
- ☐ Modeled for client the practice of:
  - ☐ Expressing emotions
  - ☐ Expressing needs/wants
  - ☐ Providing feedback
  - ☐ Seeking feedback from partner
  - ☐ Using self-compassionate and positive statements
  - ☐ Validating partner's feelings/experience
- ☐ Monitored: _____
- ☐ Normalized feelings of:
  - ☐ Anger
  - ☐ Frustration
  - ☐ Grief
  - ☐ Isolation
  - ☐ Loss
  - ☐ Overwhelm
  - ☐ Rejection
- ☐ Normalized thoughts of: _____
- ☐ Paraphrased for client regarding: _____
- ☐ Planned with client for: _____

Potential Progress Note Components (Continued)

- ☐ Practiced co-regulating with partner.
- ☐ Practiced experiential exercises to help with:
    - ☐ Avoidance
    - ☐ Emotional regulation
    - ☐ Perfectionism
    - ☐ Re-patterning reactions
    - ☐ Self compassion
    - ☐ Sense of safety
- ☐ Practiced with client:
    - ☐ Body attunement
    - ☐ Co-regulation
    - ☐ Deep breathing
    - ☐ Mind/body awareness
    - ☐ Orienting and anchoring
    - ☐ Present moment exercises
    - ☐ Positive self-talk
    - ☐ Reframing thoughts/beliefs
    - ☐ Tapping (EFT)
- ☐ Problem solved regarding: _____
- ☐ Processed fears of: _____
- ☐ Processed feelings related to:
    - ☐ Childhood experiences
    - ☐ Family of origin
    - ☐ History of abuse
    - ☐ Relationships
    - ☐ Self/Identity
    - ☐ Trauma
- ☐ Processed trauma related to:
    - ☐ Bias/marginalization
    - ☐ Bullying
    - ☐ Childhood experiences
    - ☐ Death of significant relationship
    - ☐ Divorce/separation
    - ☐ Generation/family experiences
    - ☐ History of abuse
    - ☐ Pregnancy loss
    - ☐ Racism
    - ☐ Religion
    - ☐ Sexual experience

Potential Progress Note Components (Continued)

- ☐ Work environment
- ☐ Prompted client to: _____
- ☐ Provided referral for: _____
- ☐ Questioned evidence for conclusion that: _____
- ☐ Provided psychoeducation on:
    - ☐ Addiction
    - ☐ Autonomic nervous system
    - ☐ Body responses to trauma
    - ☐ Burnout
    - ☐ Common relationship struggles
    - ☐ Differences in symptom presentation for children
    - ☐ Differences in symptom presentation for older adults
    - ☐ Dissociation
    - ☐ Distorted body image
    - ☐ Effects of chronic stress
    - ☐ Executive functioning
    - ☐ Guilt vs shame
    - ☐ Impacts of trauma experience
    - ☐ Neurodiversity
    - ☐ Patterns of interaction in families
    - ☐ Reasons for avoidance
    - ☐ Rejection sensitivity dysphoria
    - ☐ Sleep hygiene
    - ☐ Sexual experiences
    - ☐ Somatic responses
    - ☐ Time blindness
    - ☐ Types of grief
    - ☐ Types of trauma
- ☐ Provided psychoeducation on symptoms of:
    - ☐ ADHD
    - ☐ Anxiety
    - ☐ Autism
    - ☐ Complex trauma
    - ☐ Depression
    - ☐ Disordered eating
    - ☐ Grief
    - ☐ OCD
    - ☐ PTSD
    - ☐ Panic attacks

Potential Progress Note Components (Continued)

- ☐ Personality disorders
- ☐ Trauma
- ☐ Provided psychoeducation on the modality of:
    - ☐ Acceptance and Commitment Therapy (ACT)
    - ☐ Cognitive Behavior Therapy (CBT)
    - ☐ Dialectical Behavior Therapy (DBT)
    - ☐ EMDR
    - ☐ Emotionally Focused Therapy (EFT)
    - ☐ Internal Family Systems (IFS)
    - ☐ Polyvagal theory
    - ☐ Somatic experiencing
- ☐ Reassured client regarding: _____
- ☐ Redirected client when: _____
- ☐ Reflected back to client:
    - ☐ Observations on their responses
    - ☐ Patterns in their relationships
    - ☐ Their interaction with one another (for couples)
    - ☐ Their progress
    - ☐ Their strengths
    - ☐ The discrepancy in their statements
- ☐ Reframed for client:
    - ☐ Circumstances in their life
    - ☐ Negative coping as formerly necessary survival skills
    - ☐ Negative statements
    - ☐ Perceived failure
    - ☐ Their progress to date
- ☐ Reinforced behavior of: _____
- ☐ Reinforced client for: _____
- ☐ Reviewed goals with client.
- ☐ Reviewed progress toward goals.
- ☐ Reviewed results of assigned homework.
- ☐ Reviewed strategies for:
    - ☐ Communicating needs
    - ☐ Coregulation
    - ☐ Expressing emotions
    - ☐ Increasing window of tolerance
    - ☐ Managing current situation
    - ☐ Managing triggers
    - ☐ Procrastination and avoidance

Potential Progress Note Components (Continued)

- ☐ Self-compassion
- ☐ Self-soothing
☐ Role played: _____
☐ Set boundaries regarding: _____
☐ Set goals related to:
  - ☐ Areas of need
  - ☐ Current symptoms
  - ☐ Strengths and resiliency
☐ Summarized for client: _____
☐ Trained client in: _____
☐ Used behavior management for: _____
☐ Used bilateral stimulation.
☐ Used cues to: _____
☐ Used biofeedback to help with regulation.
☐ Used imagery/relaxation training to help with regulation.
☐ Used miracle question for: _____
☐ Used perspective building for communication skills.
☐ Used play therapy to practice:
  - ☐ Age appropriate social skills
  - ☐ Anger management skills
  - ☐ Asking for help
  - ☐ Communicating with others
  - ☐ Identifying emotions
  - ☐ Identifying social cues
  - ☐ Problem-solving skills
  - ☐ Regulating emotions
☐ Used somatic experiencing to assist with:
  - ☐ Coregulation
  - ☐ Decreased arousal
  - ☐ Emotional regulation
  - ☐ Grounding
  - ☐ Noticing felt sense
  - ☐ Repatterning
  - ☐ Self-regulation
☐ Used scaling to identify: _____
☐ Used supportive questioning to assist with: _____

Potential Progress Note Components (Continued)

Presentation during session (mood, affect, behavior):

- ☐ Argumentative
- ☐ Contemplative
- ☐ Dissociated
- ☐ Distracted
- ☐ Engaged
- ☐ Expressive
- ☐ Flat affect
- ☐ Focused
- ☐ Grandiose
- ☐ Hypervigilant
- ☐ Indecisive
- ☐ Insightful
- ☐ Interactive
- ☐ Irritable
- ☐ Lethargic/sluggish
- ☐ Mindful
- ☐ Quiet/passive
- ☐ Restless/fidgety
- ☐ Rigid thinking
- ☐ Sad
- ☐ Shaking/trembling
- ☐ Talkative
- ☐ Tearful
- ☐ Tired/sleepy
- ☐ Withdrawn
- ☐ Yelling/shouting
- ☐ Other: _____

Feelings expressed by client during session:

- ☐ Angry
- ☐ Anxious
- ☐ Burnout
- ☐ Confused
- ☐ Content
- ☐ Encouraged
- ☐ Excited
- ☐ Exhausted
- ☐ Fearful
- ☐ Frustrated
- ☐ Guilty
- ☐ Happy/joyful
- ☐ Hopeful
- ☐ Hopeless
- ☐ Indifferent
- ☐ Lonely
- ☐ Motivated
- ☐ Nervous
- ☐ Numb
- ☐ Overwhelmed
- ☐ Sad
- ☐ Satisfied
- ☐ Shame
- ☐ Stressed
- ☐ Suicidal (see risk assessment below)
- ☐ Unmotivated
- ☐ Worthless
- ☐ Worried
- ☐ Other: _____

Potential Progress Note Components (Continued)

Safety/Risk Assessment:

- ☐ No risk reported or observed
- ☐ Self-harming behaviors: Thoughts only (see description below)
- ☐ Self-harming behaviors: Thoughts and actions (see plan for safety below)
- ☐ Suicidality: Passive thoughts, no plan/intent (see description below)
- ☐ Suicidality: Plan and/or intent, but able to create a plan for safety (see below)
- ☐ Suicidality: Plan and intent, not able to create a plan for safety (see actions taken and rationale)
- ☐ Homicidal: Intent to harm others (see actions taken and rationale)
- ☐ Other potential risk/harm (see actions taken and rationale)

Description of thoughts/intent:

_____

Plan for client safety:

_____

Clinician rationale for plan:

_____

Risk factors:

- ☐ Access to means of self-harm
- ☐ Chronic pain or medical condition
- ☐ Delusions and/or hallucinations
- ☐ Current significant stressors
- ☐ Drug or alcohol use
- ☐ Feeling hopeless
- ☐ History of self-harm
- ☐ Lack of social support
- ☐ Previous suicide attempt
- ☐ Recent loss or trauma
- ☐ Recent change in behavior
- ☐ Stated plan for self-harm

Protective factors:

- ☐ Awareness of triggers
- ☐ Engaged in ongoing treatment
- ☐ No history of attempts
- ☐ Pet ownership
- ☐ Positive rapport with clinician
- ☐ Religious/spiritual beliefs
- ☐ Reports motivation to live
- ☐ Strong social support
- ☐ Statements about negative effect on children or others
- ☐ Willing to use safety plan and coping skills

Potential Progress Note Components (Continued)

Progress made toward goals:

Improvement in or awareness of::
- ☐ Assertion of needs
- ☐ Communication skills
- ☐ Contribution to negative patterns
- ☐ Distress tolerance
- ☐ Emotional regulation
- ☐ Establishing/being firm about boundaries
- ☐ Expression of symptoms
- ☐ Expression of emotions
- ☐ Executive functioning
- ☐ Impact of history and traumatic experiences
- ☐ Making transitions
- ☐ Problem-solving skills
- ☐ Providing feedback to partner
- ☐ Sleep hygiene/routine
- ☐ Triggers to symptoms

Managing symptoms of:
_____

Using coping skills of:
_____

Using strategies for:
- ☐ Burnout
- ☐ Conflict resolution
- ☐ Distress tolerance
- ☐ Emotional regulation
- ☐ Management of triggers
- ☐ Mindfulness
- ☐ Motivation
- ☐ Organization/time management
- ☐ Pausing/reducing impulsivity
- ☐ Reinforcing positive thoughts/behaviors
- ☐ Self-care

Continued difficulties:
- ☐ Communication in relationships
- ☐ Conflict resolution
- ☐ Distress tolerance
- ☐ Establishing/being firm about boundaries
- ☐ Expressing and asserting needs
- ☐ Expressing emotions appropriately
- ☐ Maintaining social relationships
- ☐ Managing work tasks
- ☐ Medication adherence
- ☐ Motivation
- ☐ Regulating emotions/responses
- ☐ Repetitive behaviors
- ☐ Responding to identified triggers
- ☐ Rigid beliefs/patterns
- ☐ Sleep hygiene/routine
- ☐ Understanding social cues/interactions
- ☐ Using positive coping skills

Potential Progress Note Components (Continued)

Current symptoms impacting functioning:

- ☐ Angry outbursts
- ☐ Anxiety
- ☐ Avoidance of stimuli
- ☐ Binging/purging
- ☐ Depressed mood
- ☐ Dissociative reactions
- ☐ Exaggerated arousal/reactivity
- ☐ Fear or avoidance
- ☐ Feeling worthless or guilty
- ☐ Hypervigilance
- ☐ Impulsivity
- ☐ Irritability
- ☐ Isolating from others
- ☐ Lack of motivation
- ☐ Low energy
- ☐ Negative beliefs
- ☐ Nightmares
- ☐ Panic attack(s)
- ☐ Poor concentration/focus
- ☐ Poor follow through
- ☐ Recurrent/distressing memories
- ☐ Restlessness
- ☐ Restricted eating
- ☐ Self-criticism
- ☐ Self-destructive behavior
- ☐ Sleep disturbance

Impact on Daily Activities

Symptoms impacting relationships with:

- ☐ Children
- ☐ Coworkers
- ☐ Family of origin
- ☐ Friendships
- ☐ Marriage/Partnership
- ☐ Other: _____

Symptoms negatively impacting:

- ☐ Living situation
- ☐ Physical health
- ☐ School
- ☐ Self-care
- ☐ Work
- ☐ Other: _____

Potential Progress Note Components (Continued)

Client Quote/Insights:
_____

Session Takeaways:
_____

In Session Notes:
_____
_____

Plan:

- ☐ Continue with regularly scheduled session time.
- ☐ Next session scheduled for: _____
- ☐ Client will practice skills from today's session.
- ☐ Client will complete homework: _____

- ☐ Resources/Recommendations (as applicable): _____

- ☐ General Follow-up (as applicable): _____

Progress Note Example: Simple

Progress Note (Simple)

Demographic and Insurance Info:

Client name: Moana Waialiki

Session Date: 08/13/2024

Session Time: 2pm

CPT Code: 90834

Session Location:
- ☐ In office
- ☑ Telehealth
- ☐ Telephone
- ☐ Other:

Verified Client Location for Telehealth:
- ☐ Home (address on file)
- ☐ Work (address on file)
- ☐ Other:

Statement for Telehealth:
- ☑ Client is appropriate for telehealth. Session environment, privacy risks, and emergency and disconnection protocols reviewed with client.
- ☑ Clinician used best practices for confidentiality, client safety, and security of communication.

Topics Discussed:

- ☐ Alcohol Use
- ☐ Anxiety
- ☐ Attention/Concentration
- ☐ Childhood experiences
- ☐ Communication
- ☐ Cultural experiences
- ☐ Dating
- ☐ Divorce/Separation
- ☐ Eating behaviors
- ☐ Family conflict
- ☐ Fearfulness
- ☐ Fulfillment
- ☐ Grief/Loss
- ☐ Health
- ☐ Identity
- ☑ Loneliness
- ☐ Major life changes
- ☐ Medication/side effects
- ☐ Motivation
- ☐ Overwhelm
- ☐ Parenting
- ☐ Perinatal issues
- ☐ Relationships (partner/spouse)
- ☐ Relationships (other)
- ☐ Sadness
- ☐ School
- ☐ Self harm/Intent to harm
- ☐ Sexuality
- ☐ Sleep
- ☑ Social support
- ☐ Substance use
- ☐ Symptoms management
- ☐ Thinking
- ☐ Time Management
- ☐ Trauma
- ☑ Values/beliefs
- ☐ Work
- ☑ Other: Difficulty with friends

Progress Note Example: Simple (Continued)

Interventions (2-4):

- ☐ Assessed: _____
- ☑ Assisted client in identifying:
    - ☐ Alternative behaviors
    - ☐ Boundaries
    - ☐ Coping skills
    - ☑ Effects of negative coping skills
    - ☐ Irrational thoughts
    - ☑ Needs and wants
    - ☐ Relapse prevention skills
    - ☐ Sabotaging behaviors
    - ☐ Ways of expressing anger
- ☐ Explored patterns in:
    - ☐ Communication
    - ☐ Family of origin
    - ☐ Relationships
    - ☐ Stress response
    - ☐ Ways of coping
- ☐ Practiced experiential exercises to help with:
    - ☐ Avoidance
    - ☐ Emotional regulation
    - ☐ Perfectionism
    - ☐ Re-patterning reactions
    - ☐ Self compassion
    - ☐ Sense of safety
    - ☐ Social interactions
- ☑ Practiced with client:
    - ☐ Body attunement
    - ☐ Co-regulation
    - ☐ Deep breathing
    - ☐ Mind/body awareness
    - ☐ Orienting and anchoring
    - ☐ Present moment exercises
    - ☑ Positive self-talk
    - ☑ Reframing thoughts/beliefs
- ☑ Processed feelings related to:
    - ☐ Childhood experiences
    - ☑ Family of origin
    - ☐ History of abuse
    - ☑ Relationships
    - ☑ Self/Identity
    - ☐ Trauma
- ☐ Provided psychoeducation on: _____
- ☐ Reviewed strategies for:
    - ☐ Communicating needs
    - ☐ Increasing window of tolerance
    - ☐ Managing current situation
    - ☐ Managing triggers
    - ☐ Procrastination and avoidance
    - ☐ Self-compassion

Client Quotes/Insights during session (as applicable):

"I just feel like I don't fit in with my own community."

Progress Note Example: Simple (Continued)

Presentation during session (mood, affect, behavior):

- ☐ Argumentative
- ☐ Contemplative
- ☐ Dissociated
- ☐ Distracted
- ☑ Engaged
- ☑ Expressive
- ☐ Flat affect
- ☐ Focused
- ☐ Grandiose
- ☐ Hypervigilant
- ☐ Indecisive
- ☑ Insightful
- ☑ Interactive
- ☐ Irritable
- ☐ Lethargic/sluggish
- ☐ Mindful
- ☐ Quiet/passive
- ☐ Restless/fidgety
- ☐ Rigid thinking
- ☐ Sad
- ☐ Shaking/trembling
- ☐ Talkative
- ☐ Tearful
- ☐ Tired/sleepy
- ☐ Withdrawn
- ☐ Yelling/shouting
- ☐ Other: _____

Progress Toward Goals:

Improvement or awareness of:
- ☐ Assertion of needs
- ☐ Communication skills
- ☑ Contribution to negative patterns
- ☐ Distress tolerance
- ☐ Emotional regulation
- ☐ Establishing/being firm about boundaries
- ☐ Expression of symptoms
- ☐ Expression of emotions
- ☐ Executive functioning
- ☐ Impact of history and traumatic experiences
- ☐ Making transitions
- ☐ Problem-solving skills
- ☐ Providing feedback to partner
- ☐ Sleep hygiene/routine
- ☐ Triggers to symptoms

Managing symptoms of:
_____

Using copings skills of:
_____

Using strategies for:
- ☐ Burnout
- ☐ Conflict resolution
- ☐ Distress tolerance
- ☐ Emotional regulation
- ☐ Management of triggers
- ☐ Mindfulness
- ☐ Motivation
- ☐ Organization/time management
- ☐ Pausing/reducing impulsivity
- ☐ Reinforcing positive thoughts/behaviors
- ☑ Self-care

Progress Note Example: Simple (Continued)

Continued Challenges/Impairments:

- ☐ Communication in relationships
- ☐ Conflict resolution
- ☐ Distress tolerance
- ☐ Establishing/being firm about boundaries
- ☑ Expressing and asserting needs
- ☐ Expressing emotions appropriately
- ☑ Maintaining social relationships
- ☐ Managing work tasks
- ☐ Medication adherence
- ☐ Motivation
- ☐ Regulating emotions/responses
- ☐ Repetitive behaviors
- ☐ Responding to identified triggers
- ☐ Rigid beliefs/patterns
- ☐ Sleep hygiene/routine
- ☐ Understanding social cues/interactions
- ☐ Using positive coping skills

Safety/Risk Assessment (select from dropdown and add info as needed):
No risk reported or observed ▾

- ☐ *Description of thoughts/intent*
- ☐ *Plan for client safety*
- ☐ *Clinician rationale for plan*

_____

_____

Risk factors:

- ☐ Access to means of self-harm
- ☐ Chronic pain or medical condition
- ☐ Delusions and/or hallucinations
- ☐ Current significant stressors
- ☐ Drug or alcohol use
- ☐ Feeling hopeless
- ☐ History of self-harm
- ☐ Lack of social support
- ☐ Previous suicide attempt
- ☐ Recent loss or trauma
- ☐ Recent change in behavior
- ☐ Stated plan for self-harm

Protective factors:

- ☐ Awareness of triggers
- ☐ Engaged in ongoing treatment
- ☐ No history of attempts
- ☐ Pet ownership
- ☐ Positive rapport with clinician
- ☐ Religious/spiritual beliefs
- ☐ Reports motivation to live
- ☐ Strong social support
- ☐ Statements about negative effect on children or others
- ☐ Willing to use safety plan and coping skills

Progress Note Example: Simple (Continued)

In Session Notes (as applicable):

None.

Plan:

- ☑ Continue with regularly scheduled session time.
- ☑ Next session scheduled for: 08/20/2024
- ☑ Client will practice skills from today's session.
- ☐ General Follow-up (as applicable): _____

Awesome Therapist   *08/13/2024*
_____
Therapist Signature   **Date**

Progress Note Example: Insurance

Progress Note Example (Insurance)

Demographic and Insurance Info:

Client name: Elsa Agnarrsdottir

Session Date: 09/06/2024

Session Start Time: 10:01am
Session Stop Time: 10:55am

CPT Code: 90837

Extended session time required in order to (special note for 90837):
- ☐ Address the severity of the client's symptoms and prevent the need for further escalation of care.
- ☐ Allow all individuals in the session to meaningfully participate.
- ☑ Process complex trauma and then regulate emotions effectively prior to leaving session.
- ☐ Process emotions and events with frequent redirection and encouragement to stay focused.
- ☐ Problem-solve through complex concepts and adequately practice skills reviewed in session.

Session Location:
- ☑ In office
- ☐ Telehealth
- ☐ Telephone
- ☐ Other:

Verified Client Location for Telehealth:
- ☐ Home (address on file)
- ☐ Work (address on file)
- ☐ Other:

Statement for Telehealth:
- ☐ Client is appropriate for telehealth. Session environment, privacy risks, and emergency and disconnection protocols reviewed with client.
- ☐ Clinician used best practices for confidentiality, client safety, and security of communication.

Progress Note Example: Insurance (Continued)

Topics/Themes of Session (choose 1-3):

- ☐ Alcohol Use
- ☐ Anxiety
- ☐ Attention/Concentration
- ☐ Childhood experiences
- ☐ Communication
- ☐ Cultural experiences
- ☐ Dating
- ☐ Divorce/Separation
- ☐ Eating behaviors
- ☐ Family conflict
- ☐ Fearfulness
- ☐ Fulfillment
- ☐ Grief/Loss
- ☐ Health
- ☐ Identity
- ☑ Loneliness
- ☐ Major life changes
- ☐ Medication/side effects
- ☐ Motivation
- ☑ Overwhelm
- ☐ Parenting
- ☐ Perinatal issues
- ☐ Relationships (partner/spouse)
- ☐ Relationships (other)
- ☐ Sadness
- ☐ School
- ☐ Self harm/Intent to harm
- ☐ Sexuality
- ☐ Sleep
- ☐ Social support
- ☐ Substance use
- ☑ Symptoms management
- ☐ Thinking
- ☐ Time Management
- ☑ Trauma
- ☐ Values/beliefs
- ☐ Work
- ☐ Other: _____

Client Quotes/Insights during session (as applicable):

"I keep forgetting I don't have to do everything on my own."

Presentation during session (mood, affect, behavior):

- ☐ Argumentative
- ☐ Contemplative
- ☐ Dissociated
- ☐ Distracted
- ☐ Engaged
- ☐ Expressive
- ☐ Flat affect
- ☐ Focused
- ☐ Grandiose
- ☐ Hypervigilant
- ☐ Indecisive
- ☑ Insightful
- ☐ Interactive
- ☐ Irritable
- ☐ Lethargic/sluggish
- ☐ Mindful
- ☐ Quiet/passive
- ☑ Restless/fidgety
- ☐ Rigid thinking
- ☐ Sad
- ☐ Shaking/trembling
- ☑ Talkative
- ☐ Tearful
- ☐ Tired/sleepy
- ☐ Withdrawn
- ☐ Yelling/shouting
- ☐ Other: _____

Progress Note Example: Insurance (Continued)

Interventions:

- ☐ Assessed: _____
- ☐ Assisted client in identifying:
    - ☐ Alternative behaviors
    - ☐ Boundaries
    - ☐ Coping skills
    - ☐ Effects of negative coping skills
    - ☐ Irrational thoughts
    - ☐ Needs and wants
    - ☐ Relapse prevention skills
    - ☐ Sabotaging behaviors
    - ☐ Ways of expressing anger
- ☑ Explored patterns in:
    - ☐ Communication
    - ☐ Family of origin
    - ☐ Relationships
    - ☐ Stress response
    - ☑ Ways of coping
- ☑ Practiced experiential exercises to help with:
    - ☐ Avoidance
    - ☑ Emotional regulation
    - ☐ Perfectionism
    - ☐ Re-patterning reactions
    - ☐ Self compassion
    - ☐ Sense of safety
    - ☐ Social interactions
- ☑ Practiced with client:
    - ☐ Body attunement
    - ☐ Co-regulation
    - ☐ Deep breathing
    - ☐ Mind/body awareness
    - ☐ Orienting and anchoring
    - ☐ Present moment exercises
    - ☑ Positive self-talk
    - ☑ Reframing thoughts/beliefs
- ☑ Processed feelings related to:
    - ☑ Childhood experiences
    - ☐ Family of origin
    - ☐ History of abuse
    - ☐ Relationships
    - ☐ Self/Identity
    - ☑ Trauma
- ☐ Provided psychoeducation on: _____
- ☐ Reviewed strategies for:
    - ☐ Communicating needs
    - ☐ Increasing window of tolerance
    - ☐ Managing current situation
    - ☐ Managing triggers
    - ☐ Procrastination and avoidance
    - ☐ Self-compassion

Progress Note Example: Insurance (Continued)

Progress Toward Goals:

Improvement in or awareness of:
- ☐ Assertion of needs
- ☐ Communication skills
- ☐ Contribution to negative patterns
- ☐ Distress tolerance
- ☐ Emotional regulation
- ☐ Establishing/being firm about boundaries
- ☐ Expression of symptoms
- ☐ Expression of emotions
- ☐ Executive functioning
- ☑ Impact of history and traumatic experiences
- ☐ Making transitions
- ☐ Problem-solving skills
- ☐ Providing feedback to partner
- ☐ Sleep hygiene/routine
- ☐ Triggers to symptoms

Managing symptoms of:
_____

Using copings skills of:
_____

Using strategies for:
- ☐ Burnout
- ☐ Conflict resolution
- ☐ Distress tolerance
- ☑ Emotional regulation
- ☐ Management of triggers
- ☐ Mindfulness
- ☐ Motivation
- ☐ Organization/time management
- ☐ Pausing/reducing impulsivity
- ☑ Reinforcing positive thoughts/behaviors
- ☐ Self-care

Continued Challenges/Impairments:

- ☐ Communication in relationships
- ☐ Conflict resolution
- ☑ Distress tolerance
- ☑ Establishing/being firm about boundaries
- ☑ Expressing and asserting needs
- ☐ Expressing emotions appropriately
- ☐ Maintaining social relationships
- ☐ Managing work tasks

- ☐ Medication adherence
- ☐ Motivation
- ☐ Regulating emotions/responses
- ☐ Repetitive behaviors
- ☐ Responding to identified triggers
- ☐ Rigid beliefs/patterns
- ☐ Sleep hygiene/routine
- ☐ Understanding social cues/interactions
- ☐ Using positive coping skills

Progress Note Example: Insurance (Continued)

Current symptoms impacting functioning:

- ☐ Angry outbursts
- ☐ Anxiety
- ☐ Avoidance of stimuli
- ☐ Binging/purging
- ☐ Depressed mood
- ☐ Dissociative reactions
- ☑ Exaggerated arousal/reactivity
- ☑ Fear or avoidance
- ☐ Feeling worthless or guilty
- ☐ Hypervigilance
- ☐ Impulsivity
- ☐ Irritability
- ☐ Isolating from others
- ☐ Lack of motivation
- ☐ Low energy
- ☐ Negative beliefs
- ☐ Nightmares
- ☐ Panic attack(s)
- ☐ Poor concentration/focus
- ☐ Poor follow through
- ☐ Recurrent/distressing memories
- ☐ Restlessness
- ☐ Restricted eating
- ☑ Self-criticism
- ☐ Self-destructive behavior
- ☐ Sleep disturbance

Impact on Daily Activities

Symptoms impacting relationships with:

- ☐ Children
- ☐ Coworkers
- ☐ Family of origin
- ☑ Friendships
- ☐ Marriage/Partnership
- ☐ Other: _____

Symptoms negatively impacting:

- ☐ Living situation
- ☐ Physical health
- ☐ School
- ☐ Self-care
- ☑ Work
- ☐ Other: _____

Safety/Risk Assessment (select from dropdown and add info as needed):
No risk reported or observed ▾

- ☐ *Description of thoughts/intent*
- ☐ *Plan for client safety*
- ☐ *Clinician rationale for plan*

_____

_____

Progress Note Example: Insurance (Continued)

Risk factors:
- ☐ Access to means of self-harm
- ☐ Chronic pain or medical condition
- ☐ Delusions and/or hallucinations
- ☐ Current significant stressors
- ☐ Drug or alcohol use
- ☐ Feeling hopeless
- ☐ History of self-harm
- ☐ Lack of social support
- ☐ Previous suicide attempt
- ☐ Recent loss or trauma
- ☐ Recent change in behavior
- ☐ Stated plan for self-harm

Protective factors:
- ☐ Awareness of triggers
- ☐ Engaged in ongoing treatment
- ☐ No history of attempts
- ☐ Pet ownership
- ☐ Positive rapport with clinician
- ☐ Religious/spiritual beliefs
- ☐ Reports motivation to live
- ☐ Strong social support
- ☐ Statements about negative effect on children or others
- ☐ Willing to use safety plan and coping skills

In Session Notes (as applicable):

None.

Plan:
- ☑ Continue with regularly scheduled session time.
- ☐ Next session scheduled for: _____
- ☑ Client will practice skills from today's session.
- ☐ General Follow-up (as applicable): _____

Awesome Therapist   09/06/2024
_____
Therapist Signature   **Date**

Progress Note Narrative Starter Phrases

Progress Note Narrative Starter Phrases
For SOAP, DAP, and Narrative Notes

Use the following starter phrases to write full sentences in notes more easily. Each phrase is coordinated with sections in commonly used progress note templates. Suggested sub-sections are in bold and italic.

There are multiple sentences to fit different needs. You likely only need 1-3 sentences per section.

Data or Subjective Sections
Client quote from session:

Client made improvement in their goal of:

Client showed increased ability to manage symptoms of:

Client reported using coping skills from sessions to address:

Client has been effectively using strategies for:

Client reported improvement in symptoms of:

The topics discussed in session included:

Data or Objective Sections

Therapist interventions
Use statements from the Therapeutic Interventions list in the main template.

Client presentation

Client's mood and affect were:

Client's behavior included:

Client presented as:

Progress Note Narrative Starter Phrases (Continued)

Assessment

Client progress

Client was able to incorporate strategies discussed in the session and showed interest in using them to improve symptoms and overall functioning.

Client struggled to incorporate strategies from the session, but was able to use them by the end of the session.

Client struggled with the therapist's suggestions but was able to show insight and awareness during the session.

Client showed increased awareness of:

Client continues to have difficulties with:

Continued symptoms and impairments

Client reported continued symptoms of:

Client continues to exhibit symptoms of:

Client reported new symptoms of:

Client's symptoms continue to negatively impact their relationships with:

-family members   -spouse   -coworkers   -friends

Client's symptoms continue to negatively impact their functioning:

-at home   -at work   -at school
-related to their physical health   -for self-care

Risk assessment
Use statements from the Risk Assessment section in the main template.

Progress Note Narrative Starter Phrases (Continued)

Plan
Client will practice skills reviewed during today's session over the next week.

Client will continue to reflect on insights gained from today's session.

Continue with regularly scheduled session time. Will meet next week on:

Provided the client homework to:

Provided the client with a resource:

In the next session, therapist will follow up on the topic of:

In the next session, therapist will continue to explore:

In the next session, therapist plans to introduce the concept of:

Therapist will change the focus of the next session to:

Progress Note Example: Narrative

Demographic and Insurance Info:

Client name: Pocahontas Powhatan

Session Date: 08/02/2024

Session Start Time: 10:00am
Session Stop Time: 10:54am

CPT Code: 90837
Session Location: Office

Extended session time was required in order to problem-solve through complex concepts and adequately practice skills reviewed in session.

Subjective

Client quote from session: "I really didn't believe it would work as well as it did in that situation!"

The client made improvement in their goal of increasing their use of resourcing skills. The client was able to identify positive memories and supports when feeling anxious. The client showed increased ability to manage symptoms of recurrent worry.

The topics discussed in session included a recent event at her children's school, meeting a new friend, and managing things at home.

Objective

Therapist interventions
Therapist reviewed treatment goals and progress to date with the client. Identified revisions to one treatment goal (see treatment plan). Therapist explored with the client her patterns in coping and related stress responses. Therapist introduced and practiced with client experiential exercises to further assist with emotional regulation.

Client presentation
The client's mood and affect were within normal limits.
The client's behavior included using deep breathing and hand gestures to slow themselves down when talking quickly.
The client presented as insightful and engaged.

Assessment

Client progress
The client was able to incorporate strategies discussed in the session and showed interest in using them to improve symptoms and overall functioning.

Progress Note Example: Narrative (Continued)

Continued symptoms and impairments
Client reported continued symptoms of dysregulation and difficulty managing autonomic arousal.
The client's symptoms continue to negatively impact their relationships with friends.
The client's symptoms continue to negatively impact their functioning at home.

Risk assessment
No risk reported or observed.

Plan
The client will practice skills reviewed during today's session over the next week.
Continue with regularly scheduled session time. Will meet next week on 08/09/2024.
In the next session, the therapist will follow up on the topic of using new resources.

CHAPTER 10: PROGRESS NOTE TEMPLATES

Progress Note: Child/Play Therapy Additions

Progress Note: Child/Play Therapy Additions

Location:
- ☐ Office
- ☐ Online
- ☐ Outside

Session attendees:
- ☐ Client
- ☐ Sibling(s)
- ☐ Parent
- ☐ Step parent
- ☐ Grandparent
- ☐ Aunt/uncle
- ☐ Other: _____

Collateral/Caregiver presentation during session:
- ☐ Able to practice/integrate strategies discussed
- ☐ Able to collaborate with client
- ☐ Critical toward client or clinician
- ☐ Difficulty understanding/empathizing with client
- ☐ Difficulty using strategies discussed
- ☐ Open to feedback from client
- ☐ Provided support and encouragement

Play characteristics:
- ☐ Collaborative
- ☐ Combative
- ☐ Competitive
- ☐ Creative
- ☐ Directive
- ☐ Distracted
- ☐ Egocentric
- ☐ Inflexible
- ☐ Parallel
- ☐ Performative
- ☐ Persistent
- ☐ Refusal
- ☐ Repetitive
- ☐ Solitary
- ☐ Structured

Play themes:
- ☐ Abandonment
- ☐ Aggression
- ☐ Caretaking
- ☐ Conflict
- ☐ Control
- ☐ Death
- ☐ Deception
- ☐ Discipline
- ☐ Exploration
- ☐ Family
- ☐ Fighting
- ☐ Friendships
- ☐ Helpless
- ☐ Hiding
- ☐ Illness
- ☐ Injury
- ☐ Loneliness
- ☐ Loss
- ☐ Money/finances
- ☐ Nurturance/love
- ☐ Power
- ☐ Protection
- ☐ Relationships
- ☐ Rejection
- ☐ Re-enactment
- ☐ Rescuing
- ☐ Safety
- ☐ Sexualized
- ☐ Violence
- ☐ War

Progress Note: Child/Play Therapy Additions (Continued)

Toys and/or materials used:

Art (drawing/painting)
- ☐ Chalk
- ☐ Coloring
- ☐ Crayons
- ☐ Easel
- ☐ Markers
- ☐ Paints
- ☐ Pencils
- ☐ Watercolor

Crafts
- ☐ Clay
- ☐ Glue
- ☐ Paper
- ☐ Stamping
- ☐ Stencils
- ☐ Yarn/string

Dress up
- ☐ Bags/purse
- ☐ Costume
- ☐ Glasses/sunglasses
- ☐ Gloves
- ☐ Hat
- ☐ Jewelry
- ☐ Mask
- ☐ Shoes
- ☐ Wand

Other
- ☐ Drama (performance)
- ☐ Sand tray
- ☐ Writing - stories
- ☐ Writing - songs/poetry

Games
- ☐ Basketball
- ☐ Bowling
- ☐ Card games
- ☐ Checkers
- ☐ Chess
- ☐ Connect Four
- ☐ Guess Who
- ☐ Operation
- ☐ Ring toss
- ☐ Tic Tac Toe
- ☐ Uno
- ☐ Client created a game

Other toys
- ☐ Animals
- ☐ Baby dolls
- ☐ Ball(s)
- ☐ Beads
- ☐ Building blocks
- ☐ Camera
- ☐ Cars/vehicles
- ☐ Cash register
- ☐ Dolls
- ☐ Doll house
- ☐ Figurines
- ☐ Kitchen/food
- ☐ Legos
- ☐ Medical kit
- ☐ Money
- ☐ Musical instruments
- ☐ Puppets
- ☐ Telephone
- ☐ Weapon(s)

Progress Note Example: Child

Progress Note (Child)

Demographic and Insurance Info:

Client name: Wendy Darling

Session Date: 06/08/2024

Session Start Time: 3:01pm
Session Stop Time: 3:50pm

CPT Code: 90847

Extended session time required in order to (special note for 90837):
- ☐ Address the severity of the client's symptoms and prevent the need for further escalation of care.
- ☐ Allow all individuals in the session to meaningfully participate.
- ☐ Process complex trauma and then regulate emotions effectively prior to leaving session.
- ☐ Process emotions and events with frequent redirection and encouragement to stay focused.
- ☐ Problem-solve through complex concepts and adequately practice skills reviewed in session.

Session attendees:

- ☑ Client
- ☐ Sibling(s)
- ☑ Parent
- ☐ Step parent
- ☐ Grandparent
- ☐ Aunt/uncle
- ☐ Other: _____

Session Location:
- ☑ In office
- ☐ Telehealth
- ☐ Outside
- ☐ Other:

Verified Client Location for Telehealth:
- ☐ Home (address on file)
- ☐ Other:

Statement for Telehealth:
- ☐ Client is appropriate for telehealth. Session environment, privacy risks, and emergency and disconnection protocols reviewed with client.
- ☐ Clinician used best practices for confidentiality, client safety, and security of communication.

Progress Note Example: Child (Continued)

Topics/Themes of Session:

- ☐ Anxiety
- ☐ Attention/Concentration
- ☐ Communication
- ☐ Cultural experiences
- ☐ Eating behaviors
- ☐ Family conflict
- ☐ Family separation
- ☒ Fearfulness
- ☐ Friends
- ☐ Grief/Loss
- ☐ Health
- ☐ Identity
- ☐ Loneliness
- ☐ Major life changes
- ☐ Motivation
- ☐ Overwhelm
- ☐ Parents
- ☒ Relationships (other)
- ☐ Sadness
- ☒ School
- ☐ Self harm/Intent to harm
- ☐ Sleep
- ☐ Social support
- ☒ Symptoms management
- ☐ Time Management
- ☐ Trauma
- ☐ Worry
- ☐ Other: _____

Presentation during session (mood, affect, behavior):

- ☐ Argumentative
- ☐ Dissociated
- ☐ Distracted
- ☐ Engaged
- ☐ Expressive
- ☐ Flat affect
- ☐ Focused
- ☐ Hypervigilant
- ☐ Indecisive
- ☐ Insightful
- ☒ Interactive
- ☐ Irritable
- ☐ Lethargic/sluggish
- ☐ Quiet/passive
- ☒ Restless/fidgety
- ☐ Rigid thinking
- ☐ Sad
- ☐ Shaking/trembling
- ☐ Talkative
- ☒ Tearful
- ☐ Tired/sleepy
- ☐ Withdrawn
- ☐ Yelling/shouting
- ☐ Other: _____

Play themes:

- ☒ Abandonment
- ☐ Aggression
- ☒ Caretaking
- ☐ Conflict
- ☐ Control
- ☐ Death
- ☐ Deception
- ☐ Discipline
- ☐ Exploration
- ☐ Family
- ☐ Fighting
- ☐ Friendships
- ☐ Helpless
- ☐ Hiding
- ☐ Illness
- ☐ Injury
- ☐ Loneliness
- ☒ Loss
- ☐ Money/finances
- ☐ Nurturance/love
- ☐ Power
- ☐ Protection
- ☒ Relationships
- ☐ Rejection
- ☐ Re-enactment
- ☒ Rescuing
- ☒ Safety
- ☐ Sexualized
- ☐ Violence
- ☐ War

Progress Note Example: Child (Continued)

Interventions:

- ☐ Assessed: _____
- ☐ Assisted client in identifying:
  - ☐ Alternative behaviors
  - ☐ Boundaries
  - ☐ Coping skills
  - ☐ Ways of expressing anger
- ☐ Completed art project to assist with:
  - ☐ Building rapport
  - ☐ Expressing emotions
  - ☐ Identifying emotions
  - ☐ Improving communication
  - ☐ Perfectionism
  - ☐ Problem-solving
- ☑ De-escalated client using:
  - ☑ Deep breathing
  - ☑ Experience of senses
  - ☐ Grounding exercise
  - ☐ Reflection of emotions/experience
- ☑ Introduced game to practice:
  - ☐ Age appropriate social skills
  - ☐ Anger management skills
  - ☐ Asking for help
  - ☐ Communicating with others
  - ☐ Coregulation
  - ☐ Expressing empathy
  - ☐ Flexibility in interactions
  - ☐ Identifying emotions
  - ☐ Identifying social cues
  - ☐ Planning ahead
  - ☑ Regulating emotions
  - ☐ Taking turns
- ☑ Practiced experiential exercises to help with:
  - ☐ Avoidance
  - ☑ Body attunement
  - ☐ Emotional regulation
  - ☐ Sense of safety
  - ☐ Social interactions
- ☐ Provided psychoeducation on: _____
- ☑ Reviewed strategies for:
  - ☐ Communicating needs
  - ☐ Increasing window of tolerance
  - ☐ Managing current situation
  - ☑ Managing triggers
  - ☑ Self-talk
- ☐ Set goals related to:
  - ☐ Areas of need
  - ☐ Current symptoms
  - ☐ Strengths and resiliency
- ☑ Used play therapy to practice:
  - ☐ Age appropriate social skills
  - ☐ Anger management skills
  - ☐ Asking for help
  - ☐ Communicating with others
  - ☐ Identifying emotions
  - ☐ Identifying social cues
  - ☑ Problem-solving skills
  - ☑ Regulating emotions

Progress Note Example: Child (Continued)

Toys and/or materials used:

Art (drawing/painting)
- ☐ Chalk
- ☐ Coloring
- ☐ Crayons
- ☐ Easel
- ☐ Markers
- ☐ Paints
- ☐ Pencils
- ☐ Watercolor

Crafts
- ☐ Clay
- ☐ Glue
- ☐ Paper
- ☐ Stamping
- ☐ Stencils
- ☐ Yarn/string

Dress up
- ☐ Bags/purse
- ☑ Costume
- ☐ Glasses/sunglasses
- ☐ Gloves
- ☐ Hat
- ☐ Jewelry
- ☑ Mask
- ☐ Shoes
- ☑ Wand

Other
- ☑ Drama (performance)
- ☐ Sand tray
- ☐ Writing - stories
- ☐ Writing - songs/poetry

Games
- ☐ Basketball
- ☐ Bowling
- ☐ Card games
- ☐ Checkers
- ☐ Chess
- ☐ Connect Four
- ☐ Guess Who
- ☐ Operation
- ☐ Ring toss
- ☐ Tic Tac Toe
- ☐ Uno
- ☐ Client created a game

Other toys
- ☑ Animals
- ☑ Baby dolls
- ☐ Ball(s)
- ☐ Beads
- ☐ Building blocks
- ☐ Camera
- ☐ Cars/vehicles
- ☐ Cash register
- ☑ Dolls
- ☐ Doll house
- ☐ Figurines
- ☐ Kitchen/food
- ☐ Legos
- ☐ Medical kit
- ☐ Money
- ☐ Musical instruments
- ☐ Puppets
- ☑ Telephone
- ☐ Weapon(s)

Client Quotes/Insights during session:

"She's not as scared when her mom is there." (About character during play)

Progress Toward Goals:

Improvement in or awareness of:
- ☐ Communication skills
- ☐ Distress tolerance
- ☑ Emotional regulation
- ☐ Establishing/being firm about boundaries
- ☐ Expression of emotions
- ☐ Making transitions
- ☐ Problem-solving skills
- ☐ Sleep hygiene/routine
- ☐ Symptoms management
- ☑ Triggers to symptoms

Using copings skills of:
_____

Using strategies for:
- ☐ Distress tolerance
- ☐ Emotional regulation
- ☐ Management of triggers
- ☐ Mindfulness
- ☐ Organization/time management
- ☐ Pausing/reducing impulsivity
- ☐ Reinforcing positive thoughts and behaviors

Current symptoms impacting functioning:

- ☐ Angry outbursts
- ☑ Anxiety
- ☐ Binging/purging
- ☐ Depressed mood
- ☐ Dissociative reactions
- ☑ Exaggerated arousal/reactivity
- ☐ Fear or avoidance
- ☐ Feeling worthless or guilty
- ☐ Hypervigilance
- ☐ Impulsivity
- ☐ Irritability
- ☐ Isolating from others

- ☐ Lack of motivation
- ☐ Low energy
- ☐ Nightmares
- ☐ Panic attack(s)
- ☐ Poor concentration/focus
- ☐ Poor follow through
- ☑ Recurrent/distressing memories
- ☐ Restlessness
- ☐ Restricted eating
- ☐ Self-criticism
- ☐ Self-destructive behavior
- ☐ Sleep disturbance

Symptoms are negatively impacting:

- ☐ Living situation
- ☐ Physical health
- ☐ Relationships at home
- ☑ Social relationships
- ☑ School activity/performance
- ☐ Other: _____

Progress Note Example: Child (Continued)

Safety/Risk Assessment:
No risk reported or observed ▾

☐ *Description of thoughts/intent*   ☐ *Plan for client safety*   ☐ *Clinician rationale for plan*

_____

_____

Risk factors:

☐ Access to means of self-harm
☐ Chronic pain or medical condition
☐ Delusions and/or hallucinations
☐ Current significant stressors
☐ Drug or alcohol use
☐ Feeling hopeless
☐ History of self-harm
☐ Lack of social support
☐ Previous suicide attempt
☐ Recent loss or trauma
☐ Recent change in behavior
☐ Stated plan for self-harm

Protective factors:

☐ Awareness of triggers
☐ Engaged in ongoing treatment
☐ No history of attempts
☐ Pet ownership
☐ Positive rapport with clinician
☐ Religious/spiritual beliefs
☐ Reports motivation to live
☐ Strong social support
☐ Statements about negative effect on children or others
☐ Willing to use safety plan and coping skills

Collateral/Caregiver presentation during session:
☑ Able to practice/integrate strategies discussed
☑ Able to collaborate with client
☐ Critical toward client or clinician
☐ Difficulty understanding/empathizing with client
☐ Difficulty using strategies discussed
☐ Open to feedback from client
☑ Provided support and encouragement

Other Collateral/Caregiver related notes:
None.

Progress Note Example: Child (Continued)

In Session Notes:
Negative interaction with teacher when using relaxation skills.
Consult with teacher?

Plan:

- ☑ Continue with regularly scheduled session time.
- ☐ Next session scheduled for: _____
- ☑ Client will practice skills from today's session.
- ☑ General Follow-up (as applicable): Will talk with client's mother about possible consult with teacher.

Awesome Therapist   06/08/2024
_____
Therapist Signature   **Date**

Progress Note: Couples Therapy Additions

Topics/Themes of Session:

- ☐ Communication styles
- ☐ Conflict resolution
- ☐ Cultural differences
- ☐ Family management
- ☐ Family roles
- ☐ Divorce/separation
- ☐ Gender roles
- ☐ Identity
- ☐ In-laws
- ☐ Jealousy
- ☐ Money management
- ☐ Parenting
- ☐ Patterns of interaction
- ☐ Religious beliefs/practices
- ☐ Value differences
- ☐ Sex-related discussion:
  - ☐ Desire
  - ☐ Frequency
  - ☐ Identity
  - ☐ Preferences
  - ☐ Satisfaction

Interventions:

Psychoeducation on:

- ☐ Anatomy/physiology and sex
- ☐ Attachment styles
- ☐ Common couples experiences
- ☐ Common sexual experiences
- ☐ Developmental stages of children
- ☐ Familial and generational patterns
- ☐ Impacts of trauma on relationships

Notable Patterns and Themes:

- ☐ Abandonment
- ☐ Aggression
- ☐ Caretaking
- ☐ Control
- ☐ Deception
- ☐ Helpless
- ☐ Loneliness
- ☐ Loss
- ☐ Money/finances
- ☐ Nurturance/love
- ☐ Power
- ☐ Protection
- ☐ Rejection
- ☐ Re-enactment
- ☐ Rescuing

Progress Note: Couples Therapy Additions (Continued)

Notes on Couple's Interactions:
- ☐ Able to work through conflicting opinions/values
- ☐ Collaborated to problem-solve
- ☐ Connected with physical touch
- ☐ Difficulty implementing strategies learned in session
- ☐ Difficulty understanding one another
- ☐ Engaged with one another
- ☐ Expressed feelings to one another
- ☐ Mirrored one another
- ☐ Presented information as a team
- ☐ Current strengths: _____
- ☐ Current struggles: _____

Client 1 Presentation During Session:
- ☐ Accepted and integrated feedback from partner
- ☐ Attuned to partner
- ☐ Focused on self needs
- ☐ Identified and expressed personal needs
- ☐ Listened without defending
- ☐ Rejected partner's request
- ☐ Restricted or flat affect
- ☐ Shouting/yelling
- ☐ Showed compassion/empathy
- ☐ Tearful/crying
- ☐ Turned away from partner
- ☐ Validated partner's needs

Client 2 Presentation During Session:
- ☐ Accepted and integrated feedback from partner
- ☐ Attuned to partner
- ☐ Focused on self needs
- ☐ Identified and expressed personal needs
- ☐ Listened without defending
- ☐ Rejected partner's request
- ☐ Restricted or flat affect
- ☐ Shouting/yelling
- ☐ Showed compassion/empathy
- ☐ Tearful/crying
- ☐ Turned away from partner
- ☐ Validated partner's needs

Progress Note Example: Couples

Progress Note (Couples)

Demographic and Insurance Info:

Client name: Aladdin Cassim
Client name: Jasmine bint Hamed Bobolonius

Session Date: 07/25/2024

Session Time: 4pm

CPT Code: 90847

Session Location:
- ☑ In office
- ☐ Telehealth
- ☐ Telephone
- ☐ Other:

Verified Client Location for Telehealth:
- ☐ Home (address on file)
- ☐ Work (address on file)
- ☐ Other:

Statement for Telehealth:
- ☐ Clients are appropriate for telehealth. Session environment, privacy risks, and emergency and disconnection protocols reviewed with clients.
- ☐ Clinician used best practices for confidentiality, client safety, and security of communication.

Topics Discussed:

- ☐ Alcohol Use
- ☐ Childhood experiences
- ☐ Communication styles
- ☐ Conflict resolution
- ☐ Cultural differences
- ☐ Divorce/Separation
- ☐ Family conflict
- ☐ Family management
- ☑ Family roles
- ☐ Divorce/separation
- ☐ Gender roles
- ☐ Grief/Loss
- ☐ Health
- ☐ Identity
- ☐ In-laws
- ☑ Jealousy
- ☑ Loneliness
- ☐ Major life changes
- ☐ Money management
- ☐ Overwhelm
- ☐ Parenting
- ☑ Patterns of interaction
- ☐ Perinatal issues
- ☐ Religious beliefs/practices
- ☐ Sadness
- ☐ Self harm/Intent to harm
- ☑ Sex-related discussion:
    - ☑ Desire
    - ☑ Frequency
    - ☐ Identity
    - ☑ Preferences
    - ☑ Satisfaction
- ☐ Sleep
- ☐ Social support
- ☐ Substance use
- ☐ Symptoms management
- ☐ Time Management
- ☐ Trauma
- ☐ Values/beliefs
- ☐ Work
- ☐ Other: _____

Progress Note Example: Couples (Continued)

Interventions:

- ☐ Assessed: _____
- ☐ Assisted clients in identifying:
  - ☐ Alternative behaviors
  - ☐ Boundaries
  - ☐ Effects of negative coping skills
  - ☐ Needs and wants
  - ☐ Strengths and resources
  - ☐ Ways of expressing feelings
- ☑ Explored patterns in:
  - ☑ Communication
  - ☐ Family of origin
  - ☐ Relationships
  - ☐ Stress response
  - ☐ Ways of coping
- ☑ Practiced experiential exercises to help with:
  - ☐ Avoidance
  - ☑ Emotional regulation
  - ☐ Re-patterning reactions
  - ☐ Self compassion
  - ☐ Sense of safety
- ☑ Practiced skills in session:
  - ☑ Body attunement
  - ☐ Co-regulation
  - ☐ Deep breathing
  - ☑ Mind/body awareness
  - ☐ Orienting and anchoring
  - ☐ Present moment exercises
  - ☐ Positive self-talk
  - ☐ Reframing thoughts/beliefs
- ☑ Processed feelings related to:
  - ☐ Childhood experiences
  - ☐ Family of origin
  - ☐ Relationship history
  - ☐ Relationship patterns
  - ☐ Self/Identity
  - ☑ Sexuality
  - ☐ Trauma
- ☑ Provided psychoeducation on:
  - ☐ Anatomy/physiology and sex
  - ☑ Attachment styles
  - ☑ Common couples experiences
  - ☑ Common sexual experiences
  - ☐ Developmental stages of children
  - ☑ Familial and generational patterns
  - ☐ Impacts of trauma on relationships
- ☑ Reflected back to clients:
  - ☐ Observations on their responses
  - ☑ Patterns in their relationships
  - ☐ Their interaction with one another and responses
  - ☐ Their progress
  - ☐ Their strengths

Progress Note Example: Couples (Continued)

Notes on Couple's Interactions:
- ☐ Able to work through conflicting opinions/values
- ☐ Collaborated to problem-solve
- ☐ Connected with physical touch
- ☑ Difficulty implementing strategies learned in session
- ☐ Difficulty understanding one another
- ☐ Engaged with one another
- ☑ Expressed feelings to one another
- ☐ Mirrored one another
- ☐ Presented information as a team
- ☐ Current strengths: _____
- ☐ Current struggles: _____

Partner 1 Quotes/Insights during session:

"I miss feeling really connected during sex."

Partner 2 Quotes/Insights during session:

"It's so frustrating feeling like I have to manage everything."

Client 1 Presentation During Session:
- ☐ Accepted and integrated feedback from partner
- ☐ Attuned to partner
- ☐ Focused on self needs
- ☑ Identified and expressed personal needs
- ☐ Listened without defending
- ☐ Rejected partner's request
- ☐ Restricted or flat affect
- ☐ Shouting/yelling
- ☐ Showed compassion/empathy
- ☐ Tearful/crying
- ☐ Turned away from partner
- ☑ Validated partner's needs

Client 2 Presentation During Session:
- ☐ Accepted and integrated feedback from partner
- ☐ Attuned to partner
- ☐ Focused on self needs
- ☑ Identified and expressed personal needs
- ☐ Listened without defending
- ☐ Rejected partner's request
- ☐ Restricted or flat affect
- ☐ Shouting/yelling
- ☐ Showed compassion/empathy
- ☑ Tearful/crying
- ☐ Turned away from partner
- ☐ Validated partner's needs

Progress Note Example: Couples (Continued)

Notable Patterns and Themes:
- ☐ Abandonment
- ☐ Aggression
- ☐ Caretaking
- ☐ Control
- ☐ Deception
- ☑ Helpless
- ☐ Loneliness
- ☐ Loss
- ☐ Money/finances
- ☑ Nurturance/love
- ☐ Power
- ☐ Protection
- ☐ Rejection
- ☐ Re-enactment
- ☐ Rescuing

Progress Toward Shared Goals:

Improvement or awareness of:
- ☑ Communication skills
- ☐ Conflict resolution
- ☐ Emotional regulation
- ☐ Establishing/being firm about boundaries
- ☐ Expression of emotions
- ☐ Impact of history and traumatic experiences
- ☐ Interruption of negative patterns
- ☐ Needs of self and others
- ☐ Problem-solving skills
- ☑ Providing and receiving feedback

Using copings skills of:
_____

Using strategies for:
- ☐ Conflict resolution
- ☐ Distress tolerance
- ☐ Emotional regulation
- ☐ Household management
- ☐ Improved sexual intimacy
- ☐ Organization/time management
- ☐ Pausing/reducing impulsivity
- ☐ Reinforcing positive thoughts and behaviors
- ☐ Self-care

Continued Challenges/Impairments:
- ☐ Communication skills
- ☐ Conflict resolution
- ☐ Distress tolerance
- ☐ Emotional regulation
- ☐ Establishing/being firm about boundaries
- ☐ Expression of emotions
- ☐ Impact of history and traumatic experiences
- ☑ Household management
- ☐ Interruption of negative patterns
- ☐ Mindfulness
- ☐ Needs of self and others
- ☐ Organization/time management
- ☐ Pausing/reducing impulsivity
- ☐ Problem-solving skills
- ☐ Providing and receiving feedback
- ☐ Reinforcing positive thoughts and behaviors
- ☐ Self-care
- ☑ Sexual intimacy

Progress Note Example: Couples (Continued)

Safety/Risk Assessment (select from dropdown and add info as needed):
No risk reported or observed ▼

☐ *Description of thoughts/intent*   ☐ *Plan for client safety*   ☐ *Clinician rationale for plan*

_____

_____

Risk factors:
- ☐ Access to means of self-harm
- ☐ Chronic pain or medical condition
- ☐ Delusions and/or hallucinations
- ☐ Current significant stressors
- ☐ Drug or alcohol use
- ☐ Feeling hopeless
- ☐ History of self-harm
- ☐ Lack of social support
- ☐ Previous suicide attempt
- ☐ Recent loss or trauma
- ☐ Recent change in behavior
- ☐ Stated plan for self-harm

Protective factors:
- ☐ Awareness of triggers
- ☐ Engaged in ongoing treatment
- ☐ No history of attempts
- ☐ Pet ownership
- ☐ Positive rapport with clinician
- ☐ Religious/spiritual beliefs
- ☐ Reports motivation to live
- ☐ Strong social support
- ☐ Statements about negative effect on children or others
- ☐ Willing to use safety plan and coping skills

Plan:
- ☑ Continue with regularly scheduled session time.
- ☑ Next session scheduled for: 08/01/2024
- ☑ Clients will practice skills from today's session.
- ☐ General Follow-up (as applicable): _____

Awesome Therapist   07/25/2024

Therapist Signature   **Date**

Progress Note: Group Therapy Additions

Location:
☐ Office ☐ Online ☐ Other: _____

Group Info:

Group Name: _____   Session Topic: _____

Number of group attendees: _____   Session Number: _____

Group Interventions:

Assisted group in identifying: _____

Incorporated movement to help with: _____

Assisted group in resolving conflict about: _____

Introduced an exercise to: _____

Directed group to work collaboratively on: _____

Led group discussion on: _____

Discussed the concept of: _____

Led group sharing exercise to identify: _____

Guided group members in: _____

Practiced in group: _____

Facilitated discussion about: _____

Provided psychoeducation on: _____

Facilitated group check-in regarding: _____

Reviewed homework on: _____

Identified skills to manage: _____

Reviewed progress in: _____

Individual Interventions: *Select from the broader Therapeutic Interventions List.*

Client's Interaction with Group Members:

☐ Argumentative   ☐ Creative   ☐ Insightful
☐ Collaborative   ☐ Distracted   ☐ Refused to engage
☐ Competitive   ☐ Encouraging   ☐ Self-focused

NOTES

NOTES

Chapter 11

Coordinating Care AND Ending Treatment

IN THIS CHAPTER

Ethically Coordinating Care With Other Professionals 273
Seeking Consultation and Whether or Not to Document It 277
Writing Objective and Helpful Letters for Clients 279
Considerations When Releasing Client Records 280
Documenting the End of the Therapeutic Relationship 282
Managing and Destroying Records Beyond Treatment 284
Quick Read Chapter Summary.. 285

> *There is immense power when a group of people with similar interests gets together to work toward the same goals.*
>
> *- Idowu Koyenikan*

Although often an afterthought when creating policies

and procedures, coordinating care and terminating with clients becomes paramount at specific times during psychotherapy. This chapter presents common scenarios for these events, along with guidance on how to address them with a variety of clients.

ETHICALLY COORDINATING CARE WITH OTHER PROFESSIONALS

Coordinating care with a client's other providers is becoming more standard than previously in mental health care. Interestingly, Medicare (2024) actually requires that psychologists attempt to collaborate with a client's physician, provided the client has consented to this collaboration. They do not explicitly require this for other mental health clinicians, but it is recommended as a standard of practice if you are the main source of mental health support for the client. Medicare further requires the following for psychologists:

- Document the date the patient consented or declined consultation and the consultation dates in the patient's medical (mental health) record.
- If consultations are unsuccessful, document that in the patient's record with the date and the physician notification method (doesn't apply if the physician made the original referral to the psychologist).

While this is a requirement specific to Medicare, it does highlight that managed care intends to integrate mental and physical healthcare more often. Wellness initiatives relating to holistic care are increasingly researched, accepted, and popular (Lim, Fuchs, and Touros, 2024). This integration of mental health care increases access and adherence to care, has positive outcomes for a variety of mental health conditions, reduces overall healthcare costs, and even improves provider satisfaction (APA 2022; Archer et al., 2012). However, integration also compounds ongoing issues for mental health clinicians, such as protecting client records (FTC, 2023) and maintaining confidentiality in team settings.

There are many instances in which coordinating care with another professional is helpful, necessary, or even requested by the client. Professional consultation may be helpful with other clinicians, but also with other non-mental health professionals. Some common scenarios for coordinating with other professionals include:

- Coordinating care with a previous (or newly assigned) mental health clinician,
- Coordinating care with the client's psychiatrist,
- Updating a referring physician about the client's involvement in treatment,
- Gathering information about the client's behaviors at school, or
- Reporting on treatment involvement and symptoms progress related to a referral by a county agency.

Again, we revisit the all important topic of informed consent. Always discuss with clients your coordination of care with any other professionals, or the need for consultation with anyone. Review exactly what will be discussed or shared, and have the client complete an Authorization to Release Information form (template provided in Chapter 12).

Authorization to Release Information

Although the HIPAA Privacy Rule does allow some sharing of protected health information without prior consent for the purpose of coordinating care, it is best practice to discuss this with clients beforehand if at all possible (HIPAA, 2013; AAMFT, 2015; ACA, 2014; AMHCA, 2020; APA, 2017; NASW, 2021). Another important action is documenting this discussion with clients and having them complete an Authorization to Release Information (also commonly referred to as a Release of Information form, or simply "ROI").

The purpose of completing this form is not to limit client access to records, but to clearly communicate exactly what will be shared, when, and to whom. This is an important distinction because in my own experience I have found that 1) there are clinicians in practice who use administrative tasks to make client access to records difficult, and 2) the form is meant to highlight that you value and protect client information and need authorization to share it.

When completing an Authorization to Release Information, make sure to identify all of the following:

- Contact information of the client (and parent/guardian, if relevant)
- Contact information of the person who is receiving or sending information about the client
- Specific information to be released
- The purpose of the release
- Expiration date for release (at most one year from date of completion)

This is a form that is easy for clients to quickly complete without understanding the potential ramifications. Remember, it is your job as the clinician to make sure clients understand what they are signing, while still complying with their request to access or share their records.

Some clinicians leave the dates for expiration blank or purposely enter the date for an extended time, such as a year. They do this as a way to share information more easily ongoing and without needing further permission from the client. That is certainly not the purpose of this form. Limit sharing information about clients to a one-time occurrence whenever possible and outline *why* the Authorization would be ongoing if that's the agreement.

Please note: You do NOT need an Authorization to Release Information when releasing records directly to the client. This is specifically for communicating with or sending information *about* the client to others.

Mistakes to avoid when coordinating care

Even after an in-depth discussion with the client and a signed Authorization to Release Information, there are considerations when sharing information. The most important of these is the concept of "minimum necessary" information (AAMFT, 2015; ACA, 2014; AMHCA, 2020; APA, 2017; NASW, 2021).

Minimum necessary means that although you have permission to speak with someone about a client, you still maintain confidentiality by only sharing what is relevant to the current discussion or situation. While this principle seems easy to follow on the surface, there are many common circumstances in which this quickly escalates into over sharing.

Let's review two scenarios relating to this concept.

Scenario #1
You are a clinician working in an office building with many medical professionals and as a result of your excellent networking skills, you receive referrals from many of the physicians. A physician referred a client for mental health treatment and requested confirmation that the client is receiving services. You have the client complete an Authorization to Release Information and discuss with the client that you will simply confirm they are receiving treatment "related to anxiety" and attending regular sessions. When talking with the physician they ask you what diagnosis you have given the client so the physician "can put it in my notes and follow up." They also request to know the type of psychotherapy being provided and share that the client presents in a way similar to someone they know who was sexually abused. They encourage you to discuss that information with the client.

Scenario #2
You are a school-based clinician working in a mental health clinic. Your new client is struggling at school and was recently suspended for fighting in class. The parent reports the client does not exhibit the same behaviors at home and recommends talking with the teacher. They sign an Authorization to Release Information for you to gather information about the client's "behavior at school" and to discuss "problem-solving strategies to use in the classroom."

When talking with the teacher, they describe the client's behaviors in detail and provide multiple examples of problematic behaviors as well as specific incidents that involved other children. The teacher gives you far more information than you expected, and it is very helpful for understanding the client. You ask the teacher about problem-solving and they say "I've tried everything and nothing works with this kid. It must be the parents. I don't think the child has consequences at home." However, they are very open to discussing problem-solving strategies to use in the classroom and say they are even open to you being in the classroom for observation or interventions. The teacher requests this "because that will just be easier."

In each of the above scenarios, the clinician appears to have acted ethically and within the context of what they had permission to share. However, it would be very easy to begin sharing more while in the midst of a conversation. For example, in Scenario #1, it would be appropriate to share that the client is receiving treatment related to anxiety, since that is the phrasing used in the Authorization to Release Information. However, sharing the specific diagnosis was not previously discussed with the client.

In Scenario #2, it may feel natural to discuss strategies the parents are or are not using at home since it is related to the discussion with the teacher. However, unless the parents have given permission to do so, it would not be appropriate to share this information. Remember that in these scenarios you can always say something like, "You know, I didn't talk with the client about sharing that information, but they might be happy to share if you asked them."

SEEKING CONSULTATION AND WHETHER OR NOT TO DOCUMENT IT

Consultation is a regular part of staying ethical as a clinician. Consultation differs from supervision in that consultation is egalitarian and does not comprise evaluation (Miu et al., 2022). It also may be an ongoing relationship or may be a one time meeting based on the expertise of the consultant, and conducted in either a group or one-on-one format.

Clinicians seek consultation on a variety of issues including (Beidas, et al., 2013; Nagy, et al., 2022; Nathan & Desposito, 2023):

- Differential diagnosis
- Multicultural competency and other influencing factors
- Treatment planning for complex cases
- Camaraderie and support to reduce burnout
- Improved self-awareness, clinical skills, and new perspectives
- Determining next steps for difficult cases
- Implementation of new guidelines and laws
- Ongoing support implementing new techniques after continuing education
- Managing personal issues that could impact clinical work

Most ethics codes promote consultation as a helpful practice and an ongoing expectation for clinicians, especially if they notice personal issues that may impact work or improved competence related to a current client or issue (APA 2017; Miu et al., 2022). The NASW Code of Ethics (2021) recommends discussing with the client whether or not consultation would be best, although other ethics codes leave this up to clinician determination (AAMFT, 2015; ACA, 2014; AMHCA, 2020; APA, 2017).

While having a professional network and consulting with other professionals is important, it is helpful to have certain questions in mind when seeking consultation:

- *How can I best protect my client's confidentiality?*

- *What rights does my client have in this situation?*
- *What outcome will benefit my <u>client</u> the most?*

When seeking consultation, it is also important to consider whether or not you plan to document the consultation (Nathan & Desposito, 2023), as well as whether or not such documentation belongs in the client's file or in another location. Factors influencing this decision include whether or not the consultation was due to client need or an issue specific to the clinician, and whether or not the consultation will impact treatment decisions.

For example, if a clinician starts to develop romantic feelings for a client and seeks consultation about how to manage these feelings without having a negative impact on the client, this is likely not appropriate to document in the client's file. It is an issue related to the clinician and is certainly appropriate for consultation so the clinician can remain ethical and receive support. The clinician may choose to document this consultation on their own in a separate file related to professional development.

However, if a client reveals to a clinician that the client has romantic feelings for the clinician, this is relevant and important to document in the client's file. The clinician may seek consultation to manage this issue, as well, particularly if it becomes an ongoing theme in treatment or is the first time the clinician has managed such an issue. The clinician may document this consultation, particularly if it results in changing course in treatment or introducing a new strategy.

Regardless of the decision, it is important to include information about any ongoing or planned consultation as part of the informed consent process. This looks like:

- Including information about involvement in peer consultation groups in documents such as a Consent for Services (this is included within the Consent for Services form in Chapter 5),
- Documenting conversations with clients about consultation in relevant progress notes, and
- Documenting reasons for seeking consultation, with whom, and the resulting decisions in a separate Consultation Progress Note (see the template in Chapter 12).

Generally, when in doubt about how to handle a difficult client situation, seek consultation. And generally, when seeking consultation, plan to document the consultation, both for your own professional notes and for the benefit of the client.

WRITING OBJECTIVE AND HELPFUL LETTERS FOR CLIENTS

At some point in your career, it is likely you will be asked to write a letter for a client. Writing a summary of treatment letter is not necessarily a requirement for most clinicians. However, this is often preferable to releasing the client's entire record, especially when the purpose is to provide evidence of the client's progress or involvement in psychotherapy.

It is important to consider policies ahead of time and provide information related to potential fees, lead time, etc. for writing summary letters. This should all be included in the initial Consent for Services and reviewed with clients any time the topic is introduced. Also discuss any limitations for writing the letter, the client's intentions for the request, and if the client would like to review the letter before sending it to any other party. If the client wants you to send the letter directly, have them complete an Authorization to Release Information.

It is important to state that a letter from the treating clinician is always an objective summary of treatment, *not* a recommendation, and especially not a recommendation related to custody or other court matters (AAMFT, 2015; ACA, 2014; AMHCA, 2020; APA, 2017; NASW, 2021).

Clinicians often become involved unethically, albeit with good intentions, by inappropriately making a recommendation about, or for, a client in a court related matter. To confuse matters further, it is not uncommon for attorneys to request a recommendation from the treating clinician. Some attorneys are aware this is unethical but are trying to circumvent the need for an additional clinician to be involved in the case. Do not take the bait! Ethically, another clinician needs to be appointed for specific recommendations to the court.

However, as the treating clinician, it is ethical (and also often requested) to provide a summary letter. It is important to remain as objective as possible in such letters, as well as to consider the minimum necessary standard. Stay within your realm of competence (Zuckerman, 2019), focusing only on a summary of your treatment with the client.

Communicate any concerns to the client, such as the possibility of a letter being shared with both sides in a court case. Also communicate any limitations, such as your inability to make specific recommendations if that is not within your scope or role. This comes up with both major issues such as court cases, and more minor issues such as requests for letters recommending an emotional support animal. Lastly, remember that you can choose not to provide a letter, if that seems the most appropriate.

Treatment summaries are fairly simple to write, since they are focused on objective data that you already have access to. Keep the letter simple, organized, and focused on the following (also, see the Case Summary example in Chapter 12):

- Your information and credentials
- Client name and basic demographics
- Reason for seeking treatment
- Dates of treatment
- Diagnosis (if applicable)
- People involved in treatment/type of treatment
- Treatment goals/focus
- Progress made toward goals
- Reason for termination (if applicable)

Retract any information that your client does not want included. For example, perhaps they are fine with sending their attorney a letter with dates of treatment but they do not want diagnosis or treatment goals included. Everything to be included should be listed on the Authorization to Release Information form when sending a letter directly to other entities.

There are times when adding other information is helpful to better represent the client (APA, 2017). For example, if a client was injured during your work together and had sporadic attendance for a few months due to difficulty with mobility and managing other healthcare appointments, that would be important to note so they are not misrepresented as unreliable. This is an example of using objective data that is helpful for anyone potentially reading the letter, while maintaining your dedication to doing what is best for the client.

CONSIDERATIONS WHEN RELEASING CLIENT RECORDS

As discussed in Chapter 2, clients generally have the right to request and access their records (except in extreme circumstances). However, records requests cause a sudden cortisol spike for most clinicians. It is scary to release records "into the wild" with no control over how they might be used or perceived. It is also common to feel nervous that others will judge the clinician's documentation.

When you receive a records request, first take a breath. This is normal, common, and yes, you have no control over what will happen once the records are released. But you do have control of the situation *now*. Here is what to do:

1. *If the request came in writing* (via subpoena or an email request, etc.), take the time to review it carefully. Identify specifically what is being requested and by whom. Breathe through this and read it more than once. Then move on to the next step.

2. *If the request came directly from your client* (or once you have reviewed a third party request you received), contact them to discuss the request. Express any concerns and explain other options, such as a treatment summary, if that is appropriate. It is important to understand what your client hopes to achieve with the request so you can appropriately guide them and meet their needs.

3. An optional but recommended step at this point is to contact your malpractice or liability insurance. They will provide a consultation with an attorney to discuss the request. *Do not try to read and interpret legal documents on your own*. Use this (usually free) consultation to understand the request and your responsibilities, as well as how to communicate with the requestor and/or your client.

4. Obtain an Authorization to Release Information from your client if the request is both approved by the client and requested by a third party.

5. Once you have confirmed records are to be released, go through the client file and make sure all documentation is complete and signed. If there are any pending or incomplete notes, finalize them as soon as possible. Prepare everything and identify how and to whom you will release the records.

6. If you receive a subpoena and the client does *not* want their records released, prepare the records as above. Assert privilege on the client's behalf but have the records ready in case this is ordered by the judge. Discuss this possibility with your client.

7. Remember that you are responsible to keep the client's information secure as long as it is in your possession. Use a secure method for sharing links or records and do not email records via regular means.

Fear about subpoenas and records in court

No clinician wants a client's mental health records being involved in a court case. The potential for misuse, misrepresentation, and negative consequences are nerve wracking. However, attorneys have a job to do, and hopefully one of the involved attorneys is working on behalf of your client. A good attorney can and will twist information to match the narrative they are portraying. Mental health records may or may not be involved.

Your role is not to hide anything potentially harmful, or even determine what might be potentially harmful. Your role is to protect confidentiality, inform the client of their rights, and comply with any legal requests (subpoena or client request). Your role is also to document the mental health services you provided. Regardless of what happens in any court case, you did nothing wrong if you accurately and ethically documented a client's treatment. There is simply no way for you to predict any legal outcome and you are not responsible for any legal outcome.

Clinician Spotlight: Kia

Kia booked a consultation with me immediately after receiving a records request related to a former but long-term client. She wanted to release just a summary instead of the full record and was worried about a potential subpoena. She was extremely nervous because her client dealt with some difficult experiences during treatment and she admitted that some things in the record might not reflect positively on the client.

Kia and I reviewed the request together. It was a request from the attorney, but it was not a subpoena. I recommended that Kia call the client to discuss all the options, including preparing a treatment summary for the attorney to review. We outlined some bullet points for Kia to cover in the conversation with her client so that she could manage her own anxiety about the situation, and tactfully discuss concerns with the client.

We then reviewed the client's records to determine potentially harmful information, so she could discuss this with the attorney, if necessary. We made sure the documentation was complete and up to date and also outlined what to include in a potential treatment summary.

Kia wrote me a few weeks later to say she never received a subpoena and while that was relieving, she felt so much better after discussing the request with me. She felt confident that she could ethically manage future records requests because she knew the steps to take.

DOCUMENTING THE END OF THE THERAPEUTIC RELATIONSHIP

Documentation is important when ending the therapeutic relationship. It is important to explain why psychotherapy ended and how the client will continue (with you or with someone else) if services are needed in the future. This shows that the clinician has not abandoned the client (Wiger, 2009). Also considering the potential liability if a client acted violently, whether toward themselves or someone else, clearly documenting termination has multiple potential benefits for the clinician.

This documentation can happen in either the final progress note, or in a separate note. If there is a final termination session with the client, it makes sense to document all the termination aspects there. However, if a client does not have a clear termination session, document this in a separate progress note.

In the final progress note it is important to show (Homeyer & Bennett, 2023; Zuckerman, 2019):

- The client-clinician relationship has ended.
- There was an appropriate reason for ending psychotherapy.
- The client received appropriate resources related to ending treatment.

These are important things to document even if the client stopped coming to sessions and there was not a clear termination session. If a client "no shows" it is still helpful to show that the clinician attempted follow up. This follow up may look different depending on the circumstances. For example, if you have a client with severe depression and a history of suicidal ideation, you might reach out to their emergency contact or even request a wellness check after a no show.

However, if you have a client who was experiencing work stress and attended sessions sporadically, and there is no evidence of need for safety concerns, you might attempt to reach out over phone and email before sending a final notice to the client that their file is closed and the relationship is terminated for now, along with recommendations for referrals and reaching you in the future. I should note here that I do not recommend actually using the word "terminated" in communication with the client, as it sounds a bit harsh.

A note about discharge summaries

Some agencies and clinics require a separate Discharge Summary be completed at the end of each therapeutic relationship. Certain insurance companies may also require this form. This is highly dependent on the requirements of the setting in which you work.

Discharge summaries can be useful for having a quick summary of the case to review. However, they include information that is all available elsewhere in the record, thus violating the tip from Chapter 1: *Never write anything twice.*

In a private practice setting, progress notes and other documentation are sufficient to explain the full treatment story without the need for an additional document. However, some clinicians like to complete a Discharge Summary for the purpose of having a succinct way to review cases later, if needed. The Case Summary Template in Chapter 12 can be used for this purpose, since it is a summary of treatment.

MANAGING AND DESTROYING RECORDS BEYOND TREATMENT

All states and mental health disciplines have slightly different requirements for how long to maintain records, so there is no way to offer specific guidance here (as discussed in Chapter 2). However, it is important to note that managing records does not end with the end of psychotherapy. Clinicians (or agencies or other workplaces) are required to maintain records beyond the client's treatment, and often for many years.

Practically speaking, this is much easier now with electronic records. Rather than moving a large file cabinet when moving offices, clinicians simply store the records digitally and usually do not need to think much about them. But client records are not something to forget and hang onto for years on end.

Much of this chapter reviewed potential scenarios when records may be requested or revealed to others. That potential remains as long as the records remain in your care. Therefore, it is recommended to destroy records after the legal date to keep them has expired. In this way you do not open your client up to the possibility of records being requested when they are no longer required or relevant.

Some clinicians do keep a tracking sheet of previous clients. This can be useful for a variety of reasons, but make sure that it has a purpose if you choose to do so. Also remember to limit the information in such a sheet to very basic data so that information could not potentially be harmful.

Quick Read Chapter Summary

- Coordinating care with other professionals offers many benefits for clients; however, it requires clinicians to consider informed consent and ongoing confidentiality issues, including sharing only the minimum necessary information.

- Consultation is another important aspect of professional growth and quality client care. Document consultations relevant to client treatment in a progress note.

- Writing treatment summary letters is often more beneficial for clients than releasing the entire treatment record. Keep these letters objective and fact-based, never providing an opinion or recommendation for court-related matters if you are the treating clinician.

- Clearly document the end of the therapeutic relationship as a way to provide continuity of care, but also as protection from liability.

- Securely maintain records as long as legally required, but destroy them as soon as possible so client records are not open to vulnerability.

NOTES

NOTES

Chapter 12

Forms for Coordinating Care and Ending Treatment

IN THIS CHAPTER

Guidance on Using Templates 289
Authorization to Release Information 291
Progress Note Example: Collateral Contact..293
Progress Note Example: Consultation 295
Case Summary Example 297
Letter Template: Summary of Treatment 299
Letter Template: Case Coordination 300
Letter Template: Case Closing 301

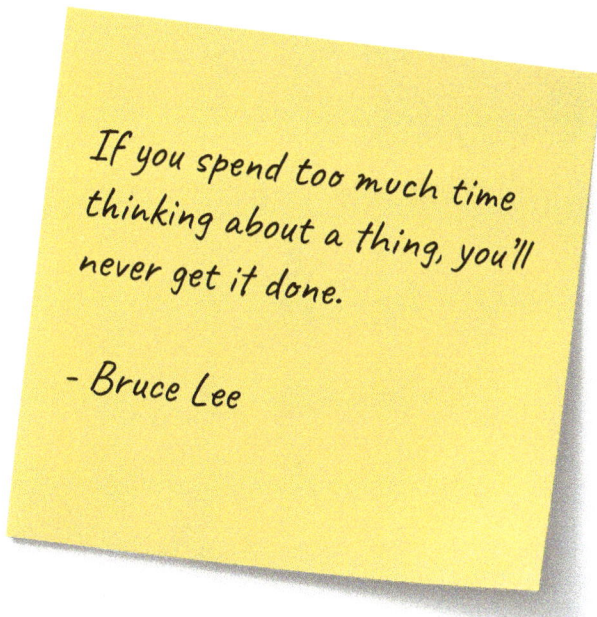

If you spend too much time thinking about a thing, you'll never get it done.

- Bruce Lee

GUIDANCE ON USING TEMPLATES

The following pages include a variety of templates and examples related to coordinating care. These include progress note templates for specific situations, as well as letter templates meant for other professionals, and templates to be used with clients. There are additional letter templates in the online resources. Modify and adapt these to your own practice.

Note that the Case Summary Example applies to both providing a summary of treatment for an open or closed case, since the same information applies whether the case is current or closed. This is discussed further in Chapter 11.

 Look for this icon to identify forms or templates meant for use with clients or others.

For students and clinicians working in a setting with prescribed forms:

Focus more on the information in Chapter 11 to better understand principles related to coordinating care and providing clients accurate information about records. However, the Case Summary Example may be especially helpful for those who work in settings that require extensive coordination of care.

For clinicians in a private practice setting with flexibility to choose their own template format:

Use all the forms that apply to your practice! Check out the video instructions at **QAPrep.com/SFD-Resources** for help with adapting the forms to your specific policies and needs.

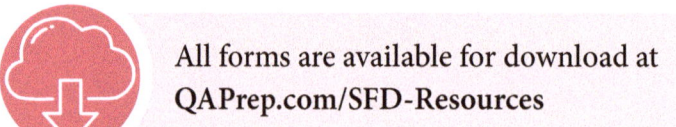 

Authorization to Release Information

Authorization to Release Information

Client Name:_____

Parent/Guardian (if applicable):_____

Information to be released:

- ☐ Client's entire record
- ☐ Dates of treatment
- ☐ Clinical test results
- ☐ Diagnosis
- ☐ Payment info
- ☐ Prognosis
- ☐ Progress notes
- ☐ Progress to date
- ☐ Summary of treatment
- ☐ Treatment Plan
- ☐ Other (described below)

_____
_____

Reason for release of information:

_____
_____

Release information to:

Name: _____

Address: _____

Phone and/or Fax: _____

Email: _____

This release to expire on the following date: _____

Authorization to Release Information (Continued)

I understand that my records are confidential information and by signing this agreement only the above described information will be released to the identified party. I have the right to revoke this agreement at any time and this revocation must be submitted in writing.

I understand that I have the right to receive a copy of this authorization.

_____
Client Signature   **Date**

_____
Parent/Guardian Signature (if applicable)   **Date**

Progress Note Example: Collateral Contact

Progress Note: Collateral

Client Name: Wendy Darling

Name of Collateral: Mary Darling

Relationship to Client: Mother

Date of Session: 06/11/2024　　**Time:** 1pm　　**Session Length:** 20 min.

- ☐ Authorization to Release Information signed by the client
- ☑ Authorization to Release Information does not apply
- ☐ Reviewed with collateral contact and the client who is the client and relevant limits to confidentiality

Reason for collateral session (check all that apply):

- ☐ Gather information for intake
- ☑ Meeting with client's parent regarding treatment
- ☐ Meeting with client's partner regarding treatment
- ☐ Reviewing and updating treatment plan and goals
- ☐ Making referrals related to client's care or collateral support
- ☐ Other: _____

Discussion:

Information gathered (if applicable):
Reviewed info regarding client's report in last session that her teacher did not let her use coping skills from sessions in class. Mother has discussed this with the teacher who seems open to learning how client can implement these without distracting classmates.

Areas of strength in supporting client:
Mother had already talked with both the client and the teacher about this issue.

Areas of need or concern:
Mother requests therapist to consult with teacher but would like to be involved so she is also aware and "everyone is on the same page."

Progress Note Example: Collateral Contact (Continued)

Interventions in Support of Client's Care:

- ☑ Created a plan to support client during times of crisis
- ☐ Gathered information about client's symptoms and needs
- ☐ Identified boundaries in support of client's goals
- ☐ Practiced co-regulation strategies
- ☑ Problem-solved current struggles
- ☐ Provided parent coaching
- ☐ Rehearsed communication strategies to use with client

- ☑ Provided psychoeducation on:
  - ☑ Behavior reinforcement
  - ☐ Client's diagnosis
  - ☐ Common responses to stress
  - ☐ Developmental stages
  - ☐ Impacts of trauma
  - ☐ Mirroring
  - ☐ Patterns in behavior
  - ☐ Self-care for caregivers
  - ☐ Symptoms presentation
  - ☐ Therapeutic modalities

Other Notes (if applicable):

None.

Plan:

- ☐ Continue with current treatment plan, no changes necessary.
- ☑ Add in coordination of care with: Client's teacher. Mother will follow up on scheduling a time.
- ☐ Adjust diagnosis: _____
- ☐ Adjust treatment plan: _____
- ☐ Made referral regarding: _____
- ☐ Other: _____

Awesome Therapist   06/11/2024

Therapist Signature   **Date**

Progress Note Example: Consultation

Awesome Therapist, LPCC
123 Main Street Long Beach CA
(999)888-7777
awesometherapist@email.com

Progress Note: Consultation

Client Name: Elsa Agnarrsdottir

Name of Consultant: Awesome Psychiatrist, MD

Date of Session: 09/13/2024 **Time:** 11am **Session Length:** 20 min.

- ☑ Release of information signed by client
- ☐ No release signed, and information kept to minimum necessary

Reason for Consultation:

- ☐ Case conceptualization
- ☑ Coordinating care
- ☐ Differential diagnosis
- ☐ Ethical dilemma
- ☑ Making a referral
- ☐ Symptom presentation
- ☑ Treatment options
- ☐ Other: _____

Consultant's expertise (if applicable):
Psychiatrist specializing in anxiety and trauma.

Discussion:

Clinical impressions and information discussed:
Reviewed the client's current symptoms and history of trauma. Discussed her difficulty managing symptoms and potential benefits of medication. Explained client's reticence about using medication.

Helpful questions and considerations (if applicable):
Emphasized the importance of discretion considering her high level position.

Suggestions for diagnosis or treatment plan (if applicable):
Therapist will review information with client and provide an official referral for the psychiatrist. If medication is prescribed, therapist will report any concerns about use, side effects, and symptom presentation to Awesome Psychiatrist.

Areas of agreement or disagreement (if applicable):
N/A

Progress Note Example: Consultation (Continued)

Other Notes (if applicable):
N/A

Plan:

- ☐ Continue with treatment plan, no changes necessary
- ☑ Add in coordination of care with: Awesome Psychiatrist in accordance with ongoing ROI.
- ☐ Adjust diagnosis: _____
- ☑ Adjust treatment plan: Will add medications to client's file if prescribed after meeting with Awesome Psychiatrist. Will check in with client regarding medication usage and effects and alert psychiatrist as needed.
- ☐ Other: _____

Awesome Therapist   09/13/2024
_____
Therapist Signature   **Date**

Case Summary Example

Case Summary

Client Name: Ariel Atlantica

☑ Contact information is the same as most recent paperwork.

☐ Contact information has changed (see updates below):

Address
_____
_____

Phone Number
_____

Email
_____

Dates of Treatment:

Treatment began on: 03/03/2024   Last day of treatment: N/A

Number of sessions attended: 12

Diagnosis (if applicable):
Major Depressive Disorder, mild, single episode

Collaterals Involved (if applicable):
None

Treatment Focus/Goals:
Treatment goals focused on reducing Ariel's symptoms of depression, increasing the frequency of interaction with her support system, and practicing self-care regularly.

Progress Made:
Ariel was able to make progress on her treatment goals quickly and continues to do so. She attends sessions regularly and is engaged in treatment. She continues to meet criteria for a depressive disorder.

Reason for Termination (if applicable):
N/A

Case Summary Example (Continued)

Resources/Referrals Provided:
I provided Ariel with a referral to a psychiatrist to consider medication. I also provided resources related to common presentations of depression and social support within the community.

Other Notes (if applicable):
N/A

Awesome Therapist   09/03/2024
_____
Therapist Signature   **Date**

Letter Template: *Summary of Treatment*

Practice Name
123 Address Street
(123)456-7890

{Name of Recipient}
{Recipient Address}
{Recipient Phone/Fax}

To Whom It May Concern:

{insert client name} participated in therapy with me from {insert beginning treatment date} through {insert current or end of treatment date} and attended a total of { x } sessions. At the time of treatment, they met criteria for {insert diagnosis}. They exhibited {insert symptoms/behaviors related to diagnosis}.

The focus of treatment was {insert goal(s)} . They made progress in {insert progress toward goals} during treatment.

Sincerely,

Letter Template: Case Coordination

Practice/Clinician Name
Address
Phone number
Email

{Name of Recipient}
{Recipient Address}
{Recipient Phone/Fax}

To Whom It May Concern

Regarding Your Patient/Client: (insert client name)

I am writing to inform you that (client name) is making significant gains in (insert broad goals and/or diagnosis). Their functioning is improving by (give one relevant example). If you have any questions, please feel free to contact me. I look forward to sending you further updates.

Sincerely,

Letter Template: Case Closing

Practice/Clinician Name
Address
Phone Number
Email

Date:

To: (Insert Client Name)
Notice of Intent to Close Case

It has been more than two weeks since your last appointment and I have been unable to contact you via phone or email.

If you would like to continue therapy, I am happy to continue working with you and to discuss your ongoing goals. However, if I do not hear from you within two weeks of this letter's date, I will consider your case closed.

If you would like to discontinue therapy, I recommend having a discussion together. I am willing to discuss any concerns you might have and also willing to conduct a final session to review your progress and what steps you might take at this point.

I am also happy to provide any referrals to another therapist, if desired, and to provide any treatment details to another provider, with a signed Authorization to Release Information as your consent.

If I can be of assistance in any way, please do not hesitate to contact me.

Sincerely,

NOTES

NOTES

APPENDIX

IN THIS SECTION

Your Documentation Journey: Where to Go From Here 305
References 306
Index 312
Acknowledgments 314
About the Author 316

Your Documentation Journey:
Where to Go From Here

If you've gotten to the back of this book, congratulations! The end of this book is the start of your documentation journey.

There is no destination to reach; there is only the journey. You already have the tools you need for success in your professional life. This book is one of those tools, and it will be tempting to constantly seek more - more templates, examples, and explanations. More validation. More reassurance.

Avoid the distraction of seeking more resources, and focus on taking action with the tools you have now.

Return to the 1-2 goals you identified in Chapter 1 and start there. Implement one strategy to help you meet these goals, evaluate how that strategy works for you, and adapt as needed. Then move on to the next step that feels most relevant for meeting your needs.

For example, trying to overhaul your entire documentation process will feel overwhelming. However, creating a list of commonly used interventions that you can reference as a cheat sheet is an example of one step in that process. That one step feels much easier to accomplish and could save hours of frustration writing progress notes over the course of a year.

Stress-free documentation happens one step at a time. Embrace the journey, focus on progress over perfection, and never forget that *any note is better than no note!*

Appendix

References

1. American Association for Marriage and Family Therapy. (2015). *AAMFT Code of Ethics.* Alexandria, VA: AAMFT.

2. American Counseling Association. (2014). *ACA Code of Ethics.* Alexandria, VA: ACA

3. American Mental Health Counselors Association. (2020). *AMHCA Code of Ethics.*

4. American Psychological Association. (2022). Behavioral Health Integration Fact Sheet [White paper]. American Psychological Association. https://www.apa.org/health/behavioral-integration-fact-sheet

5. American Psychiatric Association. (2013). *Diagnostic and statistical manual of mental disorders* (5th ed.). https://doi.org/10.1176/appi.books.9780890425596

6. American Psychological Association. (2017). *Ethical Principles of Psychologists and Code of Conduct* (Washington, DC: American Psychological Association, 2017). http://www.apa.org.ethics

7. American Psychological Association. (2021). *Professional Practice Guidelines for Evidenced-Based Psychological Practice in Health Care.* American Psychological Association. https://www.apa.org/about/policy/psychological-practice-health-care.pdf

8. American Psychological Association. (2007). Record Keeping Guidelines. *American Psychologist, 62*(9), 993–1004. https://doi.org/10.1037/0003-066X.62.9.993

9. APA Dictionary of Psychology. (2023, November 15). *Informed consent.* American Psychological Association. https://dictionary.apa.org/informed-consent

10. Archer, J., Bower, P., Gilbody, S., Lovell, K., Richards, D., Gask, L., Dickens, C., & Coventry, P. (2012). *Collaborative care for depression and anxiety problems.* The Cochrane database of systematic reviews, 10, CD006525. https://doi.org/10.1002/14651858.CD006525.pub2

11. Baldwin, D. S., Dang, M., Farquharson, L., Fitzpatrick, N. B., Lindsay, N., Quirk, A., ... & Crawford, M. (2021). Quality of English inpatient mental health services for people with anxiety or depressive disorders: findings and recommendations from the core audit of the national clinical audit of anxiety and depression. *Comprehensive Psychiatry, 104,* 152212. https://doi.org/10.1016/j.comppsych.2020.152212

12. Barnett, J. E., & Cooper, N. (2009). Creating a culture of self-care. *Clinical Psychology: Science and Practice, 16*(1), 16–20.

13. Beidas, R. S., Edmunds, J. M., Cannuscio, C. C., Gallagher, M., Downey, M. M., & Kendall, P. C. (2013). Therapists perspectives on the effective elements of consultation following training. *Administration and policy in mental health, 40*(6), 507–517. https://doi.org/10.1007/s10488-013-0475-7

14. Benjamin A. (2008). Audit: how to do it in practice. *BMJ (Clinical research ed.), 336*(7655), 1241–1245. https://doi.org/10.1136/bmj.39527.628322.AD

15. Chow, D. (2018). *The First Kiss: Undoing the Intake Model and Igniting the First Session in Psychotherapy.* Correlate Press.

16. Cure Act Final Rule: Information Blocking Exceptions. The Office of the National Coordinator for Health Information Technology. URL: https://www.healthit.gov/sites/default/files/2024-04/IB_Exceptions_Fact_Sheet_508_0.pdf

17. Darby, W. C., & Weinstock, R. (2018). The Limits of Confidentiality: Informed Consent and Psychotherapy. *Focus (American Psychiatric Publishing), 16*(4), 395–401. https://doi.org/10.1176/appi.focus.20180020

18. Fair, L. (2023, March 3). *FTC says online counseling service BetterHelp pushed people into handing over health information – and broke its privacy promises.* Federal Trade Commission. https://www.ftc.gov/business-guidance/blog/2023/03/ftc-says-online-counseling-service-betterhelp-pushed-people-handing-over-health-information-broke

19. Figley C. R. (2002). Compassion fatigue: psychotherapists' chronic lack of self care. *Journal of Clinical Psychology, 58*(11), 1433–1441. https://doi.org/10.1002/jclp.10090

20. Garrett, P. & Seidman, J. (2011, January 4). *EMR vs EHR - What is the Difference?* HealthITBuzz. https://www.healthit.gov/buzz-blog/electronic-health-and-medical-records/emr-vs-ehr-difference

21. Gehart, Diane. (2016). *Case Documentation in Counseling and Psychotherapy.* Cengage Learning.

22. Griswold, B. (2022). *Navigating the Insurance Maze* (9th ed.). Barbara Griswold, LMFT.

23. Centers for Disease Control. (2024, May 15). *Health Insurance Portability and Accountability Act of 1996 (HIPAA).* https://www.cdc.gov/phlp/php/resources/health-insurance-portability-and-accountability-act-of-1996-hipaa.html?CDC_AAref_Val=https://www.cdc.gov/phlp/publications/topic/hipaa.html

24. Homeyer, L. & Bennett, M. (2023). T*he Guide to Play Therapy Documentation and Parent Consultation.* Routledge.

25. Houston, M. (2017). *Treating Suicidal Clients & Self-Harm Behaviors.* PESI Publishing & Media.

26. Johnson, J., Hall, L. H., Berzins, K., Baker, J., Melling, K., & Thompson, C. (2018). Mental healthcare staff well-being and burnout: A narrative review of trends, causes, implications, and recommendations for future interventions. *International Journal of Mental Health Nursing, 27*(1), 20–32. https://doi.org/10.1111/inm.12416

27. Jongsma, A., Peterson, L., & Bruce, T. (2021). *The complete adult psychotherapy treatment planner* (6th ed.). John Wiley & Sons, Inc.

28. Kahn, M. W., Bell, S. K., Walker, J., & Delbanco, T. (2014). Let's show patients their mental health records. *JAMA: Journal of the American Medical Association, 311*(13), 1291–1292.

29. Khan, Y. S., Albobali, Y., & Kamal, L. F. (2022). Improving the quality of structured clinical documentation in a child and adolescent psychiatry outpatient service: Findings from an audit cycle. *Asian Journal of Psychiatry, 77*, 103268. https://doi.org/10.1016/j.ajp.2022.103268

30. Leon, A. & Pepe, J. (2012). Utilizing a continuing education workshop to increase knowledge of documentation among hospital psychosocial staff. *Journal of Social Service Research, 39*(1). 115-128. https://doi.org/10.1080/01488376.2012.724378

31. Lim, C. T., Fuchs, C., & Torous, J. (2024). Integrated Digital Mental Health Care: A Vision for Addressing Population Mental Health Needs. *International Journal of General Medicine, 17*, 359–365. https://doi.org/10.2147/IJGM.S449474

32. Los Angeles County DMH Program Support Bureau Quality Assurance Division. (2010, October 5). *Assessments* [PowerPoint slides]. https://file.lacounty.gov/SDSInter/dmh/162893_AssessmentsandMedicalNecessity10-05-10.pdf

33. Maniss, S. & Pruit, A. G. (2018). Collaborative Documentation for Behavioral Healthcare Providers: An Emerging Practice. *Journal of Human Services: Training, Research, and Practice, 3*(1).

34. Matthews, E. B. (2020). Computer use in mental health treatment: Understanding collaborative documentation and its effect on the therapeutic alliance. *Psychotherapy, 57*(2), 119–128. https://doi.org/10.1037/pst0000254

35. McCaffrey, M. (2024). *Using Artificial Intelligence (AI) as a Mental Health Clinician: Managing risk, ethics, and clinical benefits.*

36. Medicare. (2024). *Medicare and Mental Health Coverage.* Medicare Learning Network. https://www.cms.gov/files/document/mln1986542-medicare-mental-health-coverage.pdf

37. Miller, S., Hubble, M. & Chow, D. (2020). *Better Results: Using Deliberate Practice to Improve Therapeutic Effectiveness.* American Psychological Association.

38. Miu, A. S., Joseph, A., Hakim, E., Cox, E. D., & Greenwald, E. (2022). Peer Consultation: An Enriching Necessity Rather Than a Luxury for Psychologists During and Beyond the Pandemic. *Journal of Health Service Psychology, 48*(1), 13–19. https://doi.org/10.1007/s42843-021-00052-3

39. Muecke, J. (2024, April 5). *Why I Don't Do a "Thorough and Structured" Intake.* Frontiers of Psychotherapist Development. https://darylchow.com/frontiers/why-i-dont-do-a-thorough-and-structured-intake/

40. Munsey, C. (2008, April 1). How To – Stay safe in practice. *Monitor on Psychology, 39*(4). https://www.apa.org/monitor/2008/04/client-violence

41. Nagy, G.A., Cassiello-Robbins C., Anand, D., Arnold, M., Coleman, J., Nwosu, J., Singh, R., and Woodward, E. (2022). Building a multicultural peer-consultation team: Planning, implementing, and early sustainment evaluation. *Transcultural Psychiatry, 59*(6), 844-862. doi:10.1177/13634615221105117

42. Nathan, W. & Desposito, M. (2023, October). *The benefits of clinical consultation groups.* American Counseling Association. https://www.counseling.org/publications/counseling-today-magazine/article-archive/article/legacy/the-benefits-of-clinical-consultation-groups

43. National Association of Social Workers. (2021). *NASW Code of Ethics.* https://www.socialworkers.org/About/Ethics/Code-of-Ethics/Code-of-Ethics-English#principles

44. National Association of Social Workers. (2005). *NASW Standards for Clinical Social Work in Social Work Practice.* Washington, DC: NASW.

45. O'Leary, K., Heyman, R. & Jongsma, A. (2014). *The couples psychotherapy treatment planner* (2nd ed.). John Wiley & Sons, Inc.

46. Office of Minority Health, Department of Health and Human Services. (2000, December 22). National Standards on Culturally and Linguistically Appropriate Services (CLAS) in Health Care. https://www.federalregister.gov/documents/2000/12/22/00-32685/office-of-minority-health-national-standards-on-culturally-and-linguistically-appropriate-services

47. Office of the National Coordinator for Health Information Technology. (n.d.). Retrieved March 17, 2024 from https://www.healthit.gov/faq/what-electronic-health-record-ehr

48. Onyeaka, H., Ajayi, K. V., Muoghalu, C., Eseaton, P. O., Azuike, C. O., Anugwom, G., Oladunjoye, F., Aneni, K., Firth, J., & Torous, J. (2022). Access to online patient portals among individuals with depression and anxiety. *Psychiatry Research Communications, 2*(4), Article 100073. https://doi.org/10.1016/j.psycom.2022.100073

49. Peck, P., Torous, J., Shanahan, M., Fossa, A., Greenberg, W. (2017). Patient access to electronic psychiatric records: A pilot study. *Health Policy and Technology, 6*(3), 309-315.

50. *Practice Management System (PMS).* (n.d.). Definitive Healthcare. Retrieved March 17, 2024.

51. Pope, K., Vasquez, M., Chavez-Duenas, N., Adames, H. (2021). *Ethics in Psychotherapy and Counseling* (6th ed.). John Wiley & Sons, Inc.

52. Posluns, K., & Gall, T. L. (2020). Dear Mental Health Practitioners, Take Care of Yourselves: A Literature Review on Self-Care. *International Journal for the Advancement of Counseling, 42*(1), 1–20. https://doi.org/10.1007/s10447-019-09382-w

53. Sabri, B., Tharmarajah, S., Njie-Carr, V. P. S., Messing, J. T., Loerzel, E., Arscott, J., & Campbell, J. C. (2022). Safety Planning With Marginalized Survivors of Intimate Partner Violence: Challenges of Conducting Safety Planning Intervention Research With Marginalized Women. *Trauma, violence & abuse, 23*(5), 1728–1751. https://doi.org/10.1177/15248380211013136

54. Schwarz, J., Bärkås, A., Blease, C., Collins, L., Hägglund, M., Markham, S., & Hochwarter, S. (2021). Sharing Clinical Notes and Electronic Health Records With People Affected by Mental Health Conditions: Scoping Review. *JMIR Mental Health, 8*(12), e34170. https://doi.org/10.2196/34170

55. Schwitzer, A. & Rubin, L. (2015). *Diagnosis & Treatment Planning Skills* (2nd ed.). SAGE Publications, Inc.

56. Thom, R.P. & Farrell, H.M. (2017). When and How Should Clinicians Share Details from a Health Record with Patients with Mental Illness? *AMA Journal of Ethics, 19*(3): 253-259. 10.1001/journalofethics.2017.19.3.ecas3-1703.

57. US Dept. of Health and Human Services. (2006). HIPAA Administrative Simplification. Washington, DC: Author.

58. US Dept. of Health and Human Services. (2013). HIPAA Omnibus Final Rule. Washington, DC: Author.

59. van Rijt, A. M., Hulter, P., Weggelaar-Jansen, A. M., Ahaus, K., & Pluut, B. (2021). Mental Health Care Professionals' Appraisal of Patients' Use of Web-Based Access to Their Electronic Health Record: Qualitative Study. *Journal of Medical Internet Research, 23*(8), e28045. https://doi.org/10.2196/28045

60. Washington Administrative Code. WAC 246-809-035. (2017). https://app.leg.wa.gov/wac/default.aspx?cite=246-809-035

61. Washington Administrative Code. WAC 246-810-035. (2009). https://app.leg.wa.gov/WAC/default.aspx?cite=246-810-035

62. Washington Administrative Code. WAC 246-924-354 (2005). https://app.leg.wa.gov/wac/default.aspx?cite=246-924-354

63. Wiger, D.E. (2009). *The Clinical Documentation Sourcebook* (4th ed.). John Wiley & Sons, Inc.

64. Zanaboni, P., Kristiansen, E., Lintvedt, O., Wynn, R., Johansen, M. A., Sørensen, T., & Fagerlund, A. J. (2022). Impact on patient-provider relationship and documentation practices when mental health patients access their electronic health records online: a qualitative study among health professionals in an outpatient setting. *BMC psychiatry, 22*(1), 508. https://doi.org/10.1186/s12888-022-04123-7

65. Zuckerman, E. (2019). *Clinician's Thesaurus* (8th ed.). The Guilford Press.

APPENDIX: REFERENCES

Appendix

Index

A

Adolescent progress note. See Progress note, Child
Adolescent treatment plan. See Treatment plan, Child
Artificial intelligence (AI) 187–188
Assessment 71–72, 75–76
Audit 55–58, 204–207
Authorization to release information 291–292

B

Billing codes. See CPT codes
Biopsychosocial intake assessment. See Intake assessment
Burnout 210–211

C

Case coordination 273–277, 277–278, 295–296, 299, 300
Case note. See Progress note
Case summary 273–277, 297–298, 301
Catch up on notes 212–215
Collaborative documentation 185–187
Collateral involvement 73, 293–294
Consent form 111–118
Consultation 277–278, 295–296
Couples 52–55, 73, 72–74, 262–263

CPT codes 16
Cultural considerations 34–36

D

Diagnosis 45–47, 75–76, 107–108, 109
  Updates 46–48, 75–76, 109
Diagnostic assessment. See Intake assessment
Discharge summary. See Case summary

E

Electronic health record (EHR). See Practice management software
Ethics 15, 25–27, 133–135, 194–196, 273–277

G

Goals 136–139
Group therapy 269

H

HIPAA 27, 28–29, 32, 124–129, 179–180, 205–206, 274–275

I

Informed consent 49–51, 52–55, 56, 64–65, 67–68, 73, 184, 187, 191, 273–274, 278
Insurance 43–44, 51–53, 56, 68, 184

Insurance audit. See Audit
Intake assessment 69–72, 85–92, 93–100
Interventions
    Progress note 222–231
    Treatment plan 140, 154

L

Letters 279–280, 299, 300, 301

M

Medicaid 142
Medical necessity 45–48, 52–55
Medicare 44, 49–55, 273
Mental status exam 74
Minors 72–74, 93–102, 253–254
    Consent for treatment 122
    Consent to treat 121
Modalities 16

N

Notice of privacy practices 124–129

P

Parent. See Collateral involvement
Play therapy progress note. See Progress Note, Child
Play therapy treatment plan. See Treatment plan, Child
Policies 28, 64, 67–69
Practice management software 29–32, 189–190
Private practice 9–10
Process note. See Psychotherapy note
Progress note
    Amending 188–189
    Child 184, 253–261
    Content 177–178, 180–181, 203–204
    Couples 52–55, 184, 262–268
    Intake 77, 103–105
    Template 181–182, 221–236
    Types 184–185

Psychotherapy note 179–180

R

Records 28–30, 65–67
    Access to 33, 56, 205–206, 280–282, 291–292
    Destroying 284–285
Release of information 274–275, 291–292
Risk assessment 190–194, 233

S

SMART goals 138–139, 150–151
SOAP note 38, 248–250
Summary. See Case summary
Superbill 44, 49
Supervision 8
Symptoms 106, 107–108, 149, 235

T

Telehealth 119–120
Telemedicine. See Telehealth
Teletherapy. See Telehealth
Time management 207–210
Treatment goals. See Goals
Treatment plan. See Chapter 6
    Child 167–170
    Couples 171–174
    Template 149–155
    Updates 141–143

Acknowledgments

This book was made possible by Adderall (thank you to my nurse practitioner), the Eras Tour movie (played on repeat for weeks), and the work of a few dedicated individuals.

To my mom, who read to me often, frequently highlighted grammar structure, and made me diagram sentences. This book was much easier to write and required minor editing because of what you taught me. Thirty years ago I never thought I'd say this, but thank you.

To Chrissie, a rare forever friend and one of the smartest people I know. You provided guidance and feedback when I had no idea what I was doing. Who knew that two naive and goofy college girls would end up being such legit professionals?! Go us. And thank you.

To Melissa, my handler, who project-managed not only the book, but me. You offered a guiding light when I was frequently in a fog of competing priorities. Thank you.

To Dani, my Operations Guru, who took care of the important daily tasks and made it possible for me to prioritize writing, and improved multiple business systems along the way. Thank you.

To Stephen, the hottest and most dedicated designer I could ever hope to work with. You put in so many late nights and treated this book as your own. You took what I wrote and expanded the vision beyond my wildest dreams to create something beautiful that I'm proud to share with the world. Thank you.

To the Advanced Readers, who accepted the challenge of reading this book and providing feedback on short notice. You went above and beyond, and this book was greatly improved by your suggestions. Thank you.

Literally hundreds of people have impacted my work in a way that contributed to this book. Every clinician who has ever booked a consultation with me, emailed a question, or joined one of my programs has helped me improve these resources, simply by asking for help. The templates in this book would not be possible without your questions and feedback.

Thank you!

About the Author

Maelisa McCaffrey, Psy.D. is a licensed psychologist, nail design enthusiast, and documentation expert. As a clinician with ADHD, Dr. McCaffrey brings a unique perspective to clinical documentation. Unlike generic systems, her approach resonates with individuals of various organizational styles, with the goal of inclusivity and effectiveness.

After working in various clinical settings, Dr. McCaffrey started her business, QA Prep, in 2014. She is dedicated to empowering therapists across the world with comprehensive online training, consultation services, and speaking. She also facilitates weekly groups for those maintaining or catching up on paperwork.

In Stress-Free Documentation for Mental Health Therapists, Dr. McCaffrey leverages her wealth of experience, making her the perfect guide for therapists seeking effective, ethical, and hassle-free documentation practices. Explore her insightful approach and join the community of professionals benefiting from her expertise.

Visit **qaprep.com** to connect with Dr. McCaffrey and take your documentation skills to the next level.

www.ingramcontent.com/pod-product-compliance
Lightning Source LLC
Chambersburg PA
CBHW042357030426
42337CB00030B/5129